Nashville City Blues

Nashville City Blues

MY JOURNEY AS AN
AMERICAN SONGWRITER

★ ★ ★ ★ ★

James Talley

Foreword by Peter Guralnick

UNIVERSITY OF OKLAHOMA PRESS : NORMAN

This book is published with the generous assistance of the McCasland Foundation, Duncan, Oklahoma.

LIBRARY OF CONGRESS CATALOGING-IN-PUBLICATION DATA

Names: Talley, James, author.
Title: Nashville City blues : my journey as an American songwriter / James Talley.
Description: [First.] | Norman : University of Oklahoma Press, 2023. | Series: American popular music series ; volume 9 | Includes index. | Summary: "Memoir of an artist's ideals up against the Nashville recording industry, by one of Oklahoma's most important folk talents since Woody Guthrie"—Provided by publisher.
Identifiers: LCCN 2022025484 | ISBN 978-0-8061-9177-5 (hardcover) | ISBN 978-0-8061-9175-1 (paperback)
Subjects: LCSH: Talley, James. | Country musicians—United States—Biography. | Lyricists—United States—Biography. | Composers—United States—Biography. | Sound recording industry—Tennessee—Nashville. | LCGFT: Autobiographies.
Classification: LCC ML420.T1366 A3 2023 | DDC 782.421642092 [B]—dc23/eng/20220602
LC record available at https://lccn.loc.gov/2022025484

Nashville City Blues: My Journey as an American Songwriter is Volume 9 in the American Popular Music Series.

The paper in this book meets the guidelines for permanence and durability of the Committee on Production Guidelines for Book Longevity of the Council on Library Resources, Inc.

For Jan and my boys. I love you.

Nashville City Blues

People, let me tell you 'bout this Nashville town,
For twenty-five years I've watched the deal go down.
I've written every kind of song, sung every kind of tune,
Been treated every kind of way, I've had every kind of blues—
People, it's a cryin' shame—I got somethin' to say,
I've got those Nashville City Blues
And I ain't leavin' this town, people, 'till I get paid.

People, let me tell you 'bout this Nashville town,
They've taken all the music and watered it all down.
They've taken its heart, they've taken its soul,
They wouldn't know old Hank if he came walkin'
        down the road—
And old Hank had somethin' to say—
I got them Nashville City Blues
And I ain't leavin' this town, people, 'till I get paid.

People, let me tell you 'bout this Nashville town,
It will break your heart, and it will knock you down.
The glitter and the glamour, it's a big-time game, and
People, the music, it don't mean a thing—
It's all about the money that's made.
People, it's a cryin' shame—
I got them Nashville City Blues,
But I ain't leavin' this town, people, 'till I get paid.

People, let me tell you 'bout this Nashville town,
I know my music and I been around.
DeFord Bailey to Willie McTell,
Jimmie Rodgers and the Hag and Lefty Frizzel—
People I rode that train, and I know from whence I came—
I got them Nashville City Blues
And I ain't leavin' this town, people, 'till I get paid.

Well, I've paid my dues, and I put in my time,
Spent years of my life up and down the white lines,
Followin' my heart, believin' in dreams,
And I don't say nothin,' people, I don't really mean—
So, tell 'em all, get out of my way—yeah, I got somethin'
      to say—
I got them Nashville City blues,
And I ain't leavin' this town, people, 'till I get paid.

CONTENTS

FOREWORD

Peter Guralnick

I met James Talley in Memphis by the side of the road.

Well, that isn't altogether accurate, but he and Capitol Records Nashville promotion director Bill Williams picked me up in Memphis at the start of their two-man promotion tour for James's second album, *Tryin' Like the Devil.*

I was there ostensibly as a journalist (I was writing a story for the *Village Voice*) but really as a fan. I had been knocked out by James's first album, *Got No Bread, No Milk, No Money, But We Sure Got a Lot of Love,* which remains a timeless, elegiac evocation of a second-generation Okie's growing-up experience. I was now equally knocked out by his second, a more political but no less timeless statement of belief. In the words of the song that boldly proclaims its central theme, "Are They Gonna Make Us Outlaws Again?" And I don't think that question (with its built-in response) is any less immediate today than it was in 1976, when the album came out. Or, for that matter, than in the heyday of its three principal sources of inspiration, John Steinbeck, James Agee, and Woody Guthrie.

My two-plus days with James and Bill (including four hours of sleep) were a wonderful experience and taught me lessons that stay with me still. One was: Eat when you can, because you never know when or where the next meal, even if it's only M&Ms, is coming from. Another was: Lead with enthusiasm, never hold back on conviction or belief. And I don't mean this as a prescription for indiscriminate salesmanship either. I just mean: Never go out with anything less than total belief, and don't ever try to hide it either. Which was not an altogether new lesson for me, but I never saw it demonstrated more forcefully than on that first journey with James.

James was an inspiring tour guide, as we visited people and places that were the underpinning of his art. We drove to an almost deserted Mehan, the little Oklahoma town outside of Stillwater where James's grandparents Og and Mary lived when he was growing up, which provided so much of the poetic feeling of his first album. We stopped by Woody Guthrie's birthplace in Okemah at one o'clock in the morning to pay our respects. We visited with James's grandmother Mary and his Aunt Ruth, both of whom play prominent roles on *Got No Bread, No Milk, No Money*. And I listened to James retail the story of his life, his artistic inspirations and aspirations, to any number of program directors and DJs, some of whom he knew, most of whom he didn't, but every one of whom he treated with the utmost deference and respect. I felt like you could sense a little holdback on the part of one or two as they quickly scanned the new album and took in its political content. But every conversation was a model of civil discourse and what might be viewed as the careful cultivation of common ground. And it was fun, too, as host and guest recounted tales of Cain's Ballroom in Tulsa, where, James volunteered, his parents had "courted" and, in the words of the opening track of the first album (which might well get played at this point), "W. Lee O'Daniel played all night."

The trip came to an end for me in Tulsa, but the journey, of course, went on. For James, as you'll gather from the book, it was more like a crusade. And as it turned out, I was signed up for the duration. After that initial meeting, we never fell out of touch, and every conversation, every exchange we have had in the nearly forty-five years since then has been imprinted with the spirit, if not the letter, of the steadfastness that gave his second album its name. "Still tryin' like the devil," James will almost invariably sign off—at this point, it has become a kind of shorthand on which we can both agree, with no need for any further expatiation.

When, just a year after our first meeting, he was asked to play at Jimmy Carter's inauguration, James invited me along, and I got to eavesdrop on a brief but focused conversation with President and Mrs. Carter about James Agee's *Let Us Now Praise Famous Men*. It was a time of heady possibilities. Country music's "Outlaw" movement (Waylon, Willie, and the boys, including Billy Joe Shaver) was at its height, and it seemed like real change was in the air. *Tryin' Like the Devil* did not prove to be the commercial breakthrough that James and Bill Williams had been hoping for, but Johnny Cash and Merle Haggard were listening to James's songs, and it seemed, at more than one point, that Merle was on the verge of recording "Are They Gonna Make Us Outlaws Again?" Sadly, he never did (oh, man, it would have been great), but John did eventually get around to "W. Lee O'Daniel and the Light Crust Dough Boys," from that epochal first album.

James and I have been a lot of places together since then, and it's always been, well, I was going to say fun, and it has been that, certainly. But more important it's been *real*—or as Sam Phillips would say, R-E-A-L. One time James took me to meet DeFord Bailey, the first, and for over forty years the *only*, black performer on the Grand Ole Opry. James had met DeFord through a friend in the Nashville Public Health Department where James had worked in rat control for almost three years and where he made some of his closest Nashville friends. (You can see some of them on the cover of James's third album, *Blackjack Choir*, or better yet, listen to "Magnolia Boy," a beautiful, lyrical tribute to Henry Murphy, one of those pictured on the cover.)

DeFord—a small, gentle man (his growth had been stunted by a case of infantile paralysis when he was three)—visibly brightened when he came to the door of the tiny public-housing apartment where he lived and recognized James and his little boy, Reuben James. For several hours he spoke animatedly about his music, its sources and its inspiration, and the shoddy treatment he had received at the hands of the Opry, who dropped him in 1941 and for many years had virtually written him out of its history. "I never played with nobody," he told us after giving solo demonstrations on both guitar and harmonica, his trademark instrument. (DeFord's harmonica was the first sound that listeners heard on the December 10, 1927, broadcast on which the Opry was named.) "I'd like to teach your boy there, though," he said with a wink at Reuben James. "You'd see, he'd get used to me after a while."

I don't know if Reuben James, who after all, was just eight at the time, ever came back for his lessons, but for James Talley neither that connection, nor any other, was ever broken. He's held on fiercely to his past, even as he's forged on resolutely into a future that has never been guaranteed. There have been triumphs, and there have been painful disappointments, but there has never been any thought of turning back. As this book chronicles, James remains committed to his music and his ideals, and I know that will never change. I just want to hear the next album—because with every one, James has always gone someplace different. He has always set his standards high and, without fear or hesitation, exposed the beauty and the pain at the heart of his vision.

PROLOGUE

It was a warm August night in Albuquerque, New Mexico, in 1968. My friend Cavalliere Ketchum and I were scouring the used car lots on East Central Avenue for a vehicle to carry me and my worldly goods to Tennessee. I was twenty-four years old and was leaving the next week for Nashville. We found an old 1949 Willys panel truck that looked like it would get me there. I packed everything I owned in the back of it, including my 1960 Matchless motorcycle.

I drove to my parents' house to say one more goodbye to my mother. I had said goodbye to my father the night before. He was at work when I left, but my mother was an elementary schoolteacher and was still off work for the summer. Mother always cried when she said goodbye to any family member, but she was a strong woman and understood striking out to achieve a goal. As a young woman, she had courageously left the Oklahoma farm where she'd grown up and worked hard to become a teacher. She knew that to get ahead you had to reach, take some chances. With her blessing and tears of concern, I started out as other dreamers had before me. I was headed for the music capital of America—Nashville, Tennessee—in a nineteen-year-old truck.

As a young man, I thought I wanted to be a painter. I had loved drawing and painting from an early age, and I'd studied painting and art history in college. Singing and playing the guitar had been my hobby, but people kept telling me I had a good voice and kept encouraging me to be an entertainer. So I began to consider that as a possible career.

As a young painter, I was drawn to American realism. One of the books that influenced me was *The Art Spirit*, first published in 1923 by Robert Henri, a painter and teacher in the early twentieth-century Ash Can School of American realism. The book was not so much about the techniques of painting as it was about living an artistic life—seeing the world around you, thinking, exploring, observing, and developing one's vision.

I was also deeply influenced by a book I read in 1965 by Robert Shelton, then the *New York Times* music critic. It was a book of Woody Guthrie's writings called *Born to Win*. One phrase in the Guthrie book stood out for me: "The paint on your tractor is pretty to me." That there is beauty and art in the everyday things in life. There is an artistic approach to life. I knew a policeman in Albuquerque, who by the way he talked with people, with such intelligence and understanding, he was an artist. In fifteen years, he'd never had to fire his gun.

In my youth, I sang other people's songs that I enjoyed—Woody Guthrie, Johnny Cash, and Marty Robbins's gunfighter ballads. They were some of my favorites. The first song I learned to play on the guitar was from Johnny Cash's recording of, "I Got Stripes," a song he adapted from Leadbelly's "On a Monday." I always thought Cash was really a folksinger at heart. I loved his work and felt it was the most akin to my music in Nashville. I loved the modern arrangements of old folk songs that the Kingston Trio recorded. I loved the stories in those songs.

But after reading Guthrie's writings in *Born to Win*, I began to consider writing songs myself. This was something I had never thought about before. I could be a painter with words and music, and much to the disappointment of my University of New Mexico art department chairman, I abandoned my graduate work and earnestly started to develop my songwriting.

In the early fall of 1967, I was trying to figure out how to construct songs and what to write about when I got some in-person instruction in songwriting. That fall, Pete Seeger came to play a concert at the University of New Mexico, which I attended. An English professor I'd studied with knew I was writing songs, and he happened to know the people Seeger was staying with in town. Pete agreed to visit me the next afternoon and listen to some of my songs. Pete was then forty-eight and I was twenty-three.

I was renting a small house west of the Old Town Plaza in Albuquerque. I saw Pete approach out front. He must have been staying nearby because he was walking down the road with all the neighborhood dogs barking at his heels. He was informal and personable, and after some initial pleasantries he sprawled his lanky frame out on my pinewood floor, clasped his hands behind his head, and said, "Now, play me some of your songs."

I was incredibly nervous. Here was an icon of folk music in my living room, a person I admired, someone who knew Woody Guthrie. I was shaking inside, but I played him several of my songs, and as we talked, he left me with some advice that I've followed and passed on to other young writers my whole life. He said, "You have a good voice, but don't try to write folk songs like you hear coming out of New York City. You are from the Southwest. Write about the things you have seen in your life, write about your family, write about your world, write about the people here in New Mexico."

He went on, "If you think about it, that's what Woody Guthrie did. He wrote about what he saw in his life. If you do that, the rest will take care of itself." It was good advice, and I've always thought it was incredibly generous of Pete to take the time to listen to a young novice songwriter. I never forgot his advice.

★

My parents were both from Oklahoma. As young adults they lived through the Great Depression, and I heard all their Okie Depression stories. The stories held great interest for me, and I became interested in the art of the Depression era, and the photographs commissioned by Roosevelt's Farm Security Administration. The photographs of the dispossessed Okies on the road to California were stunning. They matched what I had heard from my parents and relatives in Oklahoma. I was moved by James Agee and Walker Evans's account of poor tenant farmers in Alabama, *Let Us Now Praise Famous Men*, and by Steinbeck's *The Grapes of Wrath*. Those small farmers, "tractored out" of their little tenant farms and struggling on their way to California, were part of America's painful transition from a rural to an urban society. There was no need for small tenant farmers any longer. A tractor could do the work of ten tenant farmers and their mules. This transition in our culture was poignantly documented by the FSA photographers: Dorothea Lange, Ben Shahn, John Collier Jr., Russell Lee, Walker Evans, and others.

The offspring of those Okies and tenant farmers would produce a new generation in American art and culture. As Wright Morris said in *The Inhabitants*, "They became what they beheld," as I did. The great singer-songwriter Merle Haggard, one of the people whose work I studied closely when I came to Nashville, was the offspring of those migrant Okies who settled in California. I identified with his songs as I did with Woody Guthrie's.

I was born in Oklahoma. I grew up in an Okie family with an Okie mindset, and although my working-class parents were not as desperate as the families in those FSA photographs on the road to California, they moved all over the country to find employment during the war economy of the mid-1940s. These were my early artistic influences. They are my touchstones, and they are still with me today.

★

Before moving to Nashville, to earn a living I worked for a year as a caseworker at the Bernalillo County office of the New Mexico Department of Public Welfare in Albuquerque—one of the places a young person with a fine arts degree could get a job. There I saw that thirty years after those desperate Okies were out on the road, America still had citizens who were in the same dire circumstances as the people in those 1930s photographs. I think of Haggard's song "Mama's Hungry Eyes." I saw a lot of hungry eyes. I saw suffering and despair. It was heartbreaking to witness, and I always wished I could do more for the people I served. I saw that America's safety net was inadequate, that poverty in America was by design, and I hoped that perhaps through my writing, through my songs, I could make some contribution—as I still do. This was where my philosophy, my empathy, and my approach to my songs were honed, and I started trying to write songs about those people, the *necesitados*.

★

But I didn't know where to go to achieve my music goals. I had lived in Los Angeles for a year in graduate school, and I didn't much care for the sprawl of a big, expensive town. New York City, for a young man from the Southwest, seemed like the other side of the world. Since my Okie parents had always loved country music, and its stories were akin to the folk music I loved, I thought that perhaps Nashville, a smaller town and a recording center, might be the place to go.

My socially conscious mindset from my education, my family history, and my work as a caseworker was firmly established when I arrived in Music City the last week in August 1968. To make a living I got a job as a caseworker with the Tennessee Department of Human Services, but I immediately started approaching Nashville music publishers. I had a few songs about the Hispanic families I'd served as a New Mexico caseworker, of which I was quite proud, but I had not written much else.

The trip to Nashville would begin a new life for me with many ups and downs, pleasures and pitfalls that I could never have predicted. I would be signed by Atlantic and Capitol Records. I would record fourteen albums of music—almost all, except for my Woody Guthrie tribute, *Woody Guthrie and Songs of My Oklahoma Home*, of songs that I had written. I would record with some of the greatest musicians in America, like the great Texas fiddler Johnny Gimble and blues legend B. B. King. I would perform at the Smithsonian and have dinner with President Jimmy Carter and the First Lady at the White House, where I would give a Grand Performance. I would be written about by the nation's most formidable music critics, who would do their best to spread the word about my music and songwriting in newspapers and magazines—from the *New York Times* to the *Los Angeles Times*, and publications in between, both in the United States and in Europe. I would travel across the United States, and eventually Europe, performing my songs. My songs would be recorded by other artists, including Johnny Cash, Alan Jackson, Gene Clark, Johnny Paycheck, and most improbably, the techno artist Moby, as well as others. My songs would be in movie scores and television shows. I would see the music business evolve from the days of the two-track analog tape machine to the complex digital age of recording and distribution, where my songs would be streamed by people all over the world.

There would be highs and lows. People would break my heart. I would make some bad decisions. Popular entertainment is a tough business, with each new generation demanding its own talent. No one stays on top forever. I would find the love of my life in Nashville, and we would have two wonderful sons and a grandson. I would spend a lifetime listening to people's stories, writing them down, and dreaming my dreams.

★

When I left New Mexico that bright August morning in 1968, after buying my truck I had four hundred dollars in my pocket. The old Willys, loaded with everything I owned, struggled and strained as it rolled out of Albuquerque that first morning. I stopped that first evening in Clayton, New Mexico, on the historic Santa Fe Trail—once the brutal heart of the 1930s Dust Bowl.

Leaving Clayton, I headed east into the windswept Oklahoma panhandle, where Jimmy Webb said he found the inspiration for his song "Wichita Lineman." The telephone poles along the highway were the only trees in sight and the road was straight as an arrow. The old Willys rumbled through Guymon and Fort Supply (where General Nelson Miles once headquartered his campaign against the Comanches), and on through Enid and Stillwater. I spent that second night with my maternal grandparents, Og and Mary Carr, at their home in Glencoe, Oklahoma.

The old Willys blew its head-gasket on the way, and water and antifreeze began seeping out and blowing across the side of the engine. But I kept going. I stopped at a bridge over a little creek. I let the radiator cool down, took a rag and opened the cap. I filled the radiator with my coffee pot from the creek. Then I began stopping every hundred miles to refill the radiator and keep the engine cool.

When I got to Memphis, I crossed the Mississippi River on the old Memphis Bridge. A thrill went through me as I looked down at the roiling water and the bridge's old stone piers. When I crossed that mighty river, I was in the South. I was in the town of Elvis, Beale Street, and the blues. I stopped for coffee and a sandwich at a little roadside diner. A young Black waitress poured me a cup of coffee and smiled. Her speech was slow and soft, with an accent foreign to my ears. I finished my meal and started my final push to Nashville. The stars over Interstate 40 were bright in the Tennessee night.

The next day in Nashville I started driving around the city trying to get my bearings and find a place to stay. I found a small apartment near the Hermitage, Andrew Jackson's old home east of Nashville. It was a small, new apartment and it was just leasing. I rented a one-room studio apartment for $110 a month. Thus began my journey to become a songwriter and a recording artist in Nashville. But the journey really began far from Tennessee, back in my boyhood.

Chapter 1

SONGS OF MY OKLAHOMA HOME

My father was from Welch, Oklahoma, a proud Okie born in 1911. Welch is a small town up in the northeastern corner of the state, about eight miles from the Kansas border. My father was named James Lloyd Talley, and his father was James Yancy Talley. Grandfather Talley, whose family was originally from Tennessee, lived in northwestern Arkansas, near Fayetteville.

When the family left Arkansas, they moved to Indian Territory, now the state of Oklahoma, and settled in Welch. My grandfather Talley was a merchant and operated a little general store on Main Street in Welch at the dawn of the twentieth century. He had a house in town and a couple of small homestead farms in the countryside. He was a successful businessman for his time. I was told that my father's mother, Silina Helen (Lewis) Talley, who was called Ella, was one-quarter Cherokee. She was my grandfather's second wife. His first wife had died. Ella was also from northwestern Arkansas. She died in 1926 when my father was fourteen years old. His father again remarried, this time to a widow with children, and my father took on the status of a stepson. His treatment by his stepmother left a hurt in him for the rest of his life. He always felt she was partial in all matters to her own children over him, which was perhaps natural, but after the loss of his mother he never again received the love he needed and wanted.

My father was a handsome man, slight of build, about five foot, eleven inches with curly black hair and gray eyes. As a teenager, and after high school, he clerked and helped his father in the general store. When my father was around twenty years old, his father set him up in an emerging Oklahoma industry of the time, an automobile service station. My father, though, was young and immature. He drank too much and didn't have the discipline to run a business, and the service station failed.

My father then enlisted in the US Army. During the Great Depression years, the army was probably not a bad place for a young man to be. He spent four years in the infantry, serving under Major Omar Bradley, his company commander, at Fort Sill, Oklahoma. Fort Sill was originally established during the Indian wars to subdue the Kiowa and Comanche tribes. It's the place where the Apache warrior Geronimo served out his last years as a federal prisoner and where he is buried. After four years in the infantry, my father reenlisted for two more years in the army air corps. He would say, "I spent six years and twenty-four days in the army." The food was better in the air corps, where he always slept in a bed, not sometimes on the ground as with the infantry. He always admonished me, "Son, if you ever go in the service, join the air force."

★

My mother, Florence (Carr) Talley, was born in Longton, Kansas, in 1914. She was named after her paternal grandmother, Florence Trivioli, whose family had come to America from the Italian region of Switzerland. Mother's father, Ogden Carr, was a farmer. He was the only one of five children to live past the age of eighteen, and he inherited his family's house in town and a farm near Longton. His family had been prosperous for the time, and when he met Mary Frazier from Oklahoma, she thought he had a funny name, but her family considered him a "good catch" due to his inheritance. Mary Frazier and Og Carr were married in Glencoe, Oklahoma, on April 7, 1912. Mary's family was originally from Missouri. They settled in Indian Territory during the land rush of 1889, when unassigned Native American land was opened for white settlement.

Both Og and Mary came from families who were respected in their communities. Og loved horses and purchased a harness shop in Longton in the second decade of the twentieth century, about the time everyone was beginning to drive automobiles and tractors were starting to till the farms. As there became less demand for horse harnesses, Og's business failed. The bankers foreclosed on his home and farm, which he'd used as collateral for his business loan. He felt he had been cheated by the bankers, which may have been true. I don't know all the details, but my mother said his treatment by the bankers troubled him until his dying day. Even at age eighty-nine as he was dying in a nursing home in Stillwater, Oklahoma, he was complaining about the Kansas bankers.

Broke, with no way to make a living, and with two small girls a little over one year apart—my mother and her older sister, Ruth—the family moved to Oklahoma and became dependent on Mary's family. They worked as sharecroppers on a farm owned by Mary's relatives, a few miles east of Stillwater near Glencoe. It was here my mother and her sister grew up and her younger brother by eight years, my Uncle Clyde, was born in 1922. But life was no longer easy. The family struggled to grow crops, a third of which had to go to the landowners. My grandparents were promised they would inherit the farm when Mary's father, Robert Frazier, died, but Mary's sister's husband was given control of the estate, and they were forced off the farm.

This was the last straw for my grandfather. He had worked and tended the farm as if it was his own, and this seemed to break him emotionally, my mother said. Around me as a child growing up, he kept his setbacks and disappointments to himself. However, as I grew older, I could see he was a broken man. His ambition had been stolen, first by the bankers and then by his brother-in-law. He no longer had any dreams or expectations. But I never heard him complain. He always maintained a jovial attitude, at least around me, but then I was too young to really understand his troubles. I never saw my grandfather take a drink of any kind of spirits. What he loved most was his chewing tobacco, and he always carried a pouch of Beechnut in his hip pocket.

★

When I was a boy visiting Og and Mary, their children were all grown and had left home. In 1944 they moved to Mehan, Oklahoma, an unincorporated hamlet about nine miles east of Stillwater. They purchased a four-room house there. It was on a double lot. The house was on one lot and a large garden was on the other.

I fondly remember the Mehan house from my youth. There was a small shed at the rear of the lot behind the house with a milk cow. There was a chicken coop and a fenced pen for chickens to run. There was no running water in the house, and the outhouse everyone used was in the back, behind the chicken pen. When I was a small child, the chickens would peck at me, so my grandmother taught me to hold a handful of corn kernels and toss a few kernels to the chickens as I went through the chicken pen. The chickens went after the corn and left me alone.

There was a storm cellar beside the house, with a mound of earth over it. When tornados would come, which was often in Oklahoma, my grandmother would gather us all up and we'd head for the storm cellar with our quilts and a kerosene lamp. The cellar was damp. It always smelled like rusting iron to me. The wind would howl, the rain would beat down in sheets, and the heavy metal door would rattle up and down. But my grandfather never went to the storm cellar with us. He slept through every storm.

The old house sat on sandstone blocks on an open foundation. It was unpainted wooden clapboard and had two small covered porches and a large back porch. To one side of the back porch was a small unheated room where we all took our baths in a large metal tub. The hot water was heated on the woodstove in the kitchen. On the other side of the back porch was a well, the only source of water for the house. The well water always tasted cool and sweet, with a hint of minerals. There was a bucket of water with a dipper that sat on a little table just inside the kitchen door.

My grandmother heated water for washing dishes on the woodstove. The stove could also burn coal, which burned hotter than wood. Once the wood fire was going, chunks of coal were added. The kitchen sink drained out into the grass beside the house. In the middle of the kitchen was a large table, covered with oilcloth, where the family ate.

In my grandparents' bedroom, there was a small open-flame propane heater with a ceramic grate. Other than the woodstove in the kitchen, there was no other source of heat in the house. It got extremely cold in the other bedroom, and we'd be so covered with quilts you could hardly turn over in bed. The bedsheets were made of old flour sacks sewn together.

Electricity became available in the late 1930s under Roosevelt's Rural Electrification Administration, but the house was not wired. Uncle Clyde told me that he wired the house for them when he came home from the service after World War II. It was the first house my grandparents ever lived in with electricity. In each of the four rooms, there was a bare lightbulb that hung on twisted strands from the ceiling. A crank telephone was installed on the front living room wall. Making a call entailed standing in front of it and talking into a long black mouthpiece. Cranking a little handle on the side rang the operator, who then placed the call. Anyone on that party line, if they picked up their phone, could listen to the call.

The soil in that part of Oklahoma was deep red. There were numerous creeks in the area, with rusty metal bridges across them. When it rained, the roads would turn into thick red mud that would fill the wheel wells of the old cars, which would then slip and slide through the ruts of red clay mud. Anybody getting stuck had to be pulled out with a tractor or a team of horses.

A few blocks from the house was a small grocery store that carried essentials and sundries. In the store was an old-fashioned red soda machine. The bottles sat in cold ice water. There were always a few old-timers loafing about in the store, and when I was around five years old or so, they would offer me a dime if I would sing for them. I would sing "Jesus Loves Me," and they would all clap and cheer and buy me a soda pop.

My grandfather never learned to drive a car, but a couple of blocks behind my grandparents' house a small Santa Fe train, a two-car express, passed through Mehan. It ran between Stillwater and Cushing. It did not stop unless you flagged it down. My grandparents knew the schedule, and my grandfather would stand on the tracks as he saw it coming and flag it to a stop. The small steam engine would come hissing to a halt, making loud, intimidating noises, which I feared as a child. My grandparents would take the train to Cushing to shop and buy groceries, and I would ride along with them. When they finished their day's shopping, they would ride the train back to Mehan.

★

But as my grandparents aged, they could no longer split wood for the stove, and there was still no running water in the house. The milk cow was gone, the chickens were gone, and the train between Stillwater and Cushing no longer ran. My grandfather could no longer do hard work, and he and Mary lived on old age assistance and surplus commodities from the government. So in 1958 they sold the Mehan house and moved to an old house in Glencoe, close to where they had farmed for so many years in their youth.

Glencoe is around fourteen miles east of Stillwater and a few miles north. In those days there was an old drugstore with a long soda fountain that sold ice cream, sandwiches, and soft drinks. There was a barbershop with a twisting peppermint pole in front, a small grocery store, and a few other small businesses.

On Main Street in Glencoe there were wooden benches every so often on the sidewalks. These they called loafers' benches. Each afternoon Og would walk downtown, and he and his buddies would sit on those benches, tell their stories, and chew tobacco. Og always wore baggy khaki pants that were too big for him. He held them up with broad suspenders. They gave him plenty of room for his little potbelly and for his Beechnut tobacco in his hip pockets. Og had no teeth. They had all been pulled, and his false ones apparently did not fit very well, so they sat on the windowsill over the kitchen sink. I don't think I ever saw him with his teeth in his mouth. But he loved to gum his Beechnut. He always carried a pouch in one hip pocket of his khakis, and sometimes an extra pouch in the other hip pocket.

Once, I said to my Aunt Ruth, "I wish I had a nickel for every mouthful of Beechnut that Og chewed."

My aunt said, "I wish I had a nickel for every mouthful he swallowed!"

★

My mother learned farming at an early age, working alongside her father. Farming taxed the body and the mind. It was dangerous work for a young girl of eleven or twelve years old, driving a team of horses pulling heavy farm equipment. My mother knew all the crops on a farm, and as a boy I wondered how she knew this. We would be driving through farm country and she would say, "Oh, look! There's a good-looking crop of beans." Or, "Look at all that okra or alfalfa!" Growing up, though, all I heard from my mother was how hard they worked on the farm and how poor they were—and talk of the Great Depression. My mother said sometimes she only received an orange for Christmas.

She and her older sister, Ruth, rode a "kid-wagon," to school. It was pulled by a team of horses by a local farmer, and it collected all the kids for school, like a school bus would today. My mother attended Eureka Consolidated High School, which drew from all the farms around Glencoe. Those farm girls were tough. They did hard, physical work and were athletic. My mother was a guard on her high school basketball team. In her senior year, the girls' basketball team from little Eureka High went all the way to the final-four game in the Oklahoma Women's State Basketball Championship. They lost that final game, but it was an accomplishment for a school so small even to be in the game. My mother loved basketball and followed the college and NBA teams for the rest of her life.

Mother was a determined young woman and vowed she was going to get away from the brutal work of farming. She said, "I was not going to marry some old farm boy, have a bunch of kids, and work myself to death farming."

She decided to get an education and become a teacher. She graduated high school at sixteen, worked for a year for a lady in Stillwater, and saved for her tuition. She enrolled at Oklahoma A&M University—now Oklahoma State University—in Stillwater. Her parents were not encouraging. She said they gave her no food or other help from home, as some of her other classmates received from their families, but my mother was determined to get an education.

At that time in Oklahoma, with two years of college, a person could teach in the little one-room country schoolhouses. So my mother quit school after her second year and got hired as a teacher in a one-room school near Glencoe. She taught all the grades, one through eight. Her brother, my Uncle Clyde, told me their father sold some calves to help her buy a car. She paid for half of the car, and her dad ordered a Model A Ford through the Montgomery Ward catalog. She learned to drive and took her parents around when they needed to go someplace.

It was during the Great Depression when my mother started teaching. Each morning she built a fire in the school's woodstove, and the kids would bring various fixings from home. A big pot of soup would simmer all morning on the stove, and at lunch they would all have a bowl of soup. Sometimes, she said, they would get a government surplus ham and make sandwiches. She taught a year at that first country school.

In her second year of teaching, she taught at a one-room schoolhouse on the outskirts of Stillwater. (It has now been engulfed by development and is within the city limits.) In 2001, my wife and I took her to a Eureka School Reunion in Stillwater. Any student who had ever attended Eureka was welcome. We drove her past the old country schoolhouses where she'd taught. The one near Glencoe had been turned into a barn. The doors were open, and hay and manure were scattered across the floor. The Stillwater schoolhouse, however, had been turned into a museum to show what a one-room country schoolhouse looked like back in the day. My mother was thrilled to see it so beautifully preserved. She taught one year at that Stillwater school. After those first two years of teaching, she had saved enough money to finish her degree at Oklahoma A&M.

After my mother graduated, she took a job in the elementary school in Drumright, Oklahoma. She taught there for a few years, but tension was then building toward World War II. After the attack on Pearl Harbor, when the war broke out, she switched to a munitions plant in Pryor, Oklahoma.

The plant was operated by DuPont and made gunpowder. It paid better than teaching.

It was at DuPont that my mother met my father, where he worked as a timekeeper. They were staying at the same boardinghouse. Her younger brother, my Uncle Clyde, also got a job at DuPont. They were all young then, with the energy and adventure of all youth. Pryor was not far from Tulsa, so on weekends they would drive to Tulsa, to Cain's Ballroom, and dance to the music of Bob Wills and his Texas Playboys. Uncle Clyde told me that Cain's had a hardwood dance floor laid over springs, and with hundreds of people dancing that floor was really jumping. He said, "Cain's couldn't hold all the people, so they hung speakers on the outside of the building and there would be two thousand people dancing in the street on Saturday night."

★

Pryor, Oklahoma, was where my parents were living when I was born. It is a little town named for Sargent Nathaniel Pryor of the Lewis and Clark Expedition. It is about forty-five miles northeast of Tulsa. But there was no hospital in Pryor, so I was born at the Hillcrest Hospital in Tulsa in November 1943.

In early 1944, DuPont offered some of the employees at the plant in Pryor the opportunity for better-paying jobs if they would relocate to the tri-cities area in eastern Washington State—the three towns of Kennewick, Richland, and Pasco. A nuclear reactor was being constructed north of Richland on a bend in the Columbia River. It was called the Hanford Works, or simply Hanford. The broad waters of one of America's great rivers, where Lewis and Clark braved the rapids in dugouts 140 years before, would provide the cooling water for the reactor's fuel rods. Mankind had moved from dugout canoes to nuclear technology in 140 years.

So for the opportunity of good paying jobs, my parents relocated to Washington State from Oklahoma. We lived in a large construction camp in Pasco, in small trailers that DuPont provided for their employees. It was 1944, and I was about one year old at the time. There was a common bathhouse, a laundry, and a communal kitchen. Women joined together to cook meals for everyone. The construction crews worked around the clock to complete the Hanford reactor. It took eighteen months. It was the first full-scale plutonium reactor built in the world. The plutonium from that

Hanford reactor was used in the "Fat Man" atomic bomb that exploded over Nagasaki, Japan, on August 9, 1945. After all the decades of plutonium manufacturing, over fifty million gallons of nuclear waste are still stored at Hanford. It remains the most dangerously polluted site in America. When the construction was completed on the reactor, DuPont offered my father a job in Louisville, Kentucky, so we moved there. But when the war ended, my parents quit at DuPont and moved back to Oklahoma.

My mother took a teaching job in Commerce, Oklahoma, which is in the northeastern corner of the state, not far from my father's birthplace of Welch. My father took a job in the nearby lead mines at Pitcher, Oklahoma. But it was brutal, dangerous work, and he eventually switched to a retail salesclerk job at the C. R. Anthony & Company department store in Commerce. The claim to fame of Commerce is that it's the hometown of New York Yankees baseball slugger Mickey Mantle. Whenever my father would meet people for the rest of his life, he would say, "Shake the hand that shook the hand of Mickey Mantle's hometown." Mickey was our hero. He was from Oklahoma. We were all Okies, and, of course, Yankee fans!

Work in the defense industry, especially the nuclear defense industry, paid well, and in 1947 my dad got word that Hanford was hiring again. He and another friend, whom he had worked with at Hanford in 1944, drove our 1937 Chevrolet once again to Washington State. When the school year was out in Commerce that year, my mother resigned her teaching job, and she and the wife of my dad's friend drove their car to Washington with her two small boys and me.

★

In Richland, my mother secured a teaching job at Spalding Elementary, named after Henry Spalding, the nineteenth-century Presbyterian missionary in the Pacific Northwest. My father was working in the nuclear reactor as a chemical handler. It was dangerous, intense work with no margin for error, involving the daily handling of radioactive substances. Each morning or evening, depending on the shift, my dad would shower before leaving the plant and be tested for levels of radiation. Every now and then, there would be some mishap, and he and his fellow workers would be exposed to higher-than-acceptable radiation levels.

My dad never talked much about his work at home, or for the rest of his life for that matter. It was all top secret, and he took that seriously. But back then, only the scientists truly knew the serious dangers of radiation exposure. The reactor ran twenty-four hours, and Dad worked a swing shift. He rode a company bus to work, which picked him up and dropped him off on the corner outside of our house each morning, afternoon, or evening, depending on his shift.

Because my birthday was in November, after the school year started, I was not old enough to start kindergarten with my friends. However, my mother got me enrolled in the second half of the school year, after I turned five. So I only attended kindergarten for a half year. My mother admitted later in life that she'd made a mistake in starting me so early. I was not mature enough, and I was behind in my learning for several years. I did not read at grade level until I was a sophomore in high school.

Almost every summer we would drive back to Oklahoma to see my maternal grandparents in Mehan and our other Oklahoma relatives. My Aunt Ruth lived in Stillwater and had four children, two boys and two girls—Gordon, Joe, Ruthie, and Vanita. I enjoyed playing with them when I was young, especially Joe and Ruthie, who were closest to my age.

★

Unknown to me, my father's work at Hanford had become a concern to my parents. They began to worry about how it might be impacting his health. Handling radioactive compounds day in and day out is dangerous. Sometimes my father would have nightmares about his work. I was at home with him one day, just the two of us. I was maybe seven or eight. He was sleeping restlessly. He'd been working nights and was sleeping during the day.

He began to call out, "Check the tanks! Check the tanks!" I came into his bedroom, and again, he yelled, "Check the tanks!"

I went out in the hallway and looked at the thermostat on the wall. I came back into his room, and I said, "I checked the tanks, and they are OK."

He said, "Oh, good," and greatly relieved, he fell back to sleep.

My mother's brother, my Uncle Clyde, was living in Albuquerque, New Mexico, in 1951, with his wife, Clara, and his son, Bob, and daughter, Mary Martha. My Aunt Clara was a pretty brunette with dark brown eyes, a Baptist preacher's daughter from Wichita Falls, Texas. She and Clyde met at a USO dance while he was stationed there during the war. When I was a boy, my aunt and uncle were always good to me. My cousin Bob was a couple of years younger than me. Bob and I enjoyed playing together, and we'd fight like brothers.

My parents decided to take a summer trip in 1951 to visit Clyde and Clara in New Mexico. My mother applied for a teaching job in Albuquerque and was offered a position, but my parents decided not to move that year. They were making good money in Washington, and my mother enjoyed teaching at Spalding Elementary in Richland. With all the federal dollars that supported the town, the schools were up-to-date with every aid a teacher could want, and her school was only a few blocks from our house. My dad was making good money at the nuclear reactor. They were banking my mother's teaching salary and living on my dad's income. But they continued to worry about my dad's daily exposure to radiation.

The next June, in 1952, they again decided to visit my aunt and uncle in Albuquerque. On these trips to the Southwest, we went through Navajo and Pueblo Indian country. Big red rock formations lined the highways, long blue ribbons of mountains raced across the distant horizon, and puffy white cotton-candy cloud formations were suspended in the perfect blue sky. That summer, my mother again applied to teach in Albuquerque and was offered a position, so my parents decided to move to New Mexico. I was eight years old and starting the fourth grade there in 1952.

★

Albuquerque was home to a big defense installation, the Sandia Corporation—now Sandia National Laboratories. It relies on federal defense and research contracts. There are still myriad innovations and testing ongoing for national defense at Sandia.

In the early 1950s, it was the same, an engineering and research facility. During the Cold War, it was heavily involved in nuclear deterrence projects. Atomic bombs were assembled there and stored in gigantic bunkers under the Manzano Mountains southeast of Albuquerque. Sandia was packed with engineers, PhDs, and research professionals. These professionals obviously needed support staff.

My father, who was not college educated, applied there when he arrived from Washington. In the process of applying, Sandia gave everyone a physical examination. A tumor was discovered on my dad's right lung, perhaps caused by his work at Hanford. We'll never know, but half of his right lung was removed, and thereafter my father had a long winding scar across his back and right side. Sandia held a position open for him after his recovery.

My dad's job entailed ordering supplies and equipment for the research engineers working on various projects. He held this job until his death, but his health was never quite the same after his operation. He never quit smoking or drinking, though, which did not help someone with half of a lung removed.

My sister, Mary Jo, was born in Albuquerque in 1954, so there was a significant difference in our ages. When I went away to college in 1961, my sister was only seven years old. When I graduated from college in 1965, she was eleven. I missed a lot of her growing up. But my sister was not like me. I could sit for hours building models and entertaining myself. She was a live wire, nervous like our father. She was into everything. Where I was a loner, who could care less about what clubs I belonged to in school, Mary Jo was always in the middle of everything. Where I was not that interested in joining a fraternity in college, which my parents didn't have the money for anyway, my sister joined a sorority. When our father died in 1969, she was only fourteen.

My father had three heart attacks. The first one was at age forty-five, in 1956. The second one was at Christmas in 1961. He had driven to Oklahoma to pick me up for the Christmas holidays from my first semester in college at Oklahoma State. He had a heart attack there in Stillwater. My mother took the bus to Oklahoma, and we spent that Christmas with our relatives in Oklahoma. After Christmas, I drove my parents back to New Mexico and returned to Oklahoma to complete the semester at OSU.

Despite my mother's desire to have me attend her alma mater, after my father's doctor bills they could no longer afford the out-of-state tuition at OSU. It also seemed like a good idea for me to stay closer to home, where I could help if needed. So I enrolled for the second semester of my freshman year at the University of New Mexico in Albuquerque.

My dad died after his third heart attack at age fifty-seven. In December 1968, he and my mother drove to Nashville for Christmas to meet my new wife, Jan. We had only been married a couple of weeks. Within a few weeks after returning to Albuquerque, my dad suffered another heart attack. He died the first week in February 1969. He was gone before Jan and I could travel to Albuquerque to see him. We flew back for the funeral. It was my first time on an airplane. Despite his frailties and his drinking, he was good to me growing up. Yes, he whipped me with a belt a few times when I misbehaved, which is not acceptable today, but that's the way boys were disciplined in those days. I knew he loved me, though, as I did him. He liked to buy me things, a new shirt, a coat, or perhaps a new pair of cowboy boots, the same as I enjoy buying things for my two sons. That last Christmas in Nashville, he bought me a pair of cowboy boots. I kept those boots for decades because they had come from him.

Later in his life, my dad became a Mason. It was important to him. He had wanted to be a Mason since his youth, but someone in Welch had blackballed him. In his late forties he became a Mason in Albuquerque. He bought a Masonic ring, which he wore proudly. When he died, he had a Masonic funeral, which he had wanted. He always wanted me to become a Mason, but it was simply not my inclination. It didn't mean the same to my generation.

★

My father's life was troubled, with unfulfilled aspirations. He was a hard worker, but he was not happy with his work. He never liked the job he had and often complained about it. It wasn't challenging. He had his health problems. My mother had had a hard life growing up, and even though she loved him and her children, she was not a terribly affectionate person. She was not a hugger. She had her career and could be independent. With his mother dying when he was fourteen, his unhappiness caused him to drink as a young man. It made his troubled world right for a short time, but like all alcoholics, he did not have that off switch in his brain that told him when he'd had enough. It was an issue throughout my parents' marriage. Even when they were young, my mother said that he was more interested in holding the bottle than her. I can't remember how many times she poured his whiskey down the kitchen sink trying to stop him from drinking. But that never works.

As I grew older and developed more maturity and understanding, I felt sorry for him in his unhappiness. He had a lot of love in him. He had missed his mother's love, and he needed love, which I'm not sure my mother fully understood or was capable of giving.

On the weekends, after running his weekend errands, he would sometimes not return home. My mother would know that he had stopped at a bar. She could always tell. My mother would get in her car and drive around to the neighborhood beer joints and see if she could spot his car. If she did, she would walk in and sit beside him on a barstool. He would turn and say, "Well, you caught me," and she'd say, "Let's go home." But sometimes she could not find him. The hours would go by into the evening. We would await his return, knowing the shape he would be in when he got home. My father was a binge drinker. He might not take a drop for a month, but once he sniffed the cork, he was gone.

When I was in college, a call came to the house one night from the police. They had picked up my father and wanted someone to come and retrieve him. He had been drinking across the Rio Grande in the South Valley. After work, he'd abandoned his carpool and gone to a bar with a coworker. After a few drinks, the coworker went home, but my father stayed. He met a couple of guys who offered him a ride home. But when they got him in the car, they took him out on the West Mesa, stuck a gun in his ribs, and demanded his wallet. He gave it to them, and they let him out on a lonely dirt road. A police cruiser picked him up. They called the house, and I had to go pick him up. I had to do that several times over the years.

My father always dreamed of being in business for himself—something simple, perhaps a little Tastee-Freez ice cream store. My mother understood, though, or at least she believed, that he did not have the temperament to run his own business. It was probably true. Wives know these things. He had an entrepreneurial spirit, but he was high-strung and nervous. He always lived three feet off the ground. He was the sort of guy who needed a steady paycheck. My mother would listen to his desires and then it would die down, but I don't know what they discussed between themselves.

My mother liked living in Albuquerque. She liked teaching there. So she kept teaching, and my dad kept putting one foot in front of the other and going to work each day.

★

After my father died, my mother taught several more years. She retired after nearly forty years as a teacher. My sister and I were both living in Nashville by then, and in 1984 mother moved to Tennessee. It was a hard transition for her. The topography, climate, and cultures of the two states are markedly different. She missed New Mexico. Her friends were there. She was lonely and wanted to move back, but she could not bring herself to leave her children and grandchildren. She no longer had any family in New

Mexico, and finally she resolved to stay in Nashville. She purchased a small home, not far from my sister.

As my mother reached her eighty-sixth year, she began to experience mental lapses. She was having small strokes that were not incapacitating her physically but were reducing her mental acuity. She could not keep her medications straight. My sister would prepare her medicine in little compartments for her to take each day. But instead of taking all the pills in each daily compartment, she would take one from each compartment, or however she felt she should take them. There was no telling what she was taking or not taking. She could not keep it straight. She would turn on the stove and forget she'd done it. She had been so independent, strong, and determined all her life, but she was fading, as we all do if we live long enough. She began to have more vascular dementia, and ultimately we had to place her in a nursing facility. She was angry with us. She would call my wife, Jan, whom she would say was her only friend. It was sad for all of us.

Over her last years, visiting her in the nursing home were some of the saddest days of my life. I dreaded it. I hated to go there and felt guilty if I didn't. It was painful to see her deteriorate. She had risen from poverty, gotten a hard-earned education, achieved status as an educator, and been incredibly determined. Now she could not finish a sentence. A thought would come to her, but before she could express it, it would vanish. After those visits I would leave her under a dark cloud. It was heartbreaking. My mother died in June 2006. The last evening I saw her, she was in the hospital. There were just the two of us in her room. I was sitting in a chair a few feet away, and she motioned for me to come close. I took her hand in mine and she squeezed it. I kissed her on the forehead. She could no longer speak, but she looked up at me with tired sad eyes as if to tell me: "This is it. I love you, but this will be the last time we see each other." When I left her room that night I knew I would never see her alive again. She died early the next morning. We flew her body back to Albuquerque and buried her next to my father in the plots they had purchased together many years before.

★

Mother was a tough woman. She was aloof and abrupt. She was an introvert and didn't want to be bothered with people. She could be difficult and could get her feelings hurt. She expected a lot of me. Despite her personal love for country music, she was not outwardly supportive of my music. In her mind it just wasn't serious work. I can't recall her ever coming to one of my shows, but in her own distant and personal way, I knew she was proud of me, and proud of my songs and recordings. She told me how proud my father would have been if he'd heard my recordings and seen my two sons, which of course he never did. She was never interested in remarrying. She would say, "I'm not interested in cooking and cleaning for another old man."

She came up the hard way and expected people to stand on their own two feet, but she was not unsympathetic to the disadvantaged. She understood that everyone does not have the same abilities or opportunities. She was a lifelong Democrat. She believed in our government as a force for good in our society. It was supposed to help people. Occasionally, she would express racist comments about Native Americans or Blacks when I was young, and she and my father supported George Wallace's candidacy for president, much to my dismay. But as she grew older, she evolved with the times and realized that the beliefs she'd grown up with were wrong.

She always stressed to me the importance of education. Education was the key. It was how she had escaped the farm and the poverty of her youth. I must go to college, like she did, and get an education. Education was freedom.

Looking back, I realize she put up with a lot with my father's drinking, complaining, and health problems. But my father also put up with a woman who could be cold and difficult, and who felt superior because she had a college degree. I never saw the two of them show much affection toward one another. It seemed in poor taste in their eyes to openly display it. I rarely saw them hug or embrace, and the few times I did they seemed embarrassed. She had her emotional limitations, and he had his emotional needs. Mother had no small talk. If she called you on the phone, she just launched into whatever was on her mind.

She came from a family who were not physically affectionate. She did not seem to enjoy being touched or caressed. She didn't tell me every day that she loved me. That just wasn't her. I was supposed to understand that she did. But she was strong and stable. As a boy I always knew I could depend on her. She was a disciplinarian too. There was no disobeying my mother. She was determined, and she expected the same from me. She was the only mother I had, and I loved her. I never doubted that she loved me.

Chapter 2

IN THE SPANISH SOUTHWEST

Albuquerque in my youth was a small city of around two hundred thousand people. The city was founded in 1706 as a Spanish colony along the Rio Grande valley. When I was a boy, it celebrated its 250th anniversary. The rich multicultural population of Anglos, Hispanics, and Native Americans would color my views of equality for the rest of my life. I do not fear different cultures. I appreciate people's uniqueness, and I have come to learn that people are much the same all over the world. They all have the same needs. They all want and need to be loved, and the fortunate can give love in return. They all need a roof over their head and enough to eat. They want meaningful, satisfying work. They love their children. The languages and customs may be different, but the song is the same.

Many Americans never travel far from where they grow up. They retain local prejudices and customs and carry them for a lifetime. I was fortunate as a boy, and for much of the rest of my life, to travel and see America's vastness and variety.

While I was growing up, my parents always loved dogs, and I've always been a dog person. I've had many dogs in my life, with their wonderful unconditional love. Every one of them was precious and added much to my life. As a boy, in Albuquerque, I had a little mutt named Bob. He was a black short-legged terrier mix with a natural bobbed tail, and he was with our family for over ten years. He was an ugly little dog, but he was our dog.

One weekend, our family went on a picnic in the Manzano Mountains southeast of Albuquerque. When we got ready to go home, no one could find Bob. We looked and looked, called and called, but no Bob. Finally, with everyone totally upset, we headed home. We thought perhaps some wild animal had gotten him. In about three days, however, we heard a scratching at the front door, and there was old Bob. He had traveled seventy miles on his short little legs, and with his porky little body, and found his way home from the mountains.

In my youth, I spent a lot of time alone after school, waiting for my parents to come home from work. I've never minded being alone. In fact, I enjoy it. It gives me time to think. I would busy myself building models. I purchased models with every spare cent I had. I built airplanes, ships, tanks, jeeps, cars, and other vehicles. I carefully assembled and painted them. I could sit for hours and build models. When I was around twelve, I started mowing lawns in our neighborhood for money, and I had a little shoeshine box. The price of a shine was fifteen cents. I would go door-to-door and ask people if they had any shoes they needed shined. Each time I saved up enough money I would buy another model.

My public elementary school in Albuquerque was the school where my mother taught third grade, Bel-Air. In 1952 during the Cold War, fearing a Russian nuclear attack, we had Armageddon drills. We'd all lie face down on our stomachs in the hallway, with our hands over our heads, and practice for a nuclear attack—as if that would do any good.

I don't remember most of my elementary teachers that well, except for my fifth-grade teacher, Mr. Giacci. He was from New York, and he threw chalk and blackboard erasers at us if we were talking or not paying attention. Someone would be softly whispering with a person in the desk next to them, and bam!—an eraser or a piece of chalk would come flying across the room. Mr. Giacci had a good throwing arm. He was accurate. I was the recipient of several eraser and chalk fusillades. We all thought it was funny, but that sort of teacher's behavior would probably not be tolerated today. Some parent would complain and be after his job. But my mother was a teacher, and as far as my parents were concerned, if I got into any trouble at school, it was my fault.

Albuquerque was building schools across the city in the 1950s for the oncoming post–World War II baby boomers. Both my junior high school and my high school were brand-new schools when I started in each one of them. In junior high, besides the usual core curriculum, I took shop in the seventh and eighth grades, where I learned to work with tools. I always had a keen eye for the way things were put together—perhaps from my model building. I was a good observer. Our shop teacher, Mr. Brown, had a deep booming voice and occasionally let out swearwords that would hardly be tolerated today. We all feared him. But, looking back, he was in a shop with a bunch of adolescents, power saws, lathes, sanders, and so on. If you were not careful, it was easy to get hurt, so he put up with no nonsense. I am glad that I took shop because it taught me how to handle my tools, which came in handy later in life.

When I was around twelve, I discovered my father could play the guitar. He had no guitar at home, and he had never revealed this talent to me until a friend of mine was given an inexpensive guitar for his birthday. We brought the guitar to the house, and I was amazed when my father tuned it and began to play and sing old Jimmie Rodgers songs popular in his youth—"Dear old daddy you shared my heartaches and joys, you tried to bring me up right." My father had a fine tenor voice, but I had no idea he had ever played the guitar and sang with it. He had never mentioned it.

It was around this time that my mother decided I should take piano lessons. My parents purchased a small maple spinet. A piano teacher was hired and came by the house weekly to teach me. But she was horrible, and I was not motivated. She did not make playing the piano much fun. In fact, she made it pure drudgery. I hated her and hated to practice. I learned later in life that if a child is not enjoying something and isn't motivated, he isn't going to get much out of it. I took piano lessons for several years and could not play much. Obviously, now I wish I'd been a more dedicated pupil. In hindsight, however, I did learn a lot of music theory from the piano.

In junior high school, I joined the band. Next to my father's ultimate idol, Bob Wills, he loved the big band music of trumpeter Harry James and his orchestra, so he bought me a trumpet. I played the trumpet in the junior high school band in the seventh and eighth grades. I enjoyed the trumpet much more than the piano, and I became the bugler for my Boy Scout troop.

When I was in the seventh grade, in homeroom, which was the first class of the day, I sat next to a girl named Sally. I went to school with Sally from the fourth grade through graduation at UNM. She was an artist, and quite good. Even in the fourth grade she could perfectly draw the cartoon characters from the movie *Peter Pan*.

In the seventh grade Sally sat next to me. One morning, the teacher was in front of the class talking, and Sally let out an ear-piercing shriek. She jumped up, ran across the room in front of the teacher, and up the aisle to another girl's desk. The teacher was dumbstruck, as were the rest of us. What was going on with Sally? The teacher had no idea, and neither did the rest of us. But Sally's girlfriend had an eight-by-ten publicity photograph of

Elvis Presley. She had held it up for Sally to see it, and Sally simply reacted—just the way you see the young girls behave in the old Elvis television footage. She could not contain herself. That was my first memory and awareness of Elvis Presley. I didn't know who he was until that moment. Predictably, we all grew to love him as the years went on, and we anxiously awaited each new recording he released.

In the ninth grade, I left my Boy Scout troop and joined the Explorer Scouts. Our post met at a local church. Our post advisor was a sergeant in the air force at Kirtland Air Force Base in Albuquerque. Our assistant post advisor was an amateur anthropologist and a student of Native American culture, so our post specialized in Native American dancing. We developed "native costumes" and performed at various special events. A bunch of young Anglos doing native dances would not be considered politically correct today, but it gave me a lifelong appreciation and interest in Native American culture and history.

In my ninth-grade year, the band needed a tuba player, and the band teacher asked me if I would be interested. The big sousaphone looked interesting, so I learned the bass clef notes and became the tuba player. I played the tuba through the tenth grade.

In eleventh grade, my band teacher asked me if I would be interested in being the drum major for the marching band. I was tall and thin, which was probably my qualification, so I said, "OK," and I became the drum major. But the band teacher was a tyrant. In the rehearsals on the football field no one could ever please him. He became disrespectful and demeaning of the students. I'm sure from his perspective it was like herding cats. But his outbursts of screaming and yelling upset all of us. Finally, one afternoon on the football field, in the middle of a practice, I told him off, which resulted in my being kicked out of the band and assigned a study hall for the rest of that year.

★

In high school I fell in love with the Kingston Trio's music. I loved their arrangements of old folk songs, and especially the stories in those songs. I loved their glib wit and humor. I remember when their first hit came out. My father was teaching me to drive in his old work car, his 1951 Chevy. We were on the East Mesa in Albuquerque, on a gravel road out near the Sandia Mountains. It was in that car, on that day, that I first heard "Tom

Dooley," and I was hooked. I purchased each new Kingston Trio album as it came out. My senior year in high school I had a little trio of my own. We copied the Kingston Trio. We all played guitars, wore striped shirts, and sang all the Kingston Trio's songs at school assemblies. We called ourselves the Ivy Three.

It was through the Kingston Trio that I learned of Woody Guthrie. All of Woody's songs that the trio recorded seemed to be my favorites. They spoke to me. They were poetic and powerful. They dovetailed with the Oklahoma stories my mother told me as I was growing up. Woody was an Okie, like us. His songs were about my people from Oklahoma. They were honest and reflected my heritage. I began to admire Guthrie. My exploration of Woody Guthrie led me to Pete Seeger and all the great folk music and blues on Folkways and Vanguard Records.

In high school I shifted my electives from shop to art, and I took all the art courses available. From an early age I'd enjoyed drawing and thought I was rather good at it. Evelyn Civerollo was my art teacher. She was a lot of fun, always joking with a sarcastic humor and making her classes enjoyable. I had a lot of admiration for her. Teachers who can communicate and make their classes fun inspire you. They make a difference.

I was in a couple of plays my senior year in high school, *Julius Caesar* and *Guess Who's Coming to Dinner*. I had small parts, but one of my best friends, Jim White, had the role of Julius Caesar. Jim's dad had owned a service station but had recently died from a heart attack, and Jim had been left his 1953 gold Cadillac Coupe de Ville. In 1959 it was still quite a car. Jim was proud of it and took great care of it. It was an automobile to behold. We would often sit in it at noontime and eat our sack lunches.

After Jim's father died, his mother married a construction worker. He was a crude sort, and when Jim expressed an interest in going to college, his stepfather said, "Why do you want to go to college? By the time I was your age I'd been married and divorced four times and had five trailer houses repossessed. I don't know why you want to go to college."

But Jim was intelligent, and like my mother he was determined to accomplish something with his life. He graduated from UNM with a master's degree in biology. He retired a few years ago from the Army Corps of Engineers.

I liked to have some spending money in high school to buy records and clothes, and a few bucks for dates—that is, when I got up the nerve to ask a girl out. I needed money for the movies, hamburgers, and ice cream, and to put gas in my dad's car, so I started working part-time jobs. I didn't date much in high school. I was bashful. Girls at that age were a mystery to me. Both sexes were trying to figure what they were supposed to do with all those onrushing hormones. I was never good at asking girls out. My heart always raced, and my breath grew short as I dialed their number.

At fifteen, I worked at the first McDonald's built in Albuquerque. I made one dollar an hour. There were two order windows in front and no inside seating. People took their food home or ate it in their cars. They had a big sign out front that said, "Over One Million Sold." I thought, "Wow, that's a lot of hamburgers!" I think McDonald's took those signs down when they'd sold over five hundred billion. No one had to be convinced any longer.

There was a grill man at McDonald's named Louie. He was a young guy just out of high school and was a huge Elvis fan. Each night after we closed, while we scrubbed and polished all that stainless steel, Louie would bring in his stereo and set it up in the back room. He would stack up Elvis's LPs on the auto spindle and turn the volume up loud so we could hear it all over the store. We would listen to Elvis's albums one after the other while we cleaned up at McDonald's.

During my senior year, I got a job working at Meyer & Meyer, a small men's clothier in Albuquerque. I got the job because they carried the Boy Scout line of uniforms and camping gear, which brought a lot of people into the store. They wanted a young man who was an Eagle Scout to handle that department and give advice, and someone recommended me.

The Meyers had two stores. The store where I worked was run by the Meyers' son-in-law, Sam Fine. Sam was the first person I ever met from Mississippi. The Meyers' daughter, for some reason, had gone to Old Miss and she'd picked up Sam as a husband along with her college degree. Sam was a character, right out of Faulkner. He smoked cigars all day and had a sizable repertoire of raunchy jokes, which he enjoyed sharing. He was a young man in his early twenties. He never took anything too seriously, and he seemed to enjoy life immensely. I enjoyed his colorful nature, and most of the time I was the only other person in the store to talk to anyway. I kept that job until the end of my senior year.

In my senior year I had a steady girlfriend. It was that first young love that's as deep as the stars in space. I thought she was beautiful. She was a year behind me in school, but when I graduated and went away that summer to work in the horse department at Philmont Scout Ranch in Cimarron, New Mexico, and left that fall for Oklahoma State, our young love affair ended. But that first love is the one you will never forget, and you forever carry that little dream in your heart.

I worked at Philmont Scout Ranch in the summers of 1961 and 1962 and returned again in 1967. I had loved horses since my dad first took me riding in Washington State when I was five years old. Philmont owned around two hundred horses then. Their shoes were pulled off at the end of the summer, and they ran wild in pastures all winter without shoes. But if they were to be ridden in the summer on rocky mountain trails, they needed shoes to protect their hooves.

Lawrence Sanchez was Philmont's head wrangler. We all called him "Boss." He was a veteran horseman and a dear man. I thought the world of him. He was soft-spoken, with a wry sense of humor and a little grin under his hat, and he was a great teacher. He patiently showed us how to shoe a horse properly, and we learned that shoeing two hundred head is a lot of work. After a couple of weeks of being bent over all day and wrestling with horses that had run wild all winter, most of us couldn't stand up straight.

But I loved to ride. I had palominos both summers, beautiful blonds like Roy Rogers's Trigger, with white manes, tails, and white around their cannons and fetlocks. The first year I had a mare named Missy, and the second summer a gelding named 7-11. I'd brush them down and hang a big feed bag of rolled oats over their nose. They loved it. I loved riding up in the backcountry in my free time, in those beautiful high mountain meadows. I have never forgotten the beauty of those mountain redoubts.

We were young men, lean, and strong, and drinking full of life in those dark mountains under sparkling stars. It held the same fascination and beauty for us, I'm sure, as it did for a young Kit Carson, Lucien Maxwell, or a young Jicarilla Apache from the region in their youth. The special friendships engendered there, and all those memories have lasted a lifetime. I've never felt so close to God as I did in those mountains. We're all part of the great mystery. Those summers ended too soon, and now only memories remain.

★

When I started college in 1961, I had no idea where I was headed, but my mother had always stressed education. It had given her freedom. She thought it would be wonderful if I went to her alma mater, Oklahoma State University in Stillwater, Oklahoma, so I enrolled there in 1961. But I was not well prepared for college. During high school I had spent too much time working and not enough time studying—really studying. In high school I made reasonably good grades without much effort. At OSU, though, I was up against some serious competition and some dead-serious professors, who didn't care whether I was there to learn or not. They would just as soon fail me so serious students could learn.

That first semester I had a five-hour English composition class. My professor was a mature woman with enough wrinkles to suggest she had been around the barn more than once. But she did instill in me an earnest love of language.

The first day in class, she asked us to write a one-page essay, and when we got our papers back the next day, they were so full of red ink they looked like we'd sacrificed a chicken on them. That sent me to the student bookstore for a reference on the rules of grammar and punctuation. We also had spelling tests, and I must admit, I've never been a good speller. Computer spell-check was invented for guys like me. By the end of the semester, though, she told me I was a good writer, but she could not give me a grade higher than one letter above what I'd made on my combined spelling tests—which were all Ds. So I received a C for the semester. And I was grateful. But I learned more in that first semester from this caring lady, whose name I can't now remember, than I did from any other professor in college.

I also took a four-hour humanities course that semester. It was, in college parlance, a "flunk-out" course designed to weed out those who were not serious and were wasting their time and money. It darned near was that for me. It was in a huge lecture hall with at least a couple hundred students, maybe more. The teacher lectured each day, and all of us took copious notes. We started out with our reading assignments: *The Iliad*, *The Aeneid*, the Book of Job, then Dante's *Inferno*, and we ended with *The Canterbury Tales*. I had never read any of these texts in my life. There were only two tests for the semester, the midterm and the final exam. I was struggling. I was a slow reader and there was a lot to read.

I made a D on the midterm exam. Wow! Wakeup call! There was simply no way that I could take a grade like that home to my mother, the teacher. So I resolved to get my act together and get disciplined. Each night I sat for hours at my desk in my dorm room. I outlined the entire *Inferno*. I knew every step of the descent into hell. I went to hell with Dante! I knew every river and tributary, every level of horror. I did the same with *The Canterbury Tales*. When the final exam came, my head was so full of hell and Middle English that I made a B on the final, which gave me a C for the semester. I was thankful. It was a slow start.

At the Christmas break that semester, my father had his second heart attack, and I returned to Albuquerque and enrolled for my second semester at the University of New Mexico. Since I'd always loved art and drawing, I decided I would major in art. I was interested in commercial art—something one could make a living with—but UNM did not teach commercial art, only fine art. My father was not too happy about my choice. He wanted me to be an engineer or an architect. But I have learned as a father myself that a father's dreams for his children are not their dreams. They have their own.

I needed more required coursework in English, so that semester I enrolled in Early English Literature. My family were not readers. I had no idea what early English literature was. We did not have books in the house except for a 1947 edition of World Book encyclopedias. My father read the *Albuquerque Tribune* (the Democratic Albuquerque paper) each evening when he came home from work, but that was the extent of his reading. My mother, even though she was a teacher, didn't read books either, until she retired and lived alone. Then she read romance novels. She prepared her lesson plans each night for her third graders. Books were just not a part of our lives.

In Early English Literature, we started with *The Canterbury Tales*, which I was well versed in at that point, but then we moved on to *The Faerie Queene* by Edmund Spenser, a long sixteenth-century allegorical poem. To this day my eyes glaze over just thinking about it. Then, it was on to Milton, Swift, and others. I was, as they say, above my pay grade, and certainly beyond my Okie heritage with those early English writers.

In my art classes at UNM, I took drawing as a freshman from an incredible watercolorist named Sam Smith. I was sitting on one of the little wooden benches in the drawing studio, which had a raised panel on one end to prop up your newsprint drawing pad. A woman came into the room in a bathrobe, stepped up on a platform, and dropped the bathrobe. She was stark naked, and she struck a pose. At eighteen I was not used to seeing a naked woman standing in front of me. It was a new experience. But I acted nonchalant, proceeded to follow instructions like a grown-up, and drew what was in front of me. Sam was an excellent teacher. I learned a lot from him about drawing, watercolor painting, and life.

I took courses in design, drawing, painting, sculpture, ceramics, graphics, and watercolor. I also took courses in art history. In my senior year I spent some weekends in Telluride, Colorado, where Sam and several of my professors had purchased old miners' homes for next to nothing. Telluride in those days was a sleepy little mining town in southwestern Colorado—a population of maybe a couple hundred people. It was a beautiful setting, ringed around by fourteen-thousand-foot mountains. It had not yet been discovered by real estate developers and made into the tourist destination that it is today.

Carl Paak, the UNM ceramics professor had a house there, and he enjoyed my guitar playing and singing. At night Carl and I would walk down the hill to the old Sheridan Hotel saloon on the main drag. The Sheridan was what you would expect in an old mining town, where bone-weary miners might stop to enjoy a cold beer or a few whiskeys. The patrons were grisly but joyous men—the colorful local regulars. They could tell a few tall tales, smooch and grab a little with the saloon waitresses, and find a little enjoyment in their lives. It was the dog-eared Old West, like you might see in an old black-and-white western—think Henry Fonda and *The Ox-Bow Incident*. I had a little Martin classical guitar, and Carl would encourage me to sing a few songs. After a few songs, we never had to buy another beer the rest of the night. "Here, have another one, sonny," they'd say, as they handed Carl and me another beer.

But alas, Telluride was discovered by real estate developers and that authentic character, I fear, is long gone. Though I have not been back since those years, I'm sure it looks a lot like Gatlinburg, Tennessee, or Jackson Hole, Wyoming. But the beauty of those mountains hasn't changed, I'm sure of that.

★

During college, I worked part-time at Montgomery Ward in Albuquerque. But getting hired at Wards turned out not to be easy. I went to their personnel office and asked if there were any openings. The personnel lady said, "We have nothing available right now."

I told my mother what she said, and my mother said, "Go back and see her next week." I went back the next week and still the lady said there were no positions open. Again, I told my mother what the lady said, and my mother said, "Go see her again next week."

So I went to see her the next week, and it was the same story. I told my mother that it was going nowhere. She said, "Go back and see her again next week."

Finally, on my fourth visit, the lady cracked. She said, "Young man, anyone who wants a job as bad as you do, I'm going to find them something." That was the way my mother was. She was determined, and she knew determination paid off.

After working in several areas as a floater, I wound up in the men's suit department. Harry Waldman was the department manager. He had been in the rag business his whole life. At one time he'd owned a men's clothing store in a small town in Kansas. He was around sixty-two years old then and a delight. He had been selling men's clothing his entire life, and he was terribly funny. He had a deadpan sense of humor as dry as the bottom of a martini glass. I've always appreciated people with humor. It helps with life's insanity.

Shoppers would often browse and take pants off the displays, look at them, then throw them down in a rumpled pile. We would have to fold them up again and put them back in the stack where they belonged. Harry would crack me up when people did this. As they were walking away, after leaving the clothes in a jumbled mess, he would dryly say under his breath, "Take your time going, but hurry back."

At one point a friend who worked with me at Wards told me about an opportunity—and beware of anyone who tells you they have an "opportunity" for you—to sell encyclopedias for the Collier's Encyclopedia company. He urged me to attend a sales meeting with him. He thought we could sell them on our days off from Wards. We went to the sales meeting, and they put on such a slick presentation that we saw ourselves making real money selling encyclopedias. I can't remember the entire pitch now, but it was something like, "We are looking for a few people in your neighborhood to buy these encyclopedias at a tremendously discounted price. We know that when your friends and neighbors see them, they will want a set for their children."

We would park our car at the end of the block in a residential neighborhood and start knocking on doors, looking for that special family. Now, I have heard that Paul Newman, the great actor, in his youth sold encyclopedias in college and was a top salesman, but we were sure not Paul Newman.

We spent many evenings and weekends knocking on doors on dusty streets in dusty New Mexico neighborhoods and being soundly rejected.

Once, I knocked on a door, and a man said, "Come on in, door's open." I went in and was standing in my suit and tie just inside his front door. He was sitting across the room in an easy chair. I started my encyclopedia spiel, and he listened passively for a few minutes. At a certain point in the "presentation" we were taught to reach into our coat pocket for a foldout brochure, which was a color photograph of the entire set of books displayed on a bookshelf. The picture featured their colorful red leatherette bindings and gold-leaf markings. It was sure to impress. But in this case, the man lifted the newspaper in his lap, and in his hand was a huge revolver that as Jimmie Rodgers might say, was "as long as it was tall." It seemed like the biggest pistol I had ever seen. And waving it around gently, the man said in the lowest gravelly voice imaginable, "I don't like encyclopedias, and I don't like encyclopedia people." I can't recall how long it took me to get out the door, but it wasn't long. We eventually decided to stick to our jobs at Montgomery Ward, and we gave up the encyclopedia business. Paul Newman we were not.

★

I met Cavalliere Ketchum, my coauthor of *The Road to Torreón* my senior year at UNM. He has remained a longtime friend. Cavalliere grew up in Scottsdale, Arizona. His uncles on his mother's side owned a blacksmith shop. They did ironwork for the architect Frank Lloyd Wright. He has many stories about Wright from his boyhood. Cavie had completed a degree in industrial arts at Arizona State University, and he'd taught auto mechanics in high school for a year before coming to UNM to study photography.

Cavie always loved cars, fast cars, and while we were at UNM he had a white 1957 Ford Ranchero pickup with a Thunderbird engine. It could lay a strip of rubber twenty yards long from a standing start. It was beautiful. As a teenager, though, Cavie was almost killed when he was broadsided in a 1927 Ford roadster.

Cavalliere was also a friend of New Mexico artist Georgia O'Keeffe. She liked Cavalliere because he was a young photographer. Her late husband Alfred Stieglitz was a photographer, and she liked to talk with Cavalliere about art and photography. Cavie took me to meet her at her home near Abiquiu, New Mexico. She was quite thin and dressed as you might expect in a long black dress cinched at the waist with a silver concho belt. Her silver hair was tied up in a bun at the back of her head. Her face was wrinkled from her years in the dry New Mexico air and her skin stretched tight over her cheekbones. Cavalliere and I visited with her for a while, then one of her young assistants gave me a tour of the house. After completing his MFA at New Mexico, Cavalliere was hired to start a photography program at the University of Wisconsin in Madison, where he taught until he retired as a full professor some years ago. In his years there, he trained many young American photographers.

Cavalliere and I took a graduate seminar together in research techniques from Dr. Bainbridge Bunting, an art history professor. There were only around six of us in the class. We met one evening a week at Dr. Bunting's beautiful adobe home in the North Valley. As it turned out, Dr. Bunting was quite fond of my guitar playing and singing, so I would bring my guitar to the class, and after whatever the discussion was for the evening, I would play and sing for an hour or so, and Dr. Bunting would break out the spirits. These performances seemed to be more the focus of the class than our research.

One of our research assignments was for us to study a subject and give an oral presentation on our findings. I can't recall now what my subject was, but Cavalliere's I will never forget. He walked in with an old moth-eaten Navajo rug folded under his arm for his presentation. I knew in my heart that he had done zero research on the damned thing, other than what he'd maybe learned growing up in Arizona; but he gave such an entertaining bunch of blarney about that old Navajo rug that everyone, including Dr. Bunting, was so entertained and amused that his research passed. Cavalliere and I still talk often on the telephone, and to this day he will say to me about some talk he's given, "I Navajo-rugged it," and we both know exactly what that means! I don't know how much we learned about research in that class, but we had a lot of fun.

★

After I graduated at UNM in 1965, I went to Los Angeles for a year to graduate school. The year I lived in Los Angeles, Sandy Koufax and Don Drysdale were retiring batters like knocking down bowling pins for the Los Angeles Dodgers, but there were dark clouds on the horizon. The Vietnam

War was escalating. That fall they were drafting over thirty thousand young men a month.

I did not support the war. But I figured I would soon be drafted, so taking my father's advice I signed up for officer candidate school in the air force. I signed all the paperwork and went for my physical. There were long lines of young men in their underwear and shoes snaking through a vacant floor of a Los Angeles federal building.

As we went through the line a navy corpsman held up a newspaper showing how many young men had been killed that week in Vietnam. He said, "Here's where you're headed boys." I arrived at the doctors at the end of the line and was rejected due to my injured back from my horse wrangling days. The doctor said, "I'm sorry, son, but we can't take you in the air force. The army may still call you, but we can't take you with your medical history."

★

I returned to Albuquerque that summer of 1966 and rented a little house in the North Valley. Cavalliere Ketchum came by with some record albums he'd purchased at a garage sale for one dollar each. They were recordings by a guy named Bob Dylan. I realize that in 1966 I was late in discovering Dylan's music, but I had never heard of him until Cavalliere brought those albums to share with me. He said, "I think you will like this guy." They were his early acoustic folk period recordings, and I had never heard anything like them. I thought the writing was incredible. Like so many then, who discovered him for the first time, I was blown away. I even liked the way he sang and delivered his songs. It was powerful stuff.

That summer, my friend Jim White was working on a construction job about forty miles west of Albuquerque, where Interstate 40 crossed the Laguna Indian Reservation. I needed to earn a few bucks, and Jim said, "Why don't you come and work with me." He was working as a laborer, but he said, "With your ability to handle your tools, why don't you apply as a carpenter? It pays more." So I presented myself as a carpenter and I was hired.

The job was part of the construction of Interstate 40, which crosses New Mexico. We were setting concrete forms for the culverts that run under the roadway that allow water to pass under the road. I was part of a three-man crew: two young Hispanic laborers and me. They did the shoveling, and I was constructing the forms from three-quarter-inch plywood soaked with creosote.

It was in August, hot as hell, over one hundred degrees in the shade, and there was no shade. The superintendent didn't apparently much like the hot weather or his job either. We were given no plans for what we were to build, so we had to try and figure it out ourselves. Each morning, the superintendent would come by and tell us what he wanted done, then he would head for an air-conditioned bar on nearby Route 66. He stayed at the bar until just before quitting time, then he would reappear, well lubricated, to see what had been accomplished that day. He would then chew everyone out for one reason or another. If you had a question during the day, there was no one to ask.

There was no electricity on the job and no generator, so you couldn't use power tools. All the heavy three-quarter-inch plywood had to be cut with a handsaw. After several hours cutting with a handsaw, the strength in my arm was gone, and I struggled to cut the pieces for those concrete forms.

A hole had to be dug below the sixty-inch culverts, so you could pour the footers and set the forms for the wing walls. The two laborers shoveled all day so we could set footings. They drove to the job each day from small Hispanic villages some distance away. They were jovial guys, full of jokes and banter. They had young families at home, little education, and if their health held out, they would be laborers the rest of their lives.

We worked a couple of days building the forms for the end of a culvert, and that night it rained. When Jim and I drove to the job the next morning, we saw that the water had washed all the forms down the arroyo, and the footing hole was filled with mud. The laborers worked all that day, knee-deep in mud, shoveling out the hole again. I tried to salvage what was possible of the concrete forms. The foreman came by drunk again that afternoon, chewed everyone out as usual, and headed back to the bar. We got the hole excavated and the forms about half completed by quitting time.

The next day, Jim and I were heading back to the job from Albuquerque, and as we neared the worksite, we saw big pools of standing water along both sides of the road. It had rained hard again the night before. We looked at one another and thought about the ridiculousness of the job, with no power, the drunken superintendent, and another day of wading in the mud. We decided we'd had enough. We turned the car around and headed back through Albuquerque, then up into the Manzano Mountains to the little lake at Manzano and went fishing.

★

That fall of 1966, I returned to UNM and started on a new PhD program in American Studies. I wanted to specialize in the art forms of the 1930s, the years of the Great Depression—especially the photographers of the Farm Security Administration, the writings of John Steinbeck and Woody Guthrie. But all that school year I kept thinking there were things happening out in the streets, in the real world, away from the university's cloistered environment that I needed to experience. I had been in academia and felt isolated from the world many Americans inhabited. The Vietnam War was raging. There were protests, trouble in the streets, and turmoil around every corner. The civil rights movement was in full flower. I decided I no longer wanted to study *about* America in a university. *I wanted to participate!* I was ready for a change. I had completed thirty hours of graduate work, but the thought of a career as a university academic was looking less and less attractive to me.

Reading Guthrie's writing in *Born to Win* set me on a new path. Woody was a liberal, a progressive populist as I was in my heart. I had also been listening to a lot of folk music in Los Angeles, where I discovered Odetta, Ian Tyson, more Guthrie and Pete Seeger, and any number of roots and blues singers and writers. They all had something to say about our culture, and I began to wonder: "Could I write songs too?" I had been playing Woody's songs, and other folk songs for years, but it had never occurred to me to express myself in songwriting. Music had been a sideline to my visual arts, an enjoyable hobby.

★ ★ ★ ★ ★

Chapter 3

AN OLD BRICK WAREHOUSE ON TRUMBULL STREET

That spring of 1967, I ran into a fellow UNM art student who had gone to work at the Bernalillo County office of the New Mexico Department of Public Welfare. She explained that working as a welfare caseworker was a job open to graduates with a fine arts degree. It was a place where I could earn a living (albeit a meager one) and still have some time to pursue my art. She explained her duties as a caseworker, which sounded interesting, and she encouraged me to take the civil service exam to become a caseworker. She assured me that the county director was partial to fine arts graduates because she felt they were compassionate with the poor. I took the exam and was hired to begin work that September.

The Public Welfare Office in Albuquerque was in an old brick warehouse on Trumbull Street, just off South Broadway. It was adjacent to the Santa Fe Railroad yards and across the tracks from the El Modelo tortilla factory. It was a drafty building filled with old wooden schoolteachers' desks lined up in rows across the first and second floors. The supervisors worked in individual offices built along one wall. There was a typing pool in the basement, a break room, and a snack bar run by a blind man.

This old building was full of stories. It was a history of human suffering, desperation, and abuse. Man's inhumanity to man. The latest chapters in this sad story were dictated each afternoon by caseworkers using red magnetic Dictaphone belts. The typists in the basement transcribed them, and they were added to the case histories, the latest chapters in an ongoing story of heartbreak. Some of the preserved stories were elegant, passionate, and compelling, but most were simply a recitation of dismal facts.

My supervisor was Dorothy McMurphy. She was in her late forties, caring and wise from her many years of service. As a twenty-three-year-old, I knew little about what I was doing as a caseworker, but I was ripe with empathy. I hadn't lived long enough yet to sing the blues, but I sure knew it when I saw it. I could not have been assigned to a better supervisor.

Dorothy had been at the department for many years and would retire there. She grew up on a ranch in Montana. She'd had polio as a child. One of her legs was a few inches shorter than the other, and she walked with a limp, swaying back and forth, down on one foot, and up on her toes on the other.

Dorothy had a small daughter and her husband, Bill. None of us really knew for sure what Bill did for a living. He was some sort of covert organizer and activist. He was older than Dorothy by several years, and to me he was like a character out of John Steinbeck's novel *In Dubious Battle*. There were always unusual people passing through town and sleeping over at their house. Once, I was visiting and met Rodolfo "Corky" Gonzales, the Chicano organizer and activist from Denver. His assistants (or bodyguards, as the case may be) were sleeping on couches, chairs, and the hardwood floor in Dorothy and Bill's sparsely furnished living room. Corky's sidekicks were some tough-looking dudes. Corky was one of the early organizers for Hispanic rights in Denver. Bill was obviously involved in some sort of activism, but we were left in the dark as to his official title, duties, or source of income. Dorothy and Bill were obviously not getting rich—nobody ever gets rich doing welfare work.

Dorothy was a genuinely good person. She had been doing all she could to help poor people for years. As our unit's supervisor, with her sad, knowing, brown eyes she could put you totally at ease. Those of us in her unit were her family, and we all loved her.

As a caseworker, I began thinking about all I saw: the injustice, the inequities in life, and about how the poor had no choice who their parents were, where they were born, or the color of their skin. They lacked skills, education, guidance, and opportunity—and our society certainly didn't love them. They were often stuck in generations of debilitating poverty and despair. They were not stupid. They had to be resourceful simply to survive on what they received in aid. It helped that we distributed government surplus food commodities: big sacks of flour, cornmeal, beans, powdered milk, and government surplus cheese. Those items made a lot of tacos. We did not then have food stamps in New Mexico.

I tried to understand all this and process it. I wanted to express what I was experiencing in my songwriting. But it was difficult to distill because it was so overwhelming. I was indeed no longer in academia. That was certain. I was in the street, right there where the real hurt and sorrow meet. I was learning a lot about life and our society from these poor unfortunate people.

Many of my cases were poor Hispanic families and indigent seniors. A number of my cases were in the South Valley in Albuquerque, where there was a large Hispanic population. One of my cases that I've never erased from my mind was an old woman, an *abuelita*, who lived by herself. Most of her family had moved away from the neighborhood. She could barely get out of bed or walk due to severe arthritis. Her hands were deformed, with fingers that looked like little twisted roots. She lived in a small one-room adobe with a packed-dirt floor. Her toilet was a slop jar or, if she could make it, the outhouse in the back yard. There was no running water in the little house. If her nephew did not come by to bring her water and attend to her needs, which he was not too diligent about doing, she had no water to drink. Often, her only source of water was from the condensate pan under the freezer compartment in her old refrigerator. The image of her is still with me.

Another case was a man named Solomón. He was an alcoholic. He purchased the cheapest wine he could find. He was a kind, gentle soul, with a good sense of humor. He had no education, no marketable skills. He was *flaco y débil*—thin and weak. He was not strong enough to do manual labor. His little wife had no more education or skills than he did. They had a daughter around ten years old—a beautiful, sweet child. He was only in his early forties, but he looked like he was sixty.

Normally, a woman drawing Aid to Families with Dependent Children (AFDC) was not permitted to have a man in the house, unless he was disabled. That was taboo. I never understood this. There was no sense in running the fathers away, breaking up families in order for them to receive help. Sometimes men try hard, but things don't line up for them, and they and their family need help. My song, "Does Anybody Know Why Ana Maria's Mama Is Crying?" from *The Road to Torreón* is a true story about such a man. But that was welfare policy. Solomón, however, had been approved for disability, so he could stay with his family. He was an artist. He carved delightful little *retablos* (religious reliefs) out of the wooden end-panels of old orange crates, which he obtained as scrap from a nearby grocery store. He would decorate his carvings with paint, glitter, and colored markers. They were primitive in execution but honest and beautiful. I purchased a couple of them from him, which I still have. Solomón lived on a dirt street named Hollywood, west of the Old Town Plaza in Albuquerque.

All the caseworkers, however, were not sympathetic or sensitive to their clients' plight or desperation. Some simply didn't care. My desk sat next to a grumpy old retired army colonel. He was around sixty and had retired from the service. For some unknown reason, he had taken a caseworker job. He would sit his clients down in a chair next to his desk and lecture them. They would have to change their ways! Get their act together! Shape up! They would look at him with terror in their eyes, petrified and afraid, while he harangued them.

Sometimes I would be out in the neighborhoods into the evening, calling on my caseload. If I had a lot of visits to make, I could not always get the job done in an eight-hour day. If I had been out late, my supervisor permitted me to come in a little late the next morning. One morning, after working quite late, I arrived at my desk around 10:00 A.M. and the old colonel snapped at me, "We start here at 8:00!" Well, I lost it. I told the colonel that I was not in his army, I was not one of his subordinates, and he was not my supervisor. I informed him that if he had a problem with me, he could take it up with my supervisor. He was used to people jumping when he barked, and I didn't feel like jumping. He probably had been a good soldier in his youth and served the country with dedication, but with his attitude and his tactless behavior and insensitivity to those in need, he should never have been a caseworker.

I have to confess, I have no tolerance now for anyone who complains about people on welfare, who resents their hard-earned tax dollars going to "lazy, immoral people." The immorality is in how we treat them. All I can say to the complainers is, "There but for fortune. . . . Walk a mile in their shoes and see how it feels." Perhaps those who complain have an education and talent. Perhaps those who complain have good parents who taught them, and cared for them, and loved them. Perhaps their father wasn't an alcoholic without any education. Perhaps he had a good steady job. Perhaps no one in their family was injured or disabled. Perhaps they had the brains and drive to pull themselves up by their bootstraps, like my mother. But unless the complainers have seen undiminished poverty up close, don't tell me they understand it, because they don't, and they have no right to complain about these unfortunate people. The poor are worthy of kindness. They are people too. They love their children and each other. They have feelings and dreams like the rest of us—*los necesitados.*

★

That December 1967 I met a young caseworker at the department named Sheila. I noticed her because her desk was in a back corner, and I had to pass it on my way to Dorothy McMurphy's office. I decided to ask her out. We started spending time together. We went to Colorado over New Year's. We drove my old 1957 Volkswagen to Durango, Telluride, and Ouray. It was snowing in the San Juan Mountains, and we followed the snow plough. Sheila and I became close that winter and spring. We fell in love perhaps, and we thoroughly enjoyed each other's company. She was smart, and I thought the world of her.

But at the same time my friends kept encouraging me to move to Nashville, to try my luck with singing and songwriting. There were only three music cities then—and perhaps still—where a serious recording career could be pursued: New York, Los Angeles, or Nashville. I had already spent time in Los Angeles. New York, for a guy from New Mexico, seemed like the other side of the moon. I took notice that Dylan had recorded his *Blonde on Blonde* album, still one of his best to me, in Nashville, so Nashville seemed like a place to try. It was not as expensive or intimidating as New York or Los Angeles, and I had grown up on country music with my parents' love for Bob Wills, Hank Williams, and other country artists.

As the time approached to leave for Nashville that summer in 1968, I asked Sheila if she wanted to go with me. "Are you kidding?" she said, "There's no way I would move to the South!" Well, that settled that. Our romance came to an end, because I had committed to go to Tennessee. I understood though. She was from Denver and the West. The South had been through wrenching upheavals and harrowing events: the civil rights protests, the killings, the attack dogs, the fire hoses, the bravery of the sit-ins and marches; and in April of that year, 1968, Martin Luther King Jr. had been assassinated in Memphis. Moving to the South was not an attractive proposition for a young woman raised in the rugged beauty of the Rocky Mountains. But I simply had to go, I had to try, and I was sure that not everyone in Nashville was a bigot. There are good people everywhere. So

Sheila and I went our separate ways. We'd had a lot of fun together, and we loved each other for a time. All the memories are good.

The year I spent working at the welfare department in Albuquerque changed my life forever. I saw firsthand the soft underbelly of American society. I realized that many people experience lives of suffering and deprivation. Not much had changed from the photographs of the Okies in those 1930s Farm Security Administration prints. The inequity and the poverty broke my heart, especially for New Mexico's poor Hispanic community. As a caseworker I helped a lot of people for a short time. I tried every way I could. I broke rules to help people. I still feel today that it was one of the most meaningful jobs I ever had. But I hoped that somehow I could do more with my songs, my art.

★

Cavalliere Ketchum and I remained friends after I left the university and I began working at the welfare department. We began to see that what I was trying to write about in my songs complemented his photographic work. I was trying to do as Pete Seeger had suggested Guthrie had done, to write about my world, what I saw and experienced. Cavalliere was taking photographs in the rural Hispanic villages along New Mexico Highway 14 South, in the Manzano Mountains—the little villages of Manzano, Torreón, Chilili, and Punta de Agua. They were about seventy miles southeast of Albuquerque.

Much of his work came from the village of Manzano. The people in his photographs were poor working people. They had little but love for one another. They lived in old adobe homes built by their families in generations past. They were farmers who grew a few beans and some corn on small plots, raised a few goats, chickens, and perhaps a few cattle. Some of them had a horse or two. For cash, they worked jobs in Mountainair, the largest town there in the mountains, or in Estancia, on the flatlands east of the mountains. Some drove to Albuquerque for work. Some, I am sure, received welfare assistance.

To photograph these families as intimately as Cavalliere did, he first had to gain their trust, the same as I had to do to help the people in my caseload. Cavalliere carried his camera in an old paper grocery sack. He said, "People might steal a camera bag from your car, but rarely an old, crumpled paper sack." He started by photographing the curious children in a village. He would print test strips and pass them out to the children. They would take the little photos home to show their families. Over time, he earned the families' trust enough to photograph them. He freely distributed many photographs of family members. Then, another family would see the prints and ask if he would photograph their family. Over time he made friends and gained broad access. He gave away hundreds of prints to these families for their participation as his subjects, and he became endeared to them. This went on for several years, and he would pick the best of his prints to represent them.

Cavie grew up in Arizona. He had Spanish ancestry, hence the name "Cavalliere," which was a last name on his mother's side. He was able to speak Spanish and English with his subjects, so his manner was nonthreatening. He was sincere and funny, so it was easy for people to relate to him. He was caring and disarming. It took time, but the trust he established enabled him to create some indelible portraits that revealed the soul of his subjects. Cavie once said to me, "Any photographer can take pictures of landscapes. The real challenge is photographing people."

Cavalliere always photographed in black and white, and he never carried much equipment. Most of his photographs were done with a Bronica camera in a square format. He believed in keeping it simple. The art is in the vision and the relationships, not in the equipment. His work was done with natural light. The important thing was what was before his lens, the people—capturing their essence.

I accompanied him on some of his trips to the area and met many of the people in his photographs. His rapport and relationship with the people were obvious. He was totally at ease with them, and they were completely at ease with him. He had something to say with his camera. You could see the people's entire lives in his photographs. They were ballads in black and white, outlines of lives that you could envision through them. He was doing what Woody Guthrie did, only with a camera.

Chapter 4

LEARNING THE BLUES
IN NASHVILLE

When I got to Nashville that fall of 1968, I needed a job. The four hundred dollars I'd started with wasn't going to last for long. But I figured there were poor people in Tennessee the same as in New Mexico, so I signed up to take the caseworker exam with the Tennessee Department of Human Services. That was the new nomenclature, "Human Services." All the welfare departments across the country were changing their official names to human services. It had a more appealing ring to it. After passing the civil service exam, I was hired in the Davidson County office of the Tennessee Department of Human Services in Nashville.

Welfare work in the South, however, had a much different feel to it than it did in New Mexico. The poor people weren't different. They were still the same desperate families I'd left behind in New Mexico. But instead of being mostly Hispanics, they were primarily African Americans. In New Mexico the feeling around the office was very casual and informal. The South was a much more formal place. The building was not a funky old warehouse as in New Mexico. It was a small, modern office building, and the women caseworkers dressed up much more. Most of the men caseworkers wore coats and ties, which we never did in New Mexico, and there were more women caseworkers than men. Things were done more by the book. There was not as much bending of the rules to help people as there was in New Mexico.

The county director was a sweet woman. She liked me and did all she could to help me fit in. I was in a supervisory unit with five women. Most of them were around my age. They were all conscientious and caring, and I got along well with them. However, my direct supervisor was not the experienced, wise, and empathetic person that Dorothy McMurphy was in New Mexico. She was stiff and professional, and we didn't get along that well.

But still, I did my best to help the people in my caseload. The caseworkers in the Nashville office were not used to seeing a young long-haired guy carrying a motorcycle helmet under his arm, and word got around fast about the new guy.

I stayed in that small studio apartment I'd rented in Hermitage, near Andrew Jackson's old home until October, then I moved to an apartment in Nashville. It was in an old house on Seventeenth Avenue South, near Music Row. My apartment had a small enclosed back porch with large windows. I built a big desk out of a piece of plywood and attached it to the wall under the windows. That's where I would write. I built a plywood platform for a bed, with two-by-four legs, and covered it with a four-inch-thick piece of foam rubber purchased at a salvage company. I went to a used furniture auction and purchased a used table and a few chairs for the kitchen.

I got to know the guy who lived downstairs in a musty basement apartment. His name was Owen Stratvert. There were pairs of shoes under his bed covered with mildew that needed a shave. He had attended the US Naval Academy at Annapolis for a year, but he returned to Tennessee and enrolled at Peabody College, which is now part of Vanderbilt University. He'd graduated with a degree in history and was working for the Tennessee State Library and Archives and was starting night law school. We hit it off right away. Owen was funny and smart, and over the next few weeks we polished off a few beers together as young men will do. Owen loved music, as I did, and I could hear his music from time to time upstairs. He liked rhythm and blues, which I was not that familiar with then, but it was quite popular with young people in the South. He loved Ray Charles and the Sweet Inspirations. He had one album that was a recording of a train passing through a thunderstorm—a sort of J. M. W. Turner in audio.

The engine in my old Willys had so much torque that when it started the sound reverberated and rolled around the inside in a deafening roar. The first time Owen got in the Willys with me, and I started it up, he said, "Humm, what's the brand name on this car, Okie?" From then on, the old Willys panel became known as "The Okie."

★

One morning at the welfare office, the first week in November, we were all sitting around the big table in the conference room in a staff meeting. I looked across the table and saw a beautiful young woman whom I'd never seen before at the office. She had long dark brown hair, and the darkest, brightest, brown eyes. Her skin was a dusky olive for, as it turned out, she was of Cherokee heritage on both sides of her family. She was like a song I could not turn off. She had on a printed batik dress, with little bells sewed to diamond points around the cuffs. I couldn't take my eyes off her. Who was this beautiful young woman?

After the meeting, I asked the women in my unit who she was, and they told me her name was Janice, and that she was in a work unit in another part of the building. I couldn't get her out of my mind. Finally, I decided to write her a note and ask her out, so as not to embarrass her or me in front of the other workers. I typed it out at home and persuaded one of my coworkers to deliver it to her. I told her she was beautiful, and would she consider going out with me? The answer came back that she would, though she later informed me I had misspelled a couple of words in my note!

She was twenty-four and had worked at the welfare office for two years, since graduating from Peabody College. I didn't have much cash, so I purchased a couple of steaks and some salad fixings and had her over for dinner in the big kitchen at my apartment. It wasn't much of a meal, because I'm not much of a cook, and I had reached the limits of my culinary capabilities. She agreed to a second date, and we went out to dinner, then we drove around in The Okie, stopping in Centennial Park in front of Nashville's full-sized replica of the Parthenon. It is an exact copy of the one on the Acropolis in Athens—only it's not a ruin. With my art history background, I told her that the chief architect of the Parthenon was Ictinus, and the chief sculptor was Phidias. I hoped she was impressed.

We began to see a lot of each other, almost every day for the next two weeks. I was head over heels. Then, I got sick with a horrible sinus infection and had to take a couple of days off work. She came by to see me with a new copy of the Beatles' *White Album*, which had just been released, as a gift. She loved music as much as I did, and being a Nashville native she had grown up with it. Pat Boone lived down the street when she was growing up. She'd gone to school with Eddy Arnold's daughters and Minnie Pearl's nieces. She had seen the Beatles perform in Memphis. She had a complete collection of the Kingston Trio's and Bob Dylan's albums. She knew more about music than I ever would. She was beautiful and smart. She was amazing.

We went together for a little over two weeks, and I asked her if she would marry me. She said she would, but she said, "Don't you think we should wait a little while?"

I said, "Sure."

So we waited another two weeks. We got married on Friday, December 13, 1968, at the Davidson County Courthouse. We went back to her house, told her astonished parents, and headed off to Gatlinburg and the Blue Ridge Mountains for a weekend honeymoon.

We returned to work the next week and there was much excitement as the word spread throughout the building. There's nothing like love to make everyone feel good. We moved into my funky old apartment on Seventeenth Avenue South, with the foam rubber mattress and Owen Stratvert below us playing his train in the thunderstorm album. We would be in bed at night, and here would come the train through the storm! It was funny. We were young people in love. Jan and Owen had known each other at Peabody. Both had graduated the same year, and she and Owen had been in several classes together. We all became good friends. We were young and happy, and the laughter was free.

★

Jan is a native Nashvillian and a true Tennessean. Her heart holds the same pride for Tennessee that my father's held for his native Oklahoma. She has relatives buried all over middle Tennessee. Her grandfather Campbell and two of her other grandparents were all railroad people. They worked for the L&N Railroad (Louisville and Nashville) in its heyday. Her grandfather was a bridge foreman for the L&N. He built wooden trestles and bridges all along the right-of-way. He was one-quarter Cherokee, and he was not afraid of heights. When his crew were afraid to paint the bronze statue of Mercury high atop the clock tower at Nashville's Union Station, he went up on ropes and painted it. There is Cherokee blood on both sides of the family, and Jan has always been proud of her Cherokee heritage. Jan's father worked in quality leather control at GENESCO, the General Shoe Company. He could feel a cowhide and tell you what kind of shoes could be made from it. His family came from the United Kingdom, some as early as the seventeenth century. Jan's mother played popular songs from sheet music on the piano, kindling Jan's love for music.

At Christmas in 1968, my parents decided to drive to Nashville and meet their new daughter-in-law. My father liked Jan. Of course! He loved to talk to anyone, and Jan was a good talker herself, so he had a new person to talk to!

After Christmas, my folks headed back to New Mexico. In leaving my father said it might be the last time we saw each other. I don't know why he said it, but maybe he knew something inside that we didn't. But the long drive was hard on him. He pushed himself. He died suddenly of heart failure the first week in February at age fifty-seven. It was hard on me. He was a caring man with a good heart, and I knew he loved me. I missed him. I still do.

At the Welfare Department, there was a state rule then that a husband and wife could not work in the same department. Since I had only worked at the Human Services for a few months and Jan had been there a couple of years, we decided that I would be the one to look for another job. I went to the employment office that January, in 1969, and discovered there was a new federally funded environmental health program starting under a federal grant at the Nashville Department of Public Health. There was a position available for a health educator. Well, if I could be a caseworker, why couldn't I be a health educator? The program was to control and reduce the Norway rat population in Nashville. Rats are pests. They carry and spread all manner of disease. It certainly wasn't glamorous, or where one would hope to spend one's time. But I needed a job, and somebody had to deal with those pesky rats. Of course, too, it was one of those jobs you could get with any bachelor's degree, even fine arts! So I moved over into the field of environmental health.

★

The director hired to run the rat control program was a sixty-three-year-old man from Mississippi. Our director of public health in Nashville was also from Mississippi, but I don't believe they knew each other previously. Our program director was an experienced administrator with a long history of working in government service. He had just returned to the states from Vietnam, where he had been an administrator in one of the USAID programs. He was a genial man, with a cordial but disciplined personality. He took his position seriously and was dedicated.

I liked him. He was grandfatherly. Unfortunately, though, he was disadvantaged by the Mississippi upbringing of his generation. He had not yet made it into the world of the late 1960s that followed the civil rights movement. Despite his affable managerial style, and even though I could see he was trying, it was hard for him to change his old Mississippi attitudes toward African Americans—and we had a number of African Americans in the program. Remember, this was early 1969. The South had just been through a wrenching decade of struggles for civil rights, and Martin Luther King Jr. had been assassinated in Tennessee less than a year before. There was understandably still a lot of resentment and anger in Nashville's Black community.

True to the Mississippi roots of his generation, our director could not seem to pronounce the word, "Negro." It always came out as "Nigra," or on occasion as "Niggero." This was that old white Mississippi dialect. There were many Black workers in our program, both as sanitarians and laborers working on the cleanup crews. They naturally noticed these mannerisms. They didn't say much, but they would glance at each other, and you could see in their faces and their body language how uncomfortable they were at times in the way he related to them.

In our program, we had a fleet of dump trucks, with three-man crews to each truck—all African Americans. There was a young white supervisor over the truck crews who appeared not too fond of his job and clueless in his manner. I never knew his background or how he was chosen for the position.

Sanitarians would go through a neighborhood, knocking on doors, explaining the program to the citizenry, and identifying trash to be picked up that could harbor rats. The truck crews would pick up the trash from backyards, vacant lots, and alleyways—anywhere rats could live. If rats were found, they were exterminated in their burrows with cyanide gas pumps—something that's quite dangerous and not much in use by health departments today.

The educational part of the program was intended to be implemented by health aides, who were women hired from the target communities. They would do outreach with the citizenry, going door-to-door with printed health pamphlets and informational materials. They would try to educate the citizens as to the health dangers of rats and improper sanitation. They would talk to residents and refer other health or welfare professionals as necessary to solve myriad health-related or social service issues. There were a lot of people helped by the health aid program. Oprah Winfrey was then a young local Nashville radio personality on WVOL, the soul music station in Nashville. She had the health aides on her radio show promoting the program. She was extremely helpful to us in getting the word out about our services.

As the health educator charged with implementing the educational part of the project, I oversaw the hiring, training, and administration of the health education outreach. In the summer of 1969, I was sent to Cincinnati, Ohio, for six weeks of training by the US Public Health Service. The training was done by two PhDs, contracted from the Community Development Department of Southern Illinois University in Carbondale. The training was attended by public health workers from all the cities where there was a federal rat control project. It was a good group of people. We all became friends—the instructors and the other trainees. In the evenings there was not much to do, so we mostly talked in our rooms, played cards, and drank whiskey. One of the US Public Health Service instructors said, "Wherever you can find four U.S. Public Health Service guys, you can find a fifth!"

The basic health education philosophy was that a person hired from a target community was better able to communicate with the citizenry in that community than was a professional person from outside the community. It seemed like common sense. After our training, we returned to our respective cities and conducted training sessions for our health aides. It was sophisticated training, which the health aides picked up on quickly. They were bright young women. They easily bought into this communication concept for health service delivery. The training sessions were conducted by those of us who were trained that summer in Cincinnati. An out-of-town person from another health department would come to Nashville to assist with the training of our health aides. At times, I was granted administrative leave to fly to other cities to help train their health aides with my counterparts in those cities.

I hired many of my health aides from the welfare rolls. They were eager to work. I had twelve of them; two were white women, and the rest were African Americans. They had all seen hard times. They were paid little, but they were incredibly dedicated. They worked hard and took pride in their work and their communities. They often discussed work issues they encountered among themselves and solved a lot of problems that way. They were not shy either. If they had something to say they would speak up, or get in your face, even to me. These courageous women may have lacked formal educations, but they were smart, and they wanted to help people. One of them eventually completed a master's degree in public health. A couple of others completed bachelor's degrees after the program ended.

There was a problem, however. The director of public health at that time was not supportive of the educational approach I was trained to implement; but he was only too glad to accept the federal money for the program. He once said to me, "I don't see how you expect *those people* to do what our professional public health nurses have not been able to do for years." He could not conceive that women of color, poor and lacking college degrees, could communicate better than his white public health nurses. Times had changed, but his mind was still in Mississippi. As the months and years went by, it became obvious that the health director didn't support our education program, which was mandated and a vital part of our federal grant. Here again, in rat control as in my welfare work, I saw in those target neighborhoods that people and their children were suffering, many living in poverty and in deplorable conditions.

★

One of the public health people I most admired in my Cincinnati training was an African American from Philadelphia named Rudy Sutton. Rudy was probably about twenty years older than me. He was bright and articulate, with a Philadelphia accent, and a personality that warmed your heart. Rudy once said to me, "Poverty in this country is by design." This was the first time I had ever heard of poverty discussed this way, and as a young man I was not sure I understood what he meant, but now I do. The United States is awash in wealth, but we cannot seem to distribute it equitably. We do not care for our less fortunate citizens. Our country was founded by rich slaveholders, for the benefit of rich slaveholders. It was set up for the rich and powerful to be in control, and they still are. It was—and is—by design.

Growing up in New Mexico, I was not around many Black people. (White people in New Mexico, though, were certainly capable of prejudice toward Native Americans and Hispanics.) Working at the rat control project was my introduction to Black culture. The value of my years at rat control was not what I learned about public health or controlling rats, it was what I was taught by my Black coworkers, what I learned about people, prejudice, and life.

We had some tremendous Christmas parties though. The health aides organized them and decorated the office. The truck crew guys would come in all dressed up. A record player that played 45 rpm records would be brought in by someone, and singles would be stacked up on the spindle: Bobby "Blue" Bland, B. B. King, Aretha Franklin, Otis Redding, Muddy Waters, Tyrone Davis, and other R&B artists. There would be dancing, and laughing, and telling old lies. As Richard Pryor would say, "Tell me some of them old lies of yours, so I can forget about the truth." When the party was over, little empty half-pint bottles of "100-pound" (100 proof) whiskey would be found tucked in corners here and there, and the punch bowl was always sufficiently spiked.

But there was also a sad, heartbreaking side too. One of my health aides was shot to death by a jealous boyfriend in front of a barbershop on Jefferson Street in North Nashville. I was invited to the funeral. I had never experienced anything like it—the emotion, the sorrow, the collective pain. All the suffering from so many years of racism, prejudice, and discrimination simply boiled over like a raw wound that would never heal. The death of a loved one pulled off the scab. The grieving mother was so distraught that she tried to climb into the casket with her deceased daughter to hold her one last time. There was screaming and yelling. The door was ajar in hearts that had been broken for a long time. I saw the strength the Black church renders to the Black community. People must have something strong to lean on when reality is so brutal.

Another of my aides was attacked on a lunch break by her angry ex-husband. He cut her face up with a knife. The plastic surgeon on call at the emergency room did a wonderful job. She healed amazingly well with tiny little scars that were almost unnoticeable. But what does a trauma like that do to the mind? What kind of PTSD lives on forever after that? These poor Black women were strong. They had to be. I was the one who took her downtown, with her face in bandages, to the Davidson County Courthouse to swear out a warrant for her assailant's arrest. I will never forget it as long as I live. I was still a young man in my mid-twenties, and there was a lot I had to learn, and a lot I had to deal with. Learn I did, but I could never learn enough. The buck dance banjo plays a broken tune.

Another of my health aides was a fantastic gospel singer. The church where she sang put on a special presentation honoring her. It was lively and boisterous, and the music was incredible. I had never experienced anything like this growing up in New Mexico. It was an education. It was the blues.

Later, when I had access to a recording studio in my music life, I invited her to come and record a few songs. She arrived with a small, thin, piano player dressed in a tight shiny black suit with a matching black cape. His hair was slicked and stood high in a pompadour. He wasn't Little Richard, but he looked the same. He pounded out the gospel accompaniment for her on the piano like he was driving a bulldozer, and with her husky voice from smoking two packs of Lucky Strikes a day, she stood at the microphone and belted out the old Dorothy Love Coates classic, "You Can't Hurry God"—"He may not come when you want him, but he's right on time." She was as authentic and majestic as the pyramids of Egypt. She sang in the church on Sundays and worked with me as a health aide during the week.

Some of these people I mentioned above are sitting with me on the cover of my third album for Capitol Records, *Blackjack Choir*. I didn't stage that cover. Those are the people I worked with, they're the real thing.

★

One day in January 1970, the project director told me that we'd had a cutback in our funding, and we were going to have to lay off several of our truck crew workers. That Friday a pink slip was inserted into several of their pay checks. The unlucky ones were terminated. No excuse or notice was given, and no severance compensation was paid.

That night our building burned down. One, or several, of the guys who'd been given pink slips took matters into their own hands. No one ever knew what caused the fire, but two-plus-two generally equals four.

We were given another building, an old vacant two-story house on Sixteenth Avenue South. Everything salvageable was taken from the other building and we were back up and running in a few days. But when you think of the waste, the effort, the time, the labor, the inconvenience, all because the director failed to handle the layoffs in a professional and compassionate manner, and in their anger and frustration the building was burned down. How much did all that cost? But we went on.

I had come to know one of the African American sanitarians, Henry Murphy, quite well. Murphy had grown up in Hattiesburg, Mississippi. Jan and I stopped off with Henry at his parents' home in Hattiesburg when we all attended a health conference in New Orleans. His mother cooked up a big batch of crab gumbo for us. Henry came to Nashville to attend college at Tennessee State University (TSU), a historically Black state university, established as separate but equal during the apartheid Jim Crow era in the South. TSU graduates take a lot of pride in their school, their sports teams, and their marching band. Wilma Rudolph, a TSU Tiger Belle sprinter, was the fastest woman in the world in 1960, winning three gold medals in the Rome Olympics. TSU is still primarily a Black university, but they now also accept white students. My older son, in fact, attended there for three years. It's the only state university in Nashville.

One afternoon the rat control director called me into his office. The truck crew supervisor position was open. The director asked me who I thought might handle the truck crews for us. I said, "What about Henry Murphy?"

The director furrowed his brow and looked at me like he was in deep thought. I said, "Henry Murphy is a college graduate, with a degree in political science."

"Murphy's a college graduate?" he animatedly said. As if he didn't know that all our sanitarians were college graduates. But Henry was Black, and in the director's Mississippi mind he had not imagined Murphy as a college graduate—or a potential supervisor.

I said, "You know, sir, all of the men on the truck crews are Black. Wouldn't it make sense to have a Black supervisor over the crews?"

"Oh, Jim," he said. "I don't know that Nashville is ready for that."

I was flabbergasted. Nashville's not ready! It wasn't Nashville that wasn't ready, it was him! He was having trouble wrapping his mind around a Black supervisor.

I said, "Can I be candidly honest with you, sir?"

"Sure, Jim."

"Well, I think some of the men here feel you are a little prejudiced."

"Me? Prejudiced?" he excitedly said. "I have nothing against the Nigras."

"Well, you asked me, sir, and I think it is worth considering promoting Murphy as supervisor over the truck crews. Just think it over." And I got up and left him to think.

As it turned out, he took my advice. He promoted Henry to supervisor; and as time went on, a mutual respect and friendship developed between the two of them. Henry, being from Hattiesburg, he'd been around old white Mississippians his whole life. He knew how to handle them. And the director discovered that a Black man could be a capable professional and a friend. I'm sure each of them learned some things from the other. Thirty years later, long after I left the program, the program had long been over, and the old director was no longer with us, Henry Murphy retired from the Metro Nashville Health Department as director of environmental health, overseeing all environmental aspects of the health department.

★

Henry had a 1956 black Ford Crown Victoria. There was an old oval speaker that sat on the transmission hump, with two wires that led up under the dashboard and connected it to the radio. The old speaker had a rip in it, and it sounded like a gravel road; but it was on that old crackling speaker, in Henry's old Ford, that I first heard B. B. King singing, "That's Why I Sing the Blues."

Henry and I became close friends. He educated me. We were the same age. He was young, smart, and had a lot understanding and feeling for people. He had grown up in the deep South. He had seen a lot. He knew the history and the truth. I learned a great deal from him. Henry introduced me to B. B. King's music, and I became a huge fan of the great bluesman. Henry is no longer with us, and I still miss him. I miss being able to call him and hear the gentle slowness in his speech and the wisdom in his voice.

B. B. played a date back then at the Tennessee State Prison in Nashville. Somehow, my enterprising health aides, who seemed to be able to manage any task, got us all access to watch the show from the wings at the prison. Those women could figure out about any situation if you turned them loose. It was a magnificent performance, with the prisoners, many of them Black, wildly cheering, and B. B. giving it everything he had playing the blues. I got to meet him and talk with him briefly. He was younger and thinner then, and he looked great in his spiffy double-breasted suit. Little did I know then that a few years later, he would play with me on one of my albums for Capitol Records.

Twenty years later, give or take, Henry Murphy invited me to a ceremony where he and his wife, Mary, were renewing their wedding vows. We were standing aside talking after the ceremony, and Henry said, "Jim Talley, when I met you, I was an angry young man, but you showed me there was another way. I learned a lot from you."

"Henry,' I said, "You didn't learn any more from me than I learned from you." We were both young once, and each of us had taught the other.

I stayed at rat control for almost three years, and I had developed a good reputation in the field of public health. I was offered a job with the Tennessee Department of Public Health. It was a significant increase in salary, and I simply had to take the job for my family. As I prepared to leave rat control, my health aides held a party for me. They elected a spokesperson to speak for them, and she said, "Mr. Talley, we all know you must leave us for your family's needs, but we want you to know how very much we love you. You have taught each of us so much."

Tears came to my eyes, I thanked them, but I said, "You think I have taught you, but you are really the ones who have done the teaching." That was the absolute truth. I received much more education than I ever gave. I was with the state health department for about a year, until I signed with Atlantic Records.

★

DeFord Bailey was also someone my health aides introduced me to. DeFord was an African American harmonica virtuoso—and I mean virtuoso! He was born in 1899. His mother died when he was only one year old. At age three he contracted polio. His father's sister and her husband raised him as foster parents in Smith County, Tennessee. While recovering from polio, he was given a harmonica to play in bed. His foster mother would also strap a little banjo around his neck, and he learned to play it, as well as the guitar, eventually.

DeFord was a member of the Grand Ole Opry from 1927 to 1941. The Opry show went on the air back then with DeFord playing his "Pan American Blues." He was a bona fide star on the radio. He traveled with Bill Monroe, Roy Acuff, and other Opry acts throughout the South. Bill Monroe once said, "When I started out, nobody knew who I was, but everyone knew DeFord."

In those years on the road in the 1930s, he was continually denied accommodations in all the southern hotels because of his race. He often had to sleep under a blanket in the car or the bus, or in private Black homes—if they could be found. Once, it was either sleep in a jail or a funeral home. He chose the funeral home. He said, "I told them I would quit before I'd spend the night in jail!" He told me that sometimes the white musicians would try to sneak him into a hotel, but that could be dangerous if he was discovered. He could not eat in restaurants with the white musicians. They had to bring his food out to him, and he would eat in the car or bus. Playing his music was the easy part.

My health aides knew he lived in the public housing high-rise for the indigent elderly. Knowing my interest in music, they took me to meet him. DeFord was always ready to perform if you went to see him. Each time I visited him he would play his harmonica and his guitar for me. He enjoyed playing for me because I was a musician. He'd play, "The Fox Chase," "Ain't Gonna Rain No More," "Ice Water Blues," "Pan American Blues," "Dixie Flyer Blues," and his remarkable version of "John Henry." He could play the melody of a song and keep the rhythm chugging along under it—an incredibly difficult thing on the harmonica, but effortless for him.

The polio of his youth left him with a severe curvature in his back. He was only about four feet ten inches tall. He was also left-handed, and he learned to play the guitar upside down, with the bass strings on the bottom and the treble strings on the top of the fretboard. (My friend Jim Rooney plays this same way, as did Jimi Hendrix.) He fingerpicked his guitar, like Mississippi John Hurt. He would play a song for me on his guitar, then he would say, "Now, you can't do that, can you?"

I would say, "No, I can't," and he would laugh his little cackling laugh.

DeFord felt he had been cheated and betrayed by the Opry and was quite bitter. They fired him in 1941, saying that he refused to learn new material, but this was an excuse. The songs he had been playing were signed to the American Society of Composers, Authors, and Publishers (ASCAP), but when Broadcast Music Incorporated (BMI) was established in 1939 as a rival performing rights society, they signed exclusive licensing agreements with the radio stations and went to war with ASCAP. The Grand Ole Opry station, WSM in Nashville, affiliated with BMI, and under their license they were prohibited from playing any songs licensed to ASCAP. This was all beyond DeFord's control, but DeFord's classic repertoire from the 1920s and 1930s were all licensed with ASCAP, not BMI. Finally, ASCAP and BMI settled their licensing dispute, and stations were permitted to play songs signed to either performing rights society, but the Opry did not rehire DeFord. I couldn't blame him for his bitter feelings. He loved his music as much as any musician, and the Opry took away his music and his livelihood. What was he supposed to do, create an entire new repertoire of songs in 1941? What people wanted to hear were his classic songs that were familiar to them.

For years after he was dismissed from the Opry, he ran a shoeshine stand in Nashville. My wife had been to his shoeshine stand several times with her dates in college to see him and hear him play. I took several people over the years to DeFord's little apartment. I took Peter Guralnick to see him. I took Hans Ziemann, a German journalist and author to see him. Hans was on assignment for the German magazine *Stern*. Hans was a serious student of the blues and a good blues guitarist, and he was well aware of DeFord. Someone in Nashville told Hans to contact me, that I could take him to see DeFord. I did, and Hans and I have remained friends for the rest of our lives.

But I could never get DeFord to consider doing any new recordings. He felt betrayed there as well. When Pete Seeger recorded an album in Nashville, he asked DeFord to record with him, but DeFord turned him down. He saw almost no royalties from his early Brunswick and Victor recordings from the late 1920s. Finally, David Morton, who was then with the Nashville Public Housing Authority, took a profound interest in DeFord and managed to get him to record many of his old songs on a quality tape recorder that David purchased and set up in his apartment. David authored a biography of DeFord's life, *A Black Star in Early Country Music*, and was significant in seeing him posthumously inducted into the Country Music Hall of Fame in 2005. Ken Burns featured DeFord in his 2019 series on country music, introducing him to a new audience. DeFord died in 1982 at the age of eighty-two. I played "John Henry" at his funeral and at a memorial service the following year to dedicate his tombstone. Bill Monroe and Roy Acuff were sitting behind me. Thank you, health aides, for introducing me to this southern music legend.

Chapter 5

JOHN HAMMOND, CLIVE DAVIS, AND JERRY WEXLER

While I was working in welfare and public health, I was writing songs in the evenings and trying to engage with publishers when I could get an appointment. I tried to write each night. I would take a nap after supper. Then, when Jan and our little son had gone to bed, I would write for a few hours, moving thoughts and words around on the page, then going back to bed around 2:00 A.M. and getting up again at 6:30 to get ready for work.

When I came to Nashville I was not an experienced songwriter, nor did I have any understanding of the music business. I had never been in a radio station. Most of the roots music I liked wasn't even played on the radio. I did not realize before coming to Nashville what a narrow channel the Nashville music business was navigating. There were no college programs then, like there are now at Belmont University, Middle Tennessee State University, and other schools that teach students how the music business works.

But by visiting with publishers, I quickly discovered that the Nashville music business only wanted a certain kind of song. They wanted love songs, more love songs, and more love songs. Especially, as one publisher told me, they wanted songs that put women up on a pedestal, like Charley Pride's "Kiss an Angel Good Morning." Women, I was told, were the listeners of country music radio!

Nashville sure as hell didn't want what I was writing or wanted to write. I was swimming against the current, and the current was strong. I wanted to be an artist. I wanted to write about life—all aspects of American life and our culture. I wanted to write about people and their struggles in this world. I wanted to write from the heart, not for the charts. I wanted to chronicle our society the way Woody Guthrie did. Despite the appreciation for Bob Wills that my father had instilled in me, I was still a folksinger at heart, and apparently I was in the wrong town. Bob Dylan may have come to Nashville to record several albums, but that was simply to use the high-quality studio musicians that Nashville was famous for. Dylan was not trying to be a country artist, and Nashville was not interested in any music that was not hard country. It was all geared to a Top 40 country radio format because that was the exposure and marketing vehicle that the Nashville music business used to sell records. There was absolutely no room for anything else in Nashville.

I heard John Hartford's song "Gentle on My Mind," which Glen Campbell released. I thought it was a great song and more along the line of what I was interested in writing. I learned that Glaser Brothers Publishing had published the song, so I went to see them.

The Glaser brothers were Tompall, Chuck, and Jim. Their voices blended well, and they did a lot of group backup work in Nashville. They sang the backup on the wonderful Marty Robbins album *Gunfighter Ballads and Trail Songs*, which I dearly loved. I sang those songs around the campfires at Philmont in the summers of 1961 and 1962 when I worked there. Tompall was the oldest, Chuck was the middle one, and Jim was the youngest. Tompall and Jim were good songwriters, and Chuck was doing most of the work in the publishing company, listening to songs from young writers and trying to find hits.

I took my songs to Chuck, and he began listening and critiquing them for me. I was writing about other subjects by then, beyond my New Mexico songs. I was trying to learn and find my way as a Nashville songwriter. Chuck would listen to what I brought him and teach me about constructing a song: about bridges, choruses, and hooks. How to build a song dramatically, and the importance of a good melody. He taught me the basic rules of commercial songwriting, but I kept struggling to fit that mold. I liked working with Chuck and I valued his guidance. I wound up with boxes of home-recorded tapes, but my early songs frankly were still not that good. I kept at it, though. I wanted to become a good songwriter.

Many people in Nashville cowrite. It is encouraged. It expands the sphere of influence to get them noticed and recorded. But I must confess I have never had much success writing with other people. I have tried it a few times, but nothing very satisfying ever came from it. Some of my songs have come very quickly, but most of them I work on for a long time, changing them, setting them aside, returning to them again, making sure they say what I want them to say. It takes me a long time, sometimes years.

Not long after I met them, the Glasers moved their operation to a new building they'd purchased on Nineteenth Avenue. It was a large old two-story stucco house, and they started building a recording studio on the second floor.

About this same time, Cavalliere Ketchum had moved from Albuquerque to the University of Wisconsin to teach photography. But he and I continued to keep in touch, and we were determined to try to publish our joint project with his photographs and my New Mexico songs. (This would eventually become *The Road to Torreón*, which was finally released some twenty years later in 1992. More about that later.) I felt I needed to record better demos of those songs with some quality Nashville musicians, to better present the project. The Glaser brothers' studio was still under construction, but Chuck said if I would pay for the musicians and the tape, he would record the demos for me. Paying the musicians was not easy for me then on my salary, but Jan and I had a few extra dollars from our IRS tax refund. It would be just enough. I paid the musicians their standard demo fee, and Chuck helped me record the songs. The studio was not finished, so there was no mixing board or sixteen-track tape machine. Chuck recorded the project straight to a four-track machine, setting the levels himself. The session was completed in one night with the excellent musicians that Chuck often used for his demos. The recordings sounded good when we were finished. I can't recall all the musicians now, but the one that stood out to me was the lead guitar player, Doyle Grisham.

These songs were the ones I had written from my caseworker experience in New Mexico. I was trying to follow Pete Seeger's advice from our 1967 meeting. But since the Glasers had no outlet for these New Mexico folk songs, I took the demo tapes to a few other publishers to get other opinions of them.

It was nearly impossible to see executives at the record labels. They kept themselves insulated. Young songwriters were encouraged to first seek out publishers, who would work with them and try to get their songs recorded by established artists. The publisher was the first step in the clearing process. Sometimes a publisher would pitch one of their writers to a label as an artist—especially if the writer had a good voice and a few songs already recorded by other artists. But in Nashville then, the only recording artists signed had to be hard country—which I was not.

I still felt, however, that our joint project of songs and photographs was artistically worthy. One of the publishers I took the demos to was United Artists Publishing, who also had a record label. At that time, songwriter Billy Edd Wheeler was working for United Artists Publishing and was listening to the songs young writers brought in. I had always loved Billy Edd's writing. Perhaps you are not familiar with his name, but you've probably heard his song "Jackson," recorded by Johnny Cash and June Carter. Several of his songs had been recorded by the Kingston Trio, and I had a lot of respect for him. To me, he was a folk songwriter, so I was excited when he agreed to meet with me.

We sat in Billy Edd's office and listened to the New Mexico demos, and when we finished, he said, "Well, I feel like I have been listening to sociology here. I don't know what we could do with these songs in Nashville." He said, "You have a good voice. You really should be the artist on these yourself."

So I began to try and figure out how that might happen. Who would care about the *necesitados* from the Southwest? It was becoming patently obvious to me that no one in Nashville was going to be interested in songs about poor Hispanics.

★

After Jan and I were married, we moved from my old apartment on Seventeenth Avenue to a small two-bedroom rental house on Acklen Avenue, just off Natchez Trace in Nashville. In November 1969 we brought our first son, Reuben James, whom we had named after a Woody Guthrie song, home to that little house. Our landlord and his wife lived down the street. They were good people and did what they could to make us comfortable. I built a little writing desk in the corner of the living room as I had done in my old Seventeenth Avenue apartment.

I had a 1966 Martin D-28 guitar on a stand next to the desk that I'd purchased in Albuquerque in 1967. On the desk was a small Sony reel-to-reel tape machine. I built a wooden stand to hold the microphones for recording my songs. One day, Jan was holding our son, without a diaper, and I said, "Please don't hold him over my guitar with no diaper. He might pee on my guitar."

She disgustedly said, "He's not going to pee on your guitar!" As she was saying that, however, right on cue, Reuben James was peeing all over it. A Martin guitar can take a lot.

In 1970 we purchased our first home on Cedar Lane, between Belmont Boulevard and Hillsboro Pike. The house was a one-and-a-half-story brick Cape Cod design, with the staircase in the center. Once we were in our house, however, we discovered all the things that were wrong with it. We were so naïve. We had no idea what to look out for. Right away, we discovered that the roof was leaking, but we were so poor we could not afford a new roof. We managed to finance a roof with monthly payments over two years with Sears. We also discovered that the electrical fuse panel for the entire house was only sixty amps. We had to install a new hundred-amp breaker panel. There was no air-conditioning. We went for a couple of years with two window units that were left by the sellers, and we ran a big attic fan that kept the house cool at night. The fan was so powerful it drew air down the chimney in the living room, then up the stairs, and out through the attic vents. Every now and then we had to chase a bird out of the living room that had been sucked down the chimney.

We had no furniture other than my homemade platform bed with the foam rubber mattress, the baby's bed and changing table, a couple of used chests of drawers, and the old auction furniture I'd purchased for my Seventeenth Avenue apartment. There was no furniture in the dining room or the living room for several years. We purchased two canvas director's chairs and used an old cable spool for a coffee table. We were given a long worktable that Jan's grandfather had used at his L&N Railroad shop when he'd been a bridge foreman. That became my writing table in the living room. The floors were covered with old rose-colored wall-to-wall carpet in the living room and a dark printed wall-to-wall carpet, with pink and white magnolias, in the dining room. The walls had old wallpaper in every room. We eventually steamed off all the wallpaper in the house, filled the cracks and gouges in the plaster, and painted the rooms. We lived in this condition for several years and tried to add a few furniture items as we could on my meager salary.

Shortly after we moved into our Cedar Lane home, I met Larimore Burton, a young Nashville attorney. Larry was six years older than me, around thirty-one years old. He was from a wealthy family that was in the insurance business in Nashville. His grandfather A. M. Burton was one of the founders of the Life and Casualty Insurance Company in Nashville. Larimore was one of the grandsons. He'd graduated from Vanderbilt University and Vanderbilt Law School and had worked as an assistant US attorney in Nashville under Bobby Kennedy as attorney general.

Like so many young lawyers I have met in my life, after lawyering for a while, Larry was not happy with the law as a career. I think he was bored with it and was looking for something more exciting and more challenging—and where he didn't have to bill hours. The music business seemed to offer him that possibility. He didn't know that much about how the music business worked, but he was trying to learn. He took an interest in me and began regularly coming to our house. As a lawyer by day, he always wore a business suit and tie, which often looked like he'd slept in it. Since we had little furniture, we'd sit around on the old carpet in the living room, leaning against the wall, or propped up on one elbow, and talk. Larry chain-smoked cigarettes, and we would talk about the music business and how we might conquer it. He believed in my songwriting and my voice. Larry introduced me to Ed Shea, who was then head of ASCAP in Nashville, the performing rights organization (along with BMI) that collects broadcast royalties paid to songwriters and publishers when their music was played on radio and television.

I loved Ed Shea. He had an effusive personality and was a consummate public relations guy. His enthusiasm bubbled over. Before coming to ASCAP, he had been executive director of the Nashville Chamber of Commerce. He was always looking for good young writers to sign to ASCAP. I don't know how he did it, but each year on Christmas Eve, he would knock on our door with gifts for us. Usually, it was some item with the ASCAP logo, along with candy and other items, and always a bottle of liquor of some kind. One year it was a nice ASCAP ashtray; one year, cufflinks; but every year it was something. This went on for all the years he was at ASCAP. I don't know how many young writers he visited on Christmas Eve, but Jan and I were impressed with his attention. It made us feel like he cared about us.

Ed felt that many of my songs would be perfect for Johnny Cash. I had always considered Cash a folksinger, even though his records were produced and distributed as country. He was then probably my closest kindred spirit in Nashville. Cash at that time also had his network television show. As head of Nashville's ASCAP office, Ed arranged a meeting with Cash to introduce us. We drove to nearby Hendersonville, Tennessee, about twenty miles northeast of Nashville—where Cash's office and home were located. Cash's office was run by his sister, Reba. Ed and I were instructed to first check in with Reba at the office, before proceeding to Cash's house. We got to the office and Ed went in to see Reba. He came back to the car quite upset. He said, "Reba says we can't see Johnny today." I don't know what the problem was, I never knew. But Ed was miffed at the rejection and Reba's failure to notify him in advance of the cancellation. He was a businessman, head of ASCAP in Nashville, and he was slighted. His ego was bruised. Ed had taken his time and made an effort. After that Ed wouldn't try to see Cash again. That ended my chance to meet Cash.

Johnny did eventually record one of my songs, "W. Lee O'Daniel and the Light Crust Dough Boys." It was fifteen years later, when Steve Popovich was head of Polygram and pitched it to him. But I feel that if I could have met Johnny back in the early 1970s, he would have recorded many of my songs over the years. You work hard to create your breaks, but sometimes the planets simply don't line up.

I kept writing songs and recording them at home with my guitar on my home tape recorder, but I still had not yet found a comfortable fit with any Nashville music publisher. I couldn't bring myself to fit the mold they wanted. My friend the songwriter Steve Young ("Seven Bridges Road") once said to me, "I would sell out, but I just don't know how to do it!" I was sort of the same as Steve. I left Glaser Brothers Publishing on good terms as I was never contractually signed to their publishing company. Chuck had been working and developing me, but he was understandably more devoted to his writers who were trying to write more commercial country songs. The Glasers had registered the copyrights on my New Mexico songs, but Chuck signed them back to me when I left. I had paid for the demos, and I'm sure he felt they could never do anything with them.

I was still working a day job, and I didn't have a lot of time for appointments with publishers. I also wanted to pursue the New Mexico project with Cavalliere Ketchum's photographs. As I thought about it, I wondered if perhaps John Hammond at Columbia Records in New York might be interested. He had signed Bob Dylan and Leonard Cohen, and maybe he might appreciate what Cavalliere and I were trying to do with our project. So I wrote to Hammond in New York, introducing myself, and I asked if he would meet with me if I came to New York. He wrote back and indicated that he would.

John Hammond didn't need his salary from Columbia Records. His mother was a Vanderbilt. He was simply a devoted appreciator of unique music and a tremendous talent scout. He was around fifty-seven at that time and had a long record of discovering talent, from Bessie Smith to Count Basie, Billie Holiday, Benny Goodman, Aretha Franklin, as well as Dylan, Leonard Cohen, and others. So Larry Burton and I drove to New York for my meeting with John Hammond. Larry thought it was a worthy adventure, and he footed the cost of the gas and the hotel in New York.

I went to John Hammond's office at "Black Rock," the CBS Building on Fifty-Seventh Street, for my meeting. I took the elevator to Hammond's floor and was directed to his corner office. His secretary, Liz Gilbert, greeted me. I explained that I was the guy from Nashville, and that I had an appointment. Hammond seemed delighted that I had come. I took out the box of Cavalliere's photographs and showed them to him. I explained our idea to release the photographs and songs together. John put my demo tape on his tape machine, and we listened. He liked the songs and liked the whole idea of the project.

John saw the potential of publishing the project as a book-LP combination. He had done similar things with Pete Seeger—small boxed sets. He set up an appointment for me with Aaron Asher at Holt, Rinehart and Winston publishers for the following day, to show them the photographs. Holt, Rinehart was then owned by CBS. The next day I met with Asher. He looked at the Cavie's photographs and said, "Well, if John wants to do the music, we'd love to do the accompanying book." He said he would talk with John about it.

I went back the next afternoon to see Hammond, and he had spoken with Asher. He was excited about the possibilities, and he then took me across the building to meet Goddard Lieberson, who was the chairman of CBS Records. Goddard was around sixty years old then and was set up in a gigantic corner office with white sofas and stuffed chairs, white carpets, elegant coffee tables, and paintings on the wall. It was a stunning, tasteful, office—designed to impress, and it did. Hammond introduced me to Goddard, who epitomized power, money, prestige, and class. He was extremely cordial and gracious. He was a classically trained musician and composer, who appreciated artistry—and this was an artistic project. It wasn't commercial Nashville. Hammond told him about speaking with Asher and showed Goddard Cavalliere's photographs. Everyone was excited. It seemed like a done deal. John loaded me up with a slew of albums he'd produced to take home with me,

including two from a new artist he'd recently signed named Bruce Springsteen. He laughed and told me that Springsteen was not selling well yet, but
that he knew he would. He said, Columbia wanted to drop Dylan after his
first two albums. "They said he wasn't selling, and he can't sing."

I told them, "Over my dead body, the kid's a genius and he will eventually sell millions." In parting, I told Liz Gilbert she should come and visit
Jan and me in Nashville.

Larry Burton and I drove back to Nashville. We were both excited. We
thought it had been a wonderful and worthwhile trip. In a couple of weeks,
word came from Liz in Hammond's office that Clive Davis wanted to meet
with me before any deal was finalized. Clive was then president of Columbia Records. He was under Goddard Lieberson, but above Hammond in
the pecking order. As it turned out, Clive was the real decider—not Goddard or John. They needed his support and promotion for the project to
work. Clive was scheduled to be in Memphis in a couple of weeks for the
Memphis Music Awards, and perhaps, they asked, could I meet with him
there? As it turned out, I had to be in Memphis that same week for a Tennessee health conference. I could duck out of the conference and meet
with Clive. I was at the Peabody Hotel and Clive was staying at the new,
exclusive, Rivermont Holiday Inn in Memphis. An appointment was set up
for one afternoon that week.

I didn't know what to wear to the meeting. How should I present myself?
I finally decided to wear a double-breasted blue suit. But should I wear a tie
or not? I decided I would wear an open shirt with a yellow silk ascot—not so
formal. I had no idea what I was doing, but I knew this was an extremely
important meeting. In hindsight, I'm sure I looked as ridiculous as I felt.

I carried my guitar and Cavalliere's photographs and went to the Rivermont Hotel. I took the elevator to Clive's floor, knocked on his door, and
was escorted into his suite. Clive was in his early forties then. He was there
with several of his young staff associates. They were all young guys dressed
in T-shirts and jeans with long hair. They looked at me like, "Who is this
yokel?" At least that's how I felt they were looking at me. The only thing
missing in their demeanor was that they were not all sucking on lemons!
But Clive was gracious, as you would expect an elegant and powerful president of a large company to be. He was there to pass judgment on another
of "Hammond's Follies," as Hammond's signings—Dylan, Cohen, and
Springsteen—were referred to then by some at the label.

He looked at the photographs and said kindly, "Please play us a few of the songs from your project." I was again shaking like a leaf inside, like I had been in 1967 when Pete Seeger asked me to play for him. I gently fingerpicked maybe three or four of the New Mexico songs on my guitar, and the meeting seemed to come to an end without any real exposure of feelings from Clive or his staffers. His guys were all waiting for Clive's reaction, which he was holding close. I put my guitar back in the case and got up to leave. His associates had said nothing the entire time, not a word. They just looked on sullenly, waiting for Clive's reaction.

Clive personally walked me back down the hall to the elevator, and as the car arrived, he shook hands with me and said, which I still remember to this day: "You're obviously an incredibly talented young man. Thank you for coming by and playing for us. We'll be in touch."

But somehow, I knew right then, from the way the meeting had gone, that this deal was over. It was just in my gut, and the way he said, "We'll be in touch." I'm sure he went back to his hotel room and his young cohorts said, "What was that? Another of Hammond's deals?" The big commercial groups then at Columbia were the big horn bands, Blood, Sweat and Tears and Chicago. For these young New Yorkers, who had probably never been to the state of New Mexico, these simple folk songs about poor Hispanics in the Southwest must have seemed like something from Mars. What the hell could they do with that? It wasn't rock and roll. It was the same as in Nashville. Who were going to care about the *necesitados* of rural New Mexico? That stuff isn't COMMERCIAL! Who cares what John Hammond thinks! None of his acts sell worth a damn anyway, and now he brings us this! Maybe what Pete Seeger had told me five years earlier was a recipe for disaster. No one cared. I wasn't Woody Guthrie. But I tried to keep the faith.

I called Jan at home in Nashville and told her that I didn't think the meeting with Clive Davis went well. I drove back to Nashville and began to wait for someone to "be in touch." No one called. I called Liz in Hammond's office, and she said she didn't know what was going on, which is what any good music business secretary would tell you. A few more weeks went by, and no word.

One afternoon, on a weekend, I was outside playing with the dog and my little three-year old son in our backyard. Jan came out and said there was a guy on the phone from New York. His name was Jerry Wexler.

Jerry Wexler! I knew Jerry Wexler. He was with Atlantic Records. How did he get in this picture? I went in the house and answered the phone, and in his thick New York accent Jerry said, "James, this is Jerry Wexler in New York. I want to sign you to Atlantic Records."

I later found out from Liz that John was quite upset that my signing had been nixed by Clive Davis. When John couldn't get me signed at Columbia, he sent Wexler a demo tape of four other songs that I'd left with him. They were simple demos that I had recorded at Woodland Studios in Nashville with a bass player named Jack Williams and a couple other musicians. One song was called "One Less Child." It was about a young boy who had died of a heroin overdose in Harlem. He was only eleven years old. I'd read an article about it in *Time Magazine,* and it moved me and troubled me, so I wrote a song about it. The other song was a simple demo of "Mississippi River Whistle Town," which I had written on one of my public health trips to Memphis. I had seen some old Black men fishing down on the banks of the Mississippi. They were sitting there on old wooden benches with their lines in the water. They were laughing and talking and fishing in the Mississippi. In writing songs, I would see an image like those old men, and I would use my imagination to fill in a story around that image. That's the way I always write. I'm looking for *that* image.

Jerry Wexler had listened to my four-song demo, and of course he had great respect for John Hammond. The recommendation from John and the four songs was all it took for Jerry. Based on that, he wanted to sign me and develop me as a writer and an artist for Atlantic. Jerry was then opening an Atlantic office in Nashville, but it was not yet functional. Not long before, he had signed John Prine, Doug Sahm, and Willie Nelson to Atlantic. I didn't know it then, but Jerry had developed Aretha Franklin's career after it stalled at Columbia. He freed the soul in her. He'd also produced Ray Charles, Wilson Pickett, Dusty Springfield, Willie Nelson, and a plethora of R&B talent. But Jerry also liked country music, especially singer-songwriters. I didn't know it then, but later he told me that he had gone to college at Kansas State University. His mother had wanted him to get out of New York City for college, and while at Kansas State he had developed a love for country music.

Jerry flew from New York to Nashville to meet me. He called and asked me to meet him at his hotel and gave me his room number. I went to his room and knocked on the door. Jerry came to the door dressed in a white T-shirt and white boxer shorts.

He said, "Come on in, James. I'm on the phone." So the first time I met Jerry Wexler, he was in his underwear.

Jerry asked me what I was doing, where I was working, how much were they paying me. I told him I was at the Tennessee Department of Public Health. I had just been promoted to a Health Educator III and was making $900 a month. Jerry said, "James, I am going to pay you $250 a week. I want you to quit your job and write songs for me for a year." I thought I had died and gone to heaven! Jerry didn't even mention the publishing. Maybe that was an oversight, or perhaps he just wanted me to develop as a writer and would deal with that later.

We arranged a meeting with Jerry at ASCAP in Nashville. We signed a contract and took pictures with me, Jerry, Ed Shea, Larry Burton. The contract called for me to deliver an album to Atlantic within one year. The next week a case of wine arrived at our house from Jerry. Jan and I knew nothing about wine in those days. We didn't know one grape from another. Neither of us had grown up in wine-drinking families. But here was a whole case of expensive cabernet sauvignon from Jerry Wexler in New York.

Chapter 6

AT THE OLD HOUND'S EAR STUDIO

Larry Burton, over time, had gotten deeper into the music business. He decided he needed a studio to make good presentations of the acts he wanted to develop and manage. So he purchased one of those grand old houses on Music Row. It was on Seventeenth Avenue South across the street from the ASCAP Building. He set up a recording studio there and furnished it with state-of-the-art recording equipment. The studio was on the main floor. The control room was in the large entry hall. The various other main-floor rooms were used to separate the instruments, which is essential for multitrack recording. This allows for separation of each instrument on its own individual track on the tape.

Since I had carpentry skills, I built baffles and did carpentry work at the studio in the evenings and on weekends. In exchange for my carpentry work, I was given studio time to record my songs. Larry was looking for other talent and was recording them as well. It was 1973 by now, and I started working on what would become my first album, *Got No Bread, No Milk, No Money, But We Sure Got a Lot of Love.* After my New Mexico songs had been so soundly rejected, I decided I was damn sure going to make a country album this time around! If they wanted country, I was going to deliver country!

That summer my mother and her sister, my Aunt Ruth, had come to visit Jan and me in Nashville. My mother picked up her sister in Stillwater on the way from New Mexico. I had found a stash of Bob Wills records at Buckley's Record Shop on Church Street, and I was playing them a lot. My friends would come by, and I would say, "Hey, listen to these Bob Wills recordings!" I would put them on, and play songs like "Misery," "Boot Heel Drag," or "Stay All Night, Stay a Little Longer," and before long my young friends would find some reason they had to leave. They were all listening to the Beatles, the Rolling Stones, or some other rock group. They couldn't take Bob Wills. But I loved those Bob Wills albums.

I was telling Aunt Ruth about the Bob Wills records I'd found, and she said, "Well, you should have heard him when he was playing with W. Lee O'Daniel and the Light Crust Doughboys." She explained that Wills had started out in Texas with "Pappy" O'Daniel and the Light Crust Doughboys. She said the theme song was "Pass the Biscuits, Pappy." I didn't know all this, but I thought W. Lee O'Daniel and the Light Crust Doughboys was a terrific image and would make a great title for a song. So I wrote a song about my parents, my Aunt Ruth, and their friends all going to a dance in Tulsa to hear the Light Crust Doughboys. Jan, who loves doing research, and is incredibly good at it, went to the Country Music Foundation Library and did some research on Pappy O'Daniel. As it turned out, by the time Wills left Texas and moved his operation to Tulsa, he was no longer associating with the Light Crust Doughboys. In fact, his drinking had led to a falling out with O'Daniel, but the name was so cool, I had to write it that way. Poetic license. It has been one of my most famous songs, ultimately recorded by Johnny Cash and Alan Jackson.

For my first album, I had a concept, as I had with my New Mexico songs. It would be centered around my family and where I came from, as Pete Seeger had advised: "W. Lee O'Daniel," "Got No Bread, No Milk, No Money, But We Sure Got a Lot of Love" "Mehan, Oklahoma," "Blue-Eyed Ruth and My Sunday Suit," "To Get Back Home." All those memories of my growing up with my Okie relatives—just like Woody did it—observe, listen, write.

Most country albums were produced then with what the producer felt would be two or three potential hit songs. These would be the singles. It didn't matter who wrote them or published them, so long as they were great songs. These quality compositions were slated to be released as the radio and jukebox singles. Beyond those stellar songs, the rest of the album would be filler material. The filler songs were often written by the artist, the producer, or published by the producer's publishing company, or another publisher who had strongly courted the producer. These were the "B-Sides." Every A-Side single needed a B-Side, and B-Side singles and album cuts generated the same mechanical royalties as the hits. (Mechanical royalties are the royalties record labels pay to a publisher for the right to "mechanically" reproduce the song.) If you could control the songs that went on an album, you could get rich. That's the way it was done, which was why, when you purchased a country album, you often had only two or three good songs and a bunch of mediocre filler tunes.

I hated that approach. I wanted to make a country album, like the Beatles produced their albums, where you put the needle down on the first track, listened through the entire album, and were not disappointed. Of course, to accomplish this you almost had to write your own material, and you had to be a good writer. Record labels like songwriter artists because their material fits their voices and their style. I wanted to take my time in the studio and experiment with my production and try different things. With Larry Burton owning the studio I could afford the time to do that. I was impressed with the albums that Mickey Newbury had recorded with Wayne Moss at his Cinderella studio in Madison, Tennessee. There was obviously a lot of care and time in those productions. I also loved Merle Haggard's albums, which always contained great songs and had great instrumentation and production. Of course, both of those guys were tremendous songwriters, and I learned a lot from them. They were my idols and teachers. I had also discovered from a review in *Time* magazine, The Band's second album, *The Band.* Those guys were making great albums that were listenable all the way through, with incredible musicianship—no filler!

Growing up, I had never played much with bands. I had always played as a solo act, as a folksinger, just me and my guitar, or with another guitarist or two in a duo or trio. I was unsure how to incorporate drums with my music. Then I heard the way Merle Haggard produced his tribute album to Jimmie Rodgers. That album showed me how to include drums with more simple folk style acoustic music. That was the template I used in producing my first album, and I kept it that way.

I started working on my first album in the spring and summer of 1973 at Larry Burton's studio, which he had named Hound's Ear Studio. Many young musicians love doing studio work and were eager to help. They were all guys around my age, and they were willing to play on spec (or speculation), as it was called, especially if they liked the songs and the artist. Even the major studio players would often do this for their friends. That meant they would play and record, with the hope of eventually being paid when the project was picked up and released by a record label. Personally, I was always very sparing in asking musicians to play for me for free, but on my first album I had no choice. *Got No Bread, No Milk, No Money* wasn't just a name, it was my reality. I appreciate the fact that musicians are trying to make a living from their talent, the same as me, and when I got where I could afford it, I always paid at least demo scale. If a master recording was sold to a major label, it could always be upgraded to master American Federation of Musicians (AFM) scale.

In those days, about the only way to get one's music out to the public was through the record labels. There was no Internet or social media to expose one's music. There was no digital streaming distribution. It was all tightly controlled and filtered through various gatekeepers. An artist had to pass through a lot of approvals, before his or her music was ever heard by the public. The first were usually the publishers, and then various label personnel, and then commercial radio music directors. It was all controlled by the major record labels and commercial radio—especially *Billboard* magazine's major reporting stations. The big labels had the distribution and sales networks, the radio promotion, and the national sales staffs to get an album promoted, stocked in the stores, and serviced to the major radio stations. They also had powerful press and publicity departments to garner articles in newspapers and magazines and expose their acts on television. There were thousands of people all working on an artist's behalf to get the records played and sold. The labels were also the banks. They financed it all. A lot of money was at stake, so they were selective. Not every record was a hit, in fact few were, and it could take years of investment in an act before the act turned a profit for a label.

Occasionally, someone was discovered in personal performance or by listening to a simple demo, but an artist's best chance to get signed was to produce the music the way it should sound as a master recording, or as a quality demo-master and let the label hear the finished recording. That would avoid any lack of imagination on the label's part. In that analog age, one also had to have thousands of dollars in expensive recording equipment to make a decent sounding recording. Recording it professionally, in a quality studio, was necessary for good sonic quality.

There were few people at the labels, it seemed to me, who had any real vision or imagination, who could hear the possibilities from a simple guitar and vocal demo. It was no longer the day of Hank Williams. If you recorded a quality demo, the record label might release the demo as a record. Most of the record executives were businessmen. A few of them were musicians themselves, like Owen Bradley and Chet Atkins. Many were not. They had come up through radio, or a label's sales or promotion staff. They weren't music people. There were not many John Hammonds or Jerry Wexlers in the music business.

With multitrack recording, one could record a rhythm track, with guitar, vocal, bass, drums, and sometimes piano; then other instruments could be added as frosting on the cake by later overdubbing additional parts. This was different from the old mono or two-track recording technique, where everyone had to play a song altogether, all at once, and the levels of the instruments and vocals were mixed on the spot. This multitrack system freed up the schedule of studio musicians and took up less of their time. They could come in at a convenient time and play their part with the rhythm track, using headphones.

Sometimes, live "scratch" vocals were done with the rhythm track, and once all the parts were completed, the final vocal track would be recorded to replace the scratch vocal. This gave the singer more control over the final vocal. Horn and string arrangements, and background vocals, were the last things to be added before the tracks were mixed. But I generally sang my vocals live with the rhythm track, because I was playing the guitar and singing at the same time, and there was always leakage between the vocal mic and the guitar mic. If I did need to sing a vocal again, I had to play another guitar part with the track to eliminate the vocal leakage on the original guitar track. Then I could sing another vocal, but I did not do this often.

Once all the parts had been recorded, the various instrument tracks on the two-inch multitrack master were then "mixed" by an engineer-mixer to a two-track stereo mix. You could delete parts that you didn't need or that didn't work. You could fix mistakes, change the EQ or equalization (tone) of the instruments and vocals, and you could add echo to the instruments and vocals. It was like film editing, you could enhance or destroy a production in the mix. It was important to have a good recording engineer and a good mixer. Sometimes those two were the same person. Some artists left it up to the engineer and producer to finalize their mix, but I always personally oversaw all my mixes. I was in the room and at the shoulder of the engineer for every mix.

Sequencing an album is also important. In sequencing one has to consider several things: tempo (slow, medium, and fast), key signature, instrumentation, and subject. If possible, it's not a good idea to have more than two songs in a row in the same key. There is nothing more boring than six

songs in a row in the same key. It sounds like one long song. The tempo
needs to vary too, so that a slow ballad is picked up in a listener's ear with
an up-tempo or medium tempo song. After a couple medium or fast songs,
a slow ballad gives the ear relief. The subject of the songs needs to be considered as well. Avoid several "down" songs in a row if possible. Dynamics is
important in determining a sequence. I make up paper strips with my titles
written on them. I write the title, key, and whether they are slow, medium,
or fast tempo on the strips. Then I place the strips on a table and move
them around into various sequences and I write them down. Then I make
up a trial sequence or two and listen through them until I achieve what I
feel is the optimum sequence for that group of songs for the listener's ear.
Dynamics in a sequence is so important. I even time the gaps between
songs to what I feel is optimum. I have always felt sequencing was essential
for the listening quality of an album.

★

One of the first songs I recorded for my first album was "No Opener
Needed." It started with Jan and my dear friend Owen Stratvert. Owen had
come over to our little rental house on Acklen Avenue and we were having a
Pabst Blue Ribbon beer together. In those days, the beer manufacturers
were getting away from the cans you had to open with the beer openers com-
monly called church keys. The new beer cans had pop top openers, built into
the top of the can, like what is in use today. On the Pabst Blue Ribbon can,
there was a little scroll that said, "No Opener Needed." Owen said, "That's a
good title for a song!" Well, I like writing songs for or about my friends, so
I started playing around with the idea of writing a country song for Owen
based on "No Opener Needed."

We were recording the song at the Hound's Ear Studio one afternoon,
and we were rehearsing it with the front door open to the street. Some young
guys came walking by and heard the music. They came up to the door and
asked if they could come in. They were young musicians from the West
Coast. We got to talking with them and one of them said, "Hey, can I play
on that song with you?"

We thought, as young people will do, "Why not!" One of them appeared
to be the leader of the group. He borrowed a guitar, and we started laying
down a rhythm track. I played the intro myself on my acoustic guitar, but
this young California musician played some tasty little acoustic fills around

my vocal. He said he was twenty-one and his named was John Hiatt. So I said, "I'll write your name down and keep it, and if we get this record released, I'll put your name on the record."

"Great," he said. I had no idea who he was. He was just another talented young musician, who had not yet made his reputation—but of course he later would. We were young and just having fun. After we finished recording the track, which was done in one take, we decided to add some backing vocals. So all of my musicians and John Hiatt and his cohorts all sang the background vocals. After we finished, John and his musicians walked on down the street. I don't know if he even remembers playing on the song or not, but that's how John Hiatt wound up playing and singing backup on "No Opener Needed." The song wound up on *Got No Bread*. John, of course, became famous as a singer-songwriter in his own right, and I have not seen him since.

I used two different drummers on *Got No Bread*, Karl Himmel and Gregg Thomas. There's an old cliché: If you can find a good drummer, you'd better marry him. They are that important. The same holds true for bass players because the rhythm track is the foundation of the song. A song is moved along by the rhythm, not the frills. The rhythm holds the heartbeat. The fills of the lead instruments add color, texture, and excitement and can enhance the rhythm track, but it is the rhythm that carries the recording and moves your heart. The bass player on the *Got No Bread* album on most of the tracks was Steve Mendel. He was given coproducer credit, because he helped me find some of the musicians we used, but once the rhythm tracks were done, he was not present for most of the rest of the production.

All the piano and keyboard work on the album was done by Rick Durrett, and I used him thereafter on all my Capitol albums. Most of the lead guitar work, acoustic and electric, was done by Doyle Grisham, whom I had met when I was doing my demo recordings of my New Mexico songs at the Glaser brothers' studio. Doyle also played all the pedal steel guitar and dobro parts. I continued to use Doyle on all my subsequent Nashville sessions. He is an incredible talent and for the past twenty years has been playing on the road with Jimmy Buffett.

This was also the first time I met Steve Hostak, who was simply a wonderful electric guitarist. He was very intelligent, as are most great musicians, and he had such an incredibly sensitive feel. His work was outstanding on "Take Me to the Country." He now lives in El Paso, Texas, and we still talk often.

I am from the West, and on *Got No Bread*, I wanted to capture a south-western feel on the album, and I wanted to use a lot of fiddles. I was looking for the right fiddler, who could interpret my southwestern songs. I settled on Johnny Gimble. When I learned that he had played with Bob Wills, I knew he was the fiddler I needed, because Wills only hired the best.

Johnny Gimble was from Tyler, Texas, and at the urging of various friends, he'd moved his family to Nashville in 1968, and he instantly became one of the top session players in town. After working with Johnny on all my Capitol albums, I said, "When Johnny dies every fiddle player in the world moves up a notch." He was that good. Johnny was older than the rest of us on the *Got No Bread* project. I was twenty-nine years old then, and Johnny was fifty-three. Johnny was a World War II veteran and he simply loved to play. He graciously lent his time to my project. I've played with a lot of musicians over the years, and I've never seen anyone who appeared to get greater pleasure from playing his instrument, and for whom it was so effortless.

I quickly discovered, too, that Johnny's stories were as interesting as his music. He once told of picking cotton as a teenager. He said "It was in the 1930s, I was around sixteen or so, and some guys asked me to play my fiddle at a dance on Saturday night. They paid me $25 for playing that night. That was more money than I'd made all week picking cotton. Man, I really started practicing that fiddle!"

When Johnny came to the studio, we ran through all the songs I wanted to add fiddle to, which were most of them, and I have never seen a musician who was so fast at picking up a song, or more creative at interpreting his part. By the time we finished that long session with Johnny, our jaws were on the floor. It's hard to truly express how good he was; amazing doesn't adequately describe him. Like B. B. King, who later would play on my third Capitol album, both he and Johnny had picked cotton in their youth. Picking cotton in the hot sun will certainly give you soul, and they both had it. As Johnny was playing one of his parts, Steve Mendel said, "Boy, that's a lot of heads shaved." Steve was referring to Johnny's work as a barber at the Veterans Hospital in Waco. Johnny worked there after the war as a barber to add steady income between musical opportunities. It's not easy to make a living as a musician when you're young and starting out, and even those who become the greatest start out poor and unknown at some point. Everything you do in life, every sacrifice you make, every head shaved, every experience reveals itself through your instrument. That's where the magic comes from—the humility, the humanity, the passion. No one starts out being great.

We finished all the tracks with Johnny that night, and I recalled a poem I had once read by Carl Sandburg. It was about an old-time fiddlers' contest. The first prize was "Turkey in the Straw with Variations," and the second-place song was "Sweet Potatoes Grown in Sandy Land." I asked Johnny if he knew a song called "Sweet Potatoes Grown in Sandy Land." He said, "No, but I know a song called 'Big Taters in the Sandy Land.'" I said, "Would you play a little of that for us?" We hastily threaded up the two-track machine and patched it into the mixing console. Doyle Grisham was in the studio with Johnny, and I said, "Doyle, pick up that acoustic and give Johnny a little rhythm." In the control room, we pressed record, the red recording light came on in the studio, and Johnny said, "OK, the machine's goin,' the people are on the floor, and here's 'Big Taters in the Sandy Land.'" That was the end of the long, and wonderful night that was my first session with Johnny Gimble. What a treat it was.

Johnny also played his four-string electric mandolin on several songs, and talk about driving the rhythm: listen to him on "Give Him Another Bottle." It really doesn't get any better. I called Johnny on the next three albums I recorded for Capitol Records. Shortly after my fourth Capitol album, *Ain't It Somethin'* in 1977, Johnny decided to move back to Texas with his family and he started touring some with Willie Nelson and Merle Haggard and playing on *A Prairie Home Companion* radio show. He told me, "James, CBS wants me to record another album for them"—he had recorded *Fiddlin' Around* in 1969 for CBS—"but they want me to play old standards and play the melody line with my fiddle. That just isn't fiddlin' to me." Johnny made his mark in Nashville, along with a lot of session money for his family. His reputation was so established that if they wanted him on a session, they could fly him in—which many did, including Merle Haggard.

The *Got No Bread* album was mixed by Richie Cicero and Tony Lyons. Tony did most of the recording and mixing. He was originally from Kentucky and had just returned from a deployment in Vietnam. Tony was a musician himself, an acoustic guitar player and a good singer. He had done some radio work in the army, fortunately switching from a rifle company to Armed Forces Radio. He had a good ear and feel for the music. He later opened an Irish pub in downtown Nashville. Unfortunately, he is no longer with us, but I have fond memories of our work together.

★

I was still under contract with Atlantic Records in 1973 when I recorded *Got No Bread, No Milk, No Money, But We Sure Got a Lot of Love*, but Larry Burton and I had heard nothing from Jerry Wexler or anyone at Atlantic Records in months. They had released the single of my demo of "One Less Child," with "Mississippi River Whistle Town" as the B-side. But we'd had no contact or talk of a budget for the required album. Their office in Nashville was floundering, and we had no contact there anyway. I had been signed directly by Jerry out of New York. He was my contact at the label. So I went to New York to try and find out what was going on. As it turned out, when I got to Atlantic's offices, Jerry was out of town. I spoke with his assistant, Mark Meyerson, and Mark said, "If you can figure out what Jerry is doing, please let us know. I wish he would get back into the music business." That was disconcerting.

As it turned out, the issue with Jerry was that he was undergoing a midlife crisis. He was fifty-five years old then, had divorced his wife of twenty-five years, and married his attractive twenty-seven-year-old secretary, Renee. The marriage lasted only about three years, but right then Jerry was in love and was AWOL from the record business and many of the acts he'd signed. With Jerry's share of the sale of Atlantic Records to Warner Brothers he certainly didn't need money. He was in love, and God bless him. He was going around the country spending money on his new bride and doing only what was absolutely necessary at Atlantic.

Under the circumstances, though, there didn't seem much point in me presenting my *Got No Bread* album to Atlantic. Larry Burton and I were disappointed, and Larry encouraged me not to send anything more to Atlantic. One must understand, record labels are like people, they are run by people, and sometimes they have their act together and sometimes they don't. But as an artist you are at their mercy. An artist must have a key person of authority at the company who is their direct advocate, a person responsible for them within the organization. Jerry was my guy at Atlantic, and he had his head elsewhere at the time. In hindsight, though, if we had sent *Got No Bread* to Jerry, he might well have gotten behind it, because when it did come out on Capitol two years later, Jerry and I reconnected at my shows at the Lone Star Cafe in New York, and he absolutely loved the album. I didn't tell him until sometime later that it could have been his at Atlantic.

The deal with Atlantic died a slow death because of Jerry's new love and neglect. Atlantic continued to pay me my $250 a week for the rest of the year, but when that year was over, I was broke; $250 did not leave any surplus, and nothing had been done to create any income stream from my music during the year. I did have a big backlog of songs, because I tried to write every night while Jerry paid me. Larry Burton also began to lose interest in the music business after the Atlantic debacle. I think he saw how flaky and capricious it could be. Hard work wasn't enough. The business couldn't be counted on, and it was becoming an awfully expensive hobby for him. Even a wealthy man has his limitations. Larry wound up selling or returning the recording equipment, selling the studio building, and we eventually drifted apart with no animosity. But I will forever hold a place in my heart for him for the way he tried to help me. I had the master to *Got No Bread*, but there were independently produced masters sitting on shelves, unsold, all over Nashville.

When my contract with Atlantic Records ended in 1973, without what I had hoped it would accomplish, I was having a hard time. I was broke, but I kept telling myself, "If I can just hang on a little longer something good will happen." I had irons in the fire, but nothing in the music business ever moves quickly enough. I called my mother and asked her if she would loan me five hundred dollars. She agreed on the phone, but apparently as she began to think it over she must have had second thoughts. When a check arrived from her, it was not for five hundred dollars, but for fifty dollars, and with it a curt note that said, "Buy some groceries for your family and go get a job." Tough love. She would have been happy if I had become a school-teacher like her. It had been a good life for her. She was proud she was a teacher, and she could not understand why it would not be good enough for me or anyone else.

★

While Hound's Ear Studio was still going, and after my album was completed, I produced an album for the folk singer Odetta. Rick Durrett had once played piano in Odetta's band. She'd come to Nashville to play a show at the Exit-In and we hooked up with her. We told her we had a studio available and asked if she would like to record some music. One thing led to another, and we found ourselves working with Odetta to record an album. She showed up the first day with a case of Old Fitzgerald whiskey, which she could well handle in those days. We finished the album, and I sent the master up to Odetta. It was a good recording, but I don't think she ever got it released.

Some years later, when I was on Capitol Records, I saw Odetta again in New York, and we went to a show together at Lincoln Center to see the Paul Butterfield Blues Band. After the show we went to a party at the house of Peter Yarrow, of Peter, Paul, and Mary fame, where I met one of my guitarist idols, Amos Garrett. In 2000, Jan and I were invited to a Woody Guthrie tribute concert in Memphis. Odetta was on the show. We were really looking forward to seeing her, but we discovered that she had declined considerably. She was in the early stages of dementia and could not remember me or the Nashville album. It was sad. I still have the safety copy tape of the project at my home in New Mexico. It has never been released.

$\star$ $\star$ $\bigstar$ $\star$ $\star$

Chapter 7

WORKING FOR WAGES AGAIN
IN NASHVILLE

At the end of 1973 I was broke. My Atlantic money was gone. Our second son, Justin Louis, had been born, and I had to find a job. I couldn't bring myself to go back to public health work. I just couldn't face it. So I gathered up my carpentry tools and started visiting construction sites. That's the thing about construction work. There are no applications, no resumes. One just shows up on a job with his tools and asks the superintendent if he needs a carpenter. If he does, he might ask a few questions to determine a person's qualifications, and if he's satisfied, and he needs a carpenter, he puts them to work. It's quick and fast.

One of the first jobs I got was with Nashville's Bell Construction—Ray Bell's company. They were putting up a telephone building on the east side of Dickson, Tennessee, about forty miles west of Nashville. It was in February. The days were short, and it was cold as hell. We had to be on the job at sunup and work until it was dark. "Kin' to Kaint" it is called—from when you first "kin" see, until you "kaint."

We were building steel mats for the footings to support concrete columns. They were incredibly heavy, like lifting a car. We'd set them with a backhoe. I was thirty years old, and I was not in good shape. It nearly killed me. I still had back problems, and I was not used to such heavy work. This was not really carpentry; it was concrete form work done by carpenters. Heavy construction it is called.

I got up every morning at 5:00 A.M. to be at the job by 7:00 A.M., about the time the sun came up in February in Tennessee. We would sit in our cars until it was light enough to work. Our younger son was only about six months old. I'd arrive back home around 7:00 P.M. after dark. I worked at that job for about one month and then got a job closer to home with Buchanan Construction.

Buchanan was building a new tennis building at the Belle Meade Country Club in Nashville. It was a metal building, but it had an elaborate Colonial-style façade on the front. The carpenter foreman on the job liked to play five-card stud poker every day at lunch. The games were short as we only had thirty minutes. It seemed like he lost a dollar or two every day. I figured he did that just so we would keep playing with him. He also chewed tobacco. If he was on a scaffold above you, you did not want to work directly below him.

One Friday, the young superintendent on the job asked me to come in on Saturday for some extra time and help him hang some interior doors. He was a young guy, only a few years older than me. He asked me if I knew how to hang doors. I said, "Well, sort of."

He said, "Well, you come in on Saturday and I will teach you the proper way to hang a commercial door"—this was commercial work, fitting a door to the metal doorjamb. The superintendent showed me the entire process. He was patient and was happy to teach me. We hung eight doors that Saturday.

I finished the Buchanan job and went to apply for a job at a big eleven-story high-rise hotel that was under construction in Nashville by the Joe M. Rodgers Company. It was at Briley Parkway and Interstate 40. It was then a Rodeway Inn, one of their top-of-the-line hotels. Today it is the Preston Hotel.

I went to the superintendent's trailer to apply, and the first thing he asked me was, "Can you hang doors?"

I said, "Yes."

He said testily, "Tell me how you hang a door."

I explained all the steps I had been taught just a couple of weeks before, and he said, "Well, you sound like you know how to hang a door; how many have you hung?" He was really grilling me.

I said, "I don't know how many I've hung, I don't keep track, maybe 500?" I had only hung eight, but I figured they're all the same after the first one and I needed a job.

He said, "OK, you be here in the morning at 7:00 A.M. I'm gonna put you with someone who can tell me right away whether you know how to hang a damned door!"

I went home and worried all night, "What kind of old crusty SOB is he going to put me with in the morning, who can tell him whether or not I can hang a door?" I didn't know what I would encounter the next morning. I was at the job at 7:00 A.M. after tossing and turning and worrying half the night about what I was going to face.

I was directed down to the basement of the building, where we were to start with the door hanging. An old carpenter named Frank Campbell was there. He was a red-headed Scotsman, and the red hair was getting gray and thinning on top. He was fifty-three years old, a World War II veteran who'd fought in Burma. He had forgotten his reading glasses and was holding the instructions for assembling a Stanley door hinge template out at arm's length. It just so happened that the template was the same one I'd used on the Buchanan job. I took it from him, and I said, "Frank, it goes together like this," snap, snap, click, click, and it was assembled.

Frank said, "Well, by god Talley, you and I are going to get along just fine." What a relief!

As it turned out, Frank was a treat to work with. He was funny, always cracking jokes and telling stories. Ridiculous stuff. We would be working along, and he would say, "Did I ever tell you about the time that me and Bob Dylan went up the Amazon together?"

I said, "Frank, you don't even know who the hell Bob Dylan is!" We'd laugh and carry on with this sort of ridiculous banter all day long.

In those days, there were no battery-powered tools, like everyone uses today, and elevators are the last thing to be completed in such a building. Every morning we would climb the stairs to whatever floor we were working on with a one-hundred-foot extension cord over each shoulder and carrying our heavy toolboxes and power tools. Frank and I got good at hanging doors, though; our record was fifty-three doors, fitted, planed, and hung in one day. It took three months for me and Frank to hang all those doors and lock them.

This was a big job. There were many carpenters on the job, plus all the subcontractors. Some of them were driving in from smaller towns around middle Tennessee. With the travel and the ten-hour days we were working, it made a long day. There were a couple of guys on the job missing fingers on one hand or the other, among the consequences of carpentering and not paying attention to what you are doing. Power tools are unforgiving, and as a guitar player I was always mighty mindful of those dangers. I have always gotten a great deal of satisfaction out of building things. There is simply something pleasing about standing back from a job you have completed and seeing the finished product.

The men on these jobs, for the most part, were not highly educated, but they were smart about their work. Good carpentry is a skill and requires a great deal of care and precision if done right. There was always a lot of banter on these jobs. One old salt carpenter said, "Hell, all a workin' man can hope for in this country today is to keep a little food on his table, a roof over his head, and make the payment on his truck. We're all just tryin' like the devil, ain't we?" I never forgot what I heard the men say on these jobs, and I would write it down. Like Pete said Woody did, I put what I heard into my songs.

I had several more construction jobs in those years—some good, some not so good—but I wound up as a punch carpenter on a big condominium project on the east side of Nashville, called Nashboro Village. As people would buy the condominiums, if they found something wrong when they moved in—which they always did—I would repair the shoddy work. This kept me quite busy.

Working with me on the Nashboro job was a carpenter in his early fifties named Jerry LeRoy. Jerry was from Rochester, New York, and he had moved south to get away from the brutal winters up north. Jerry was a true master carpenter. I always had my eye open for the techniques these experienced carpenters used. I watched them, and I learned from them. And I was always thankful for Mr. Brown, my seventh- and eighth-grade shop teacher.

★

During my Nashville carpentry years of 1974 and 1975, I was still trying to find a record label to pick up my *Got No Bread* album, but I had no access to the executives at the big record labels. I had no contacts, no entree. I played it for one retired record executive at the Hound's Ear Studio, and he said it was not slick enough. It was too country. Too country! I couldn't believe I was hearing this, but at the time many of the country productions in Nashville did have a lot of syrup in them. Lots of string arrangements were added to make them more cosmopolitan. The rough organic roots of the old 1930s country sound were no longer popular, except with some of us youngsters. My record was a different sound for Nashville.

I had this theory, as I thought about it, that there were then three generations of country music that had developed over time. The first generation was more acoustic and folk-oriented. It was Jimmie Rodgers, the Carter Family, and up through early Bob Wills and Hank Williams. It was more earthy, organic music, and more in touch with the rural America of the 1930s and 1940s and going back to the early days of radio.

But as people the age of my parents went off to fight in World War II, they learned there was another, larger, world out there beyond their immediate rural localities. They saw large cities, which were quite different from the small towns and farms where many of them had grown up. As Hank Williams said in "Honky Tonk Blues," "I left my home down on the rural route."

People from New York met people from Alabama. People from Texas met people from San Francisco. They exchanged ideas; they exchanged music; they exchanged life's experiences. Their perspectives were broadened and changed. They saw other cities and cultures in Europe and the South Pacific. People like my parents moved from Oklahoma to Washington State for defense jobs. Travel was educational and enlightening. They saw how other people lived their lives. People were exposed to different cultures and experiences.

The government's defense production for World War II improved the nation's economy and people's pocketbooks. Consumer spending lifted the economy. As that generation became more affluent, their tastes changed. They no longer wanted the simple rough and rowdy ways of Jimmie Rodgers. They wanted something more polished, more sophisticated, something that reflected their new status. My own father began to like Harry James and Glenn Miller, along with Bob Wills. The songwriting evolved too because songwriters write about life. The arrangement and production of the music evolved, along with improvements in recording technology, and a more polished urban radio format evolved to reflect this as well.

A new second generation of country music came into being. Artists like Patsy Cline, who was produced by Owen Bradley, had strings and background vocals added to their recordings. Embraced by radio, a smoother, more polished style became popular. Think of Jim Reeves or Eddy Arnold, for instance. It was much more cosmopolitan, fewer steel guitars and fiddles and more string arrangements. This became the new "Nashville Sound" production. It survived into the 1980s with producers like Billy Sherrill at CBS Records in Nashville. Think of Tammy Wynette's recording of the wonderful Red Lane song, "I'm Gonna Keep on Falling in Love 'til I Get it Right." Even an artist like George Jones, who was rough as a cob in his early years, was smoothed out—although the producers had their hands full with old Possum. But listen to the string arrangements on "He Stopped Loving Her Today," released in April 1980 and produced by Billy Sherrill. The string crescendo brings the emotional moment to the song, along with Jones's expressive voice. That was not Roy Acuff fiddling the "Wabash Cannonball." It was something else. Music had evolved.

Many young songwriters of my generation in the 1970s were hungry for a return to the more folksy, rawer, more organic sound—more fiddles, more steel guitars. Simpler arrangements, like Willie Nelson's *Red Headed Stranger* album, Waylon Jennings singing "I Don't Think Hank Done It This Way," or the *Will the Circle Be Unbroken* album by the Nitty Gritty Dirt Band. It was an eclectic appreciation of a simpler recorded sound that could be more easily reproduced with a road band. It was a generational retro shift to a third generation of country music. However, the old second-generation style didn't abruptly go away. That style persisted in parallel with the simpler sound of the third generation. That third-generation sound was the one popular with young listeners. It became what we now classify as Americana music. Today, however, I would say we have transitioned to a fourth generation of country music, which is more driven by rock and roll influences.

It was a shock to many country radio programmers when my simpler music came out. They weren't ready for that kind of honesty. In my heyday, the late 1970s, the country music audience was still dominated by older Americans, a more conservative radio listener, and the way music was produced and presented then was designed to appeal to those listeners.

Younger music lovers, the baby boomers, were still listening to rock and roll, and it was selling in the millions of units. But everybody gets older, and as those rock audiences grew older in the decade or two after my recordings, the late 1980s and 1990s, their lives had changed. They aged, they had a few of life's setbacks and experiences. They took real jobs and they lost real jobs, they married and started families, they got divorced, they bought houses, they had children, they bought minivans, they had responsibilities. They grew up! They began to understand and appreciate the heartbreak stories of life and the honesty in country music lyrics. But they still weren't that old. They still had some drive, and they had not given up the energy of rock and roll.

It wasn't a conscious decision, necessarily, but younger music producers came of age too, and the productions evolved to fit a new and younger
audience. All popular music is generational and driven by demographics.
There were still fiddles and steel guitars, but there were also fuzztone
rock guitar sounds, heavier drums, digitized sampled sounds, and syn-
thesizers. Recording technology evolved. Technology could do wonders
with digital mixing and editing. People will tell me that they can tell the
difference between digital recording and analog recording. I don't
believe them, unless in digital they mean they can't hear the annoying
needle crackles and pops on a vinyl LP. A lot of listening is done in cars
and on portable devices. The audio signal is squashed by broadcast signal
limiters and the compression of the MP3 format. Whose ears can really
tell the difference?

Radio plays the lowest common denominator of what the greatest
potential audience wants to hear. Country radio programmers evolve to
accommodate each new sound. As the older radio guys retired and died
off, newer, younger radio guys were more receptive to the more rock-
sounding country music. The life stories in the song lyrics were still there,
but the music had changed to fit a younger audience. The music was simply
a reflection of that youthful, different audience. The baby boomers were so
numerous, country music began to sell like rock music had a couple of
decades previous. It sold in the millions with artists like Garth Brooks and
his peers. Garth was the right age, in the right place, with the right thing,
at the right time. His shows were like rock concerts, which was what his
audience was used to attending. He slid down poles. He flew over the audience in a harness. He put on an event, not just a performance. He didn't
just stand in front of a microphone and sing like Willie Nelson. There was
smoke and light shows and pyrotechnics.

But the song was—and still is—the foundation. A song can be produced in many ways with different arrangements, but if the song isn't good,
if its lyrics, melody, and production do not move you, it doesn't matter how
it's produced. Songwriters, regardless of how they are abused or under-
paid, still rule the world artistically.

★

In the fall of 1974, for some reason I can't now recall, I was at the Capitol
Records Office in Nashville. A record producer was there, Audie Ashworth

(who also managed J. J. Cale). Audie said to me, "James, aren't you a carpenter?"

"Yes," I said.

Audie then said, "Frank Jones, Capitol Records' new vice president of their country division, is moving back to Nashville from Los Angeles. He's purchased a home in West Meade, and he needs some work done on it before he arrives. Is that something you could handle?"

I said, "Well, when is he due to arrive? I would have to do it on the weekends, because I have a full-time job during the week."

As it turned out, Frank wasn't due for about six weeks. So over the next several weekends, Jerry LeRoy and I did some minor repairs at the house. We painted and redecorated it, and made it ready for Frank and his family.

Not long before this time, several friends of mine had put up a few thousand dollars to help me with the *Got No Bread* album. I designed and printed up covers and pressed a thousand copies of the album on my own Torreón Records label. Clark Thomas, a young Vanderbilt student and photographer, whom I had helped when he was editor of the Vanderbilt yearbook, took the cover photograph at a little country grocery store near White Bluff, Tennessee. The store had a big RC Cola sign on the side that said, "Talley's Grocery." Our four-year-old, Reuben James, and Jan were in the photograph with me. Jan was then eight months pregnant with our second son, Justin Louis. Clark's photograph perfectly captured the spirit of *Got No Bread, No Milk, No Money, But We Sure Got a Lot of Love*. Once the album cover design was ready, I manufactured the albums and hired a small independent promotion company in Nashville to mail the records to the radio stations to see if we could generate some interest.

Jerry and I were finishing up our work on Frank's house one weekend and Frank was in town. He came by to check on how things were going. When Frank arrived, Jerry enthusiastically said, "Frank, you should hear Jim's album, it's really fantastic!"

Frank, being a very gracious and polite Canadian, said, "Why, I would love to hear it." Jerry, jumped up, ran out to the trunk of the car, and brought an album in the house and gave it to Frank.

Frank Jones had been in the music business for many years before he got the top job at Capitol's country division. He had been a staff producer with Columbia Records, where he had been involved with Johnny Cash's career and other CBS acts. I told Frank about what John Hammond had tried to do for me at Columbia in New York, and about how my deal had died on the vine with Jerry Wexler at Atlantic. He was familiar with those kinds of stories with his years in the business, but I think it also piqued his interest in at least listening to the album—which is always the first step.

At this same time, a copy of *Got No Bread* had reached WKDA Radio in Nashville, then the Top 40 AM country station in town. A copy had also reached WSIX-FM, the easy-listening country station then in Nashville. The program director at WKDA, Mike Hanes, simply loved the album and was playing my song, "Give Him Another Bottle" in heavy drive-time rotation. WSIX-FM was playing "Red River Memory" and the ballad "Take Me to the Country."

Frank Jones arrived in Nashville from Los Angeles and moved into his house. He told me that each morning when he woke up to his clock radio, it would be playing "Red River Memory," and as he drove to the office, WKDA would be playing "Give Him Another Bottle," during drive time. In a week or so, Frank called me and said he really liked the album.

He said, "Let me get settled in the office here for a few weeks, and I will call you and we can talk more about your album." Jan and I were excited. I had finally reached a record executive through the back door with my carpentry.

Three weeks went by, and Frank called me. We set up an appointment at his Capitol office. Frank said he had played the album for Bill Williams, who was then director of country promotion at Capitol Nashville. He said Bill liked the album too and wanted to meet me. Frank said he needed Bill and his promotion staff to get behind it if Capitol was going to release it. Frank then asked me what I wanted for the album. Naturally, I knew nothing about that sort of thing, but here I had a shot, and I didn't want to blow it. I wanted to make a deal, and I wanted to minimize any risk Frank might have in signing me. Invariably, the first person who mentions money in a negotiation is the one who leaves money on the table, but at that point in my life I was a young artist, and I knew nothing about money or the business of record companies.

I said, "Frank, it will take five thousand dollars to pay union master scale to all the musicians who played on the album. I can let you have it for five thousand dollars."

There was no money in the deal for me, no vocal session fees for me through AFTRA (American Federation of Television and Radio Artists, the singers' union), but I had my carpenter job to pay my bills. I am sure this offer thrilled Frank. As it turned out, I had forgotten about the FICA payments for the musicians, their Social Security payments. I wound up having to borrow five hundred dollars from my mother to pay those fees. It left no money for me or my family, or for any other costs, like studio time and tape. But it minimized the risk for Frank to take a chance on me, so if there was any doubt, or lack of success in signing me, he didn't have much of his hide to lose, and I was on a major record label!

I was sure Larry Burton would not mind the studio time. Larry would have never wanted to hold me back. But if I had known then what I know now, I would have asked for more money, or I would have said, "Frank, let me review my expenses and come up with a number for you." Or, I might have simply leased the master to Capitol, rather than selling it to them—a business practice I was not familiar with in those days.

When the meeting ended, Frank said, "You can tell John Hammond he's not the only one with ears." Frank had known Hammond from when he'd worked at Columbia. I think he felt a little pride in following John's lead.

★ ★ ★ ★ ★

Chapter 8

HOW CAN IT BE ANY GOOD? WE DIDN'T PAY ANYTHING FOR IT

Capitol's director of promotion in Nashville, Bill Williams, set up a meeting with me. We met on a crisp fall day in Nashville's Centennial Park. We sat on a bench near the big eight-driver-wheel steam engine in the park and talked. We hit it off right away. It was obvious that Bill loved the album. Bill was only a couple of years older than me, and he had recently come to Capitol from Columbia Records, where he had promoted many of CBS's artists to stardom. Before leaving CBS, he had established Charlie Rich as a star, along with many others. Bill was an honest guy, a straight-shooter. He had great marketing ideas, and he worked extremely hard. He was a breath of fresh air in the music business. He was from Waco, Texas, where his parents owned a small record store. This was his kind of country music. He was truly a visionary, and he loved sincere artists who believed in what they were singing about.

He said, "I want you to be an artist. Your job is to make the best music you can, and our job is to promote it."

This was music to my ears. He just wanted to meet me and see if my head was screwed on straight, and he soon realized he could not have found anyone more eager or more dedicated to do his part. I asked him about my publishing, and he said, "No, you keep your publishing. I'm not interested in that. I'm interested in you as an artist." It was the same as Jerry Wexler back in 1972. Just keep writing. Bill and I became great friends and even though he eventually left the music business, we are still friends to this day.

With Bill's blessing, Frank Jones said he would buy the album. By then, the year 1974 was rapidly vanishing in the rearview mirror and we were heading into 1975. It seemed to take Capitol's lawyers forever to get the contract ready, but finally, in April 1975, the contract arrived, drafted by their head of business affairs, Bob Young.

Larry Woods, a young attorney was living across the street from Jan and me on Cedar Lane. I took the contract over to Larry and asked him if he would look it over for me. Larry reviewed the contract and basically said, "This isn't a great contract, Jim. It's the 'Iowa Farm Boy Contract.' But you are a new artist, and you aren't dealing from a position of strength. If the album does well, Capitol will pick up their options for more albums (there were options for three more albums in the contract), and if not, it will be over. But what choice do you have? You want it released, don't you?"

I did indeed want it released, and signed the "Iowa Farm Boy Contract," with a paltry royalty rate. And then I waited for the release date. In the meantime, I kept pounding nails. It took several months for Capitol to get the album into their release schedule. They used the same cover Clark Thomas and I designed, but it had to be reprinted with Capitol's logo. The record had to be manufactured, and a marketing, promotion, and sales plan set in motion. Finally, in late June the record was released. The first single was "W. Lee O'Daniel and the Light Crust Dough Boys." On my way home each day from my carpentry job in my old 1964 Chevy pickup (the one on the cover of my second album, *Tryin' Like the Devil*), I would hear my song played on the radio. The old radio in the truck went in and out with a lot of static, and I would pound on the dashboard when the signal would falter. What a thrill it was, driving to and from my construction job and hearing my song on the radio.

When the album and the first single hit radio, Bill Williams called me and said, "I need you to come in the office and call radio stations."

I said, "Bill, I can't come in and call radio stations, I have to work. I still have my carpenter job and I've got a family to support."

I had no understanding of how any of this worked, so Bill said, "Let me think about this. I'll call you back."

I got another call from Bill, and he said, "How much do you make a week at your carpenter job?"

I said, "Two hundred dollars a week."

He said, "If I could pay you two hundred dollars, could you get a week off?"

I said, "Let me check." I went to the Nashboro Village office and told Bruce Smith, the project manager, what Bill wanted me to do.

Bruce was a country boy himself who had grown up on a farm in Livingston, Tennessee. He loved the album and was quite proud that one of his carpenters had a record out. He said, "Of course you can have the time off. Go call the radio stations." I called Bill Williams back and told him I would be in Monday morning to call radio stations.

I came in that Monday to call radio stations. Bill gave me a check for two hundred dollars and I said, "What do you want me to do when I call a station?" I had never been in a radio station. I knew how to make music, the artistic part, but I had no understanding of the business of promoting a record.

Bill said, "Just ask for the music director; here is a list of stations and their music directors' names, and phone numbers. Ask them if they have received your album, to be sure they have it. If they have it, then ask them if they've had a chance to listen to it. If they have not yet listened, tell them you would sure appreciate it if they would give it a listen. If they have already listened, thank them, and take the conversation wherever they want to go with it. They may want to ask you some questions about it, or about your life. Just ingratiate yourself with them."

I started calling radio stations. Some of the music directors were great guys, and we had some good rapport. Some of them seemed like arrogant jerks who didn't want to be bothered with a new young artist who wasn't yet a star. I was not Merle Haggard. But I did the best I could. It was all new to me.

As part of the promotion of *Got No Bread*, Bill had what I've always thought was a brilliant idea to introduce me to radio and the press. He contracted with Mike Hanes, the program director at WKDA in Nashville, who had been playing the tar out of the record, to record an interview album with me about my life. I was then thirty-one years old. Mike was about six years older than me and had been in radio a long time. He had one of those beautiful, deep, resonant, radio voices. He was intelligent and was an experienced interviewer. We went into a small independent production studio one night shortly after I signed the Capitol contract, and he interviewed me for a couple of hours. Then he edited the interview down to a length that would fit on an LP record and delivered it to Bill. He did a first-class professional job. Bill had Capitol press a thousand copies of the interview album and mail them out in a plain white cover along with *Got No Bread* to radio and the press. It was my first interview. Mike's questions were probing and caught me off guard at times, but the interview was poignant and honest.

When a thirtieth-anniversary CD edition of *Got No Bread* was released in 2005, a copy of that interview was included on a separate CD with the release. I gave a copy to my friend Tim Niarhos, a young Nashville attorney. He listened to it and said, "Thirty years, and you haven't changed a bit."

Even now, I can still abide by what I said all those years ago in that little production studio. I will always have a place in my heart for Mike Hanes for all he did to help me in the beginning. If you create something that moves people, they want to help you share it.

After the first week of calling radio stations, Bill Williams said, "Can you get another week off? I need you to keep calling the stations." I was able to get another week off and I called the stations for another week. At the end of those two weeks Bill said, "This is ridiculous. We sign an act and don't give them any support. I can't promote this record with you working as a carpenter. How are we supposed to make this work? You get some more time off next week. We are flying to Los Angeles Sunday to get you some money!" Sunday afternoon, I was on a plane with Bill flying to Los Angeles. It was only my second time on an airplane—the first being when my father died. Bill used his company account for the tickets and said, "I can fly first class if I am flying with one of our artists." So we flew first class!

The next morning Bill and I went to the Capitol Tower in Hollywood. Bill took me to the president's office and introduced me to Brown Meggs, the distinguished writer who was then president of Capitol Records. Bill said to Brown, "We've signed this new artist, his record is out and is getting incredible notices, and I need some money for him to live. He's working as a carpenter, and I need him to be working to promote this record."

Meggs said, "How much do you need?"

Bill said, "How about ten thousand dollars?"

Brown said, "OK, you guys go to lunch and come back, I'll have a check ready for you." So Bill and I went down the street to the Brown Derby Restaurant, a famous Hollywood landmark close to Capitol, and had lunch.

We flew back to Nashville, and my mind was much more at ease. I could easily live for a year then on ten thousand dollars. I had some security for my family, and I didn't have to go back to the carpenter job.

Then Bill decided he would take me to see Frances Preston, who was head of BMI in Nashville. Frances was a lovely woman with brains and charm, who had worked her way up from a secretary to the head of BMI in Nashville. Eventually, she would head the entire organization from New

York. Frances and I developed a good friendship, the kind of relationship she had with many of her writers. I had been an ASCAP writer—but Ed Shea, my mentor there, was no longer at ASCAP, and I had no relationship with his replacement.

Bill said to Frances, "James is one of our new artists. We have his first album out; it's doing quite well, and Capitol is picking up its option for a second album. He writes all his own material. He has been with ASCAP, but his contract is up with them. He would be willing to switch to BMI, but he needs some money."

Frances said, "How much do you need, Bill?"

Bill said, "How about ten thousand dollars?"

I thought, "Wow, ten thousand dollars must be the magic number!"

Frances said, "How about if I give you five thousand dollars now, and another five thousand after the first of the year? You won't have to pay so much in taxes." That obviously sounded pretty savvy to me. I was finally getting paid again for my music.

When the reviews started coming in on *Got No Bread, No Milk, No Money, But We Sure Got a Lot of Love*, I was amazed, and so was Capitol in Hollywood. The first one was from the rock critic Greil Marcus, in the *Village Voice* in New York City. It was placed across the centerfold from the review of Willie Nelson's *Red Headed Stranger* album, Willie's first release after switching from Atlantic to Columbia. On August 11, 1975, Greil wrote:

> James Talley is a country (western swing) (cowboy) (folk) singer out of Oklahoma who has on his first try produced an album that may well become a classic. . . . Talley's album is being marketed as country, but it has little to do with what came out of the Nashville machine . . . there's not a cliche on it. Every note sounds as if it was played—and what is more, felt—by a living human being. . . . It is as finely tuned as that of a mid-60s Donovan album, and as unobtrusive as anything you might be hearing from Bob Dylan. Talley's album is modest, yet it grows stronger, more interesting each time it is played. Its tension, like everything else about it, is subtle. In the vein of the Band's second album, it is an affirmation. It is by its end, disquieting; and it sounds much better at night than in the daytime.

More glowing reviews came in from Bob Christgau at the *Village Voice*, Chet Flippo in *Rolling Stone*, Peter Guralnick in the *Village Voice Music*

Supplement, Robert Hilburn in the *Los Angeles Times,* Nat Hentoff in *Cosmopolitan,* Larry Rohter at the *Washington Post,* Roxy Gordon in *Country Music,* and papers from Los Angeles to Boston, and points in between. They were coming from the rock critics as well as the country reviewers. We were getting more play on the new progressive FM stations that broadcast in stereo than we were with the AM country stations. Young listeners liked the album. Capitol in Los Angeles didn't know what to make of it. The head of publicity at Capitol was looking like a star with all the reviews that were coming in. The head of sales at Capitol in Los Angeles, Dennis White, said, "How can this album be any good; we didn't pay anything for it."

★

Popular music is generational. My music in the late 1970s was being marketed to the older demographic that was then the majority of country music listeners. That was the business model at the time. But we were being reviewed by rock critics, and our audience was as much the youth of the baby boom generation as it was the older country listener. In fact, it probably appealed more to the young FM listeners. Progressive stereo FM stations were a new format then and were on the rise. They played my music mixed in with their rock programming.

But it soon became apparent that the country division at Capitol was a stepchild within the company. Bill Williams had to beg Capitol to release my albums in the new cassette tape format, because that is what my young listeners wanted, not the cranky old eight-tracks that shifted gears in the middle of a song, which the label released to older country audiences. Every effort, every expense was made by the label for rock music because that was the greatest demographic, where most of the record buyers were. It is a business of demographics. That is the money. The biggest act on Capitol's country division then was Merle Haggard, and I was told he was selling around 125,000 copies of each album release. He made his money on the road, in concerts, not from his record sales.

Capitol had regional promotion people in every major market, but they all reported to the head of pop promotion in Hollywood. They were instructed to work and promote the country product, to get the records to the country stations, but if they let it slide no one in Hollywood's promotion section much cared. Bill Williams, as head of Capitol's country promotion in Nashville, had no real authority over the regional promotion guys. All he could do was to keep as much pressure on them as possible, begging them to work his country releases. I once went to Charlotte, North Carolina, on a promotion tour, and the regional rep there took me to two country stations he had not visited in over a year. The guys at the stations chided him, "Hey man, where you been?" He didn't seem to be too embarrassed by it.

I was performing in Atlanta with my band at the Great Southeast Music Hall after my second Capitol release, *Tryin' Like the Devil*. Atlanta was the largest record market in the South, and there were no press interviews set up, no radio interviews, no in-store promotions. Nothing was being done to promote the show or promote the new album. I was still just being discovered by music audiences, so venue owners were paying me almost nothing as an opening act. It was certainly not enough to cover expenses, and I was using my recoupable tour support advances from Capitol to pay my musicians. They were all young guys with families and small children like me, and I felt a responsibility to them. The cost of touring—hotel rooms, gasoline, meals—was all part of that original ten thousand dollars Capitol had advanced me, and "advanced" means all those dollars are charged against any future royalties due. Until all the costs of producing the album, all the advances for living expenses, and all the tour support money was recouped, I would not see a dime in royalties from the label. Indeed, I never did—as is the case with most recording artists.

In Atlanta I was so irritated that nothing had been done for us that I called the president of the label in Los Angeles, who by then was Don Zimmerman. I said to him, "Don, we're out here trying to promote this album, in the biggest market in the South, and nothing is being done to help us!" Suddenly, the next day, here was the regional promotion rep in my hotel room: there were press interviews set up, radio station appointments set up, an in-store visit to Peaches Records, radio spots advertising our performance. Obviously, the local promotion guy had been jacked-up by someone. The problem was, he still reported to the head of pop promotion in Hollywood, who didn't give a hoot whether he did anything to promote a country artist or a country record, or whether he rendered any assistance to the country division at all. The head of promotion in Nashville had no authority over him.

I was beginning to wonder how this was supposed to work. How were my records supposed to sell without any promotion and without them being stocked in stores? The result of my raising hell with Capitol's president was that, after we left town, that Atlanta rep never did another thing to help us. My irate call to the president of the label didn't accomplish a thing. It just pissed off the local rep. His expense account and his company baseball jacket—which all the promo guys wore then—were in no way threatened. He was not required to work our Nashville-based product, so he simply didn't.

I realized later that Merle Haggard was hiring his own independent promotion person, in addition to Capitol's staff, to work his records. Merle knew the ropes, which I'm sure he'd learned the hard way too. Frank Mull in Nashville was Merle's promotion guy. Frank Mull was a great guy, and we later became good friends. He was the first promotion guy in Nashville to use computers. This was the late 1970s, and Frank had an office with an early Apple computer to keep up with his radio station tracking, chart action, and promotion. But I didn't have the money to add my own promotion people to help me. I had to live or die by what the label could do for me. If I had known how it worked, I would have appealed to Capitol for the money to hire an independent like Frank. Bill Williams and his little two-man team in Nashville worked extremely hard for me, but he did not have all the tools he needed from the company. I recently spoke with Bill, and after all these years later he said to me, "Capitol was a horrible record label." In the 1970s the demographics simply were not there yet for them to give much of a damn about country music.

★

In the decades that followed, as the young music listeners matured from their rock addiction and began to appreciate country product, more money and promotion was devoted to country music and country artists. Country records began to sell in larger numbers. But this didn't happen for another decade after my releases. Willie Nelson, heavily promoted by Columbia Records, did sell in the millions in the late 1970s and 1980s, but he was also selling to a younger demographic that would explode ten years later. Willie was hip enough with his outlaw image and simple production to appeal to young audiences. He had two great albums on Atlantic, produced by Jerry Wexler, and when Columbia signed him, they worked hard for him. It was a long road for Willie to get to the top, but he finally made it, and deservedly so. I loved Willie.

Jimmy Bowen was a flamboyant music producer and record executive who saw the demographic shift in young record buyers that was coming in the 1980s. He took over Capitol Nashville in 1989. Before that he had been at other Nashville labels, including MCA Records and Elektra Records, where he'd promoted Hank Williams Jr. Bowen told the Nashville labels that if they wanted to have million-sellers, they needed to improve their recordings and spend the same money making them that they spent on their rock acts. He also told them they needed to spend the same money promoting and marketing their country acts as they did their rock performers. He was right, and he took several Nashville labels, including Capitol, to the top before he retired in 1995. When the labels started spending money on their country acts, they started selling millions.

★ ★ ★ ★ ★

Chapter 9

IT'S ALL ABOUT THE MONEY
THAT'S MADE

Capitol picked up its option for a second album in the fall of 1975, and I prepared a budget for musicians and studio time of eighteen thousand dollars to record my second album. It would be tight. Frank Jones was still head of Capitol's country division, and he approved my budget. With studio time, tape, and musicians, it was barely enough to record ten songs. We had to keep the production simple. The album would eventually be called *Tryin' Like the Devil*, after one of the songs on the album. Again, I chose a loose concept for the album. It would be about the working people I'd come to know in my various jobs, and it would be dedicated to them. Tom Smucker, writing for *In These Times* in New York commented that my first album showed people where I came from, and my second album told them what I stood for. I don't disagree with that.

For my second album, I had plenty of songs backlogged, thanks to Jerry Wexler paying me to write back in 1972, and Frank Jones had been pleased with my production on *Got No Bread, No Milk, No Money*, so he wanted me to keep producing my own albums. There was no money for a producer in my contract or my budget anyway. An artist producing themselves was quite unusual then, as it still is today. But I had total freedom within my budget. I could record at any studio I chose, I could use any musicians I wanted, and I could record whatever songs I wanted.

Since Larry Burton's Hound's Ear Studio was no longer in operation, I went looking for a new studio and engineer. I had always liked the way Merle Haggard's albums and mixes sounded, and I learned that he worked a lot in Nashville at Jack Clement's studio (now Sound Emporium), with Jim Williamson as his engineer. So I set up an appointment to meet with

Williamson. Jim was easy to work with in the studio, and he had vast sound engineering experience.

Musicians who travel on the road are on their way up and still developing. They are the second-tier players in Nashville. They are often not quite as good as the A-Team studio players. They lack the studio arranging experience of the top players. Many of them become seasoned studio musicians as they gain more experience. No one starts out at the top, and work on the road gives them experience and a chance to develop and get better. Wherever possible, though, if they were good enough, I wanted to reward the guys that had driven up and down the highway with me by using them in the studio. I also felt an obligation to use the guys who had played on spec for me on my first album.

Therefore, on *Tryin' Like the Devil*, I used many of the players I'd used on my first album. Some of them would eventually go on tour with me, some would not. I did not have the money to pay the top session guys what they required to travel. Except for Johnny Gimble and Josh Graves, who were close in age, the musicians I used were younger guys, about my age. It meant a great deal to these young players to be used in the studio. I used Doyle Grisham again, of course, after the stellar work he did on my first album. I loved Uncle Josh Graves's work on the dobro. I had met him at the Smithsonian Folk Life Festival in 1974, along with the songwriter Steve Young and his brother Kim Young who were his backing band. Josh was a bluegrass veteran with Flatt and Scruggs and was simply legendary on the dobro. He was a great blues player. In fact, Josh told me that the first record he ever owned was Blind Boy Fuller's "Step It Up and Go." Naturally, after what he'd done, speccing for me on *Got No Bread*, I could not make a record without Johnny Gimble and his fiddle. Charlie McCoy, another Nashville studio legend, was called in for some harmonica work. Jerry Shook, also one of the superlative Nashville studio guitarists and "head" arrangers (who could arrange in his head, on the spot, during the session), for whose interpretive imagination I had incredible respect, played some additional acoustic guitar and harmonica.

We recorded the sessions, using a lot of first takes. I like first takes, if they work and have no glaring mistakes. Successive takes when singing and playing guitar risk losing some of the vocal feeling. Before recording the first take, one has generally run the song down with the musicians several times anyway so they can get their parts. But since I do my vocals live with my guitar, I like to get it right the first time if possible. With too many takes, you also risk the musicians starting to play on autopilot. They can lose their feeling too.

Johnny Gimble's stories were again a welcome treat to all of us in the studio. As we were recording my song, "Are They Gonna Make Us Outlaws Again?" I asked Johnny if he heard a fiddle part on the song. He said, "James, you're askin' the wrong guy. I never heard a song yet that I didn't hear a fiddle part."

There was a wonderful camaraderie in those sessions, which is how I like to record. We had great times in the studio. Frankly, for a songwriter, it doesn't get any better than taking his or her songs into a quality studio, with talented musicians, and putting an arrangement around them. It's like putting the frame around a painting. It sets it apart as something special, unique, and separate in the world.

I delivered the completed *Tryin' Like the Devil* master recording to Capitol in the fall of 1975, for a release in February 1976. The cover was another photograph that Clark Thomas had taken, this time when I was working as a carpenter at Nashboro Village. Jerry LeRoy is sitting up on the back of my old 1964 Chevy pickup, and Henry Huddleston—a wonderful, gentle man who was our laborer helper—is sitting on the running board. I am standing beside them. The back photo was a picture of me with all the waitresses at the Skyline Restaurant, where we often ate lunch. They were salt of the earth, beautiful people.

Tryin' Like the Devil was released the first week of February 1976 and once again the reviews astonished me. Nat Hentoff wrote in *Cosmopolitan*: "This is an honest man making honest music." John Rockwell reviewed it in the *New York Times*. Robert Hilburn wrote a full-page review in the *Los Angeles Times*. Even in the Canadian newspapers the reviews were tremendous. I felt so encouraged.

But there was something I learned much later, perhaps too late for my own good, and that is that a person needs a team around them. Jack Tarver in Atlanta, who was a big supporter of my music, and owned the Great Southeast Music Hall in Atlanta, once told me: "There are only two reasons why people will help you: Either they like you, or they can make money off of you." It is important to let others make money from one's talent. An artist cannot do this all by himself. The record company is not enough. An artist needs strong management and a devoted booking agent, people who believe in an artist's talent and who will work extra hard to keep them working and earning through thick and thin—whether you have a record out or not. And an artist needs a record company that has its act together.

★

We finished *Tryin' Like the Devil* in October 1975. I still did not have a booking agent or a manager. Bill Williams was working himself to death for me, but Capitol Records in Hollywood was still totally devoted to their pop and rock acts. That was their money spigot. After the album was released in February 1976, I was again calling radio stations. Bill decided we should take an in-person promotional tour to radio stations so I could meet face-to-face with the guys who would be playing my records. It took a couple of weeks. We drove through Arkansas, Oklahoma, Texas, Mississippi, Alabama, and back to Nashville.

Our first stop was Memphis. We checked into the Rivermont Holiday Inn, where I'd had my infamous meeting with Clive Davis back in 1972. We met the music writer Peter Guralnick in Memphis. He would join us on the road for a few days to write a story for the *Village Voice Music Supplement.* We all joked around with each other during the trip. Bill had used Peter's talent to profile other artists when he was at CBS Records in Nashville, especially Charlie Rich, whose music Peter dearly loved. I had never met Peter before, but he turned out to be down-to-earth and humble, and with a great sense of humor. He wasn't famous then as he is now, but we became friends for life on that trip.

We went to Okemah, Oklahoma, where we stopped at the old burned-out Woody Guthrie house. We stopped at a pay-phone booth in front of the Okemah library, and I called Greil Marcus in Berkeley to tell him that Peter and I were in Okemah together. We drove on to Tulsa and left Peter to fly back through Fort Smith to Memphis for some other interviews. Peter included portions of the story he wrote from this trip in his book *Lost Highway.* For years Peter and I have signed off our correspondence with "Keep the Faith!" He has been a faithful friend.

When we left Nashville on that trip, the newly released single from the album, the title song, "Tryin' Like the Devil," was at Number 79 with a bullet on the *Billboard* Country Radio Chart. Every week Bill tediously tracked all the *Billboard* reporting stations for their chart positions, so before we left Nashville Bill knew the single would jump up ten points on the chart the next week.

Bill was looking for his first breakthrough single from the album, and everything looked good. However, when we got to Memphis, *Billboard*'s chart for the following week was published and the record had dropped to Number 99. What was this!? Bill was livid. He called *Billboard* and said "Hey, what's going on with you guys? Capitol has been tracking the same reporting stations as you. This record should be going up the charts, not down! What is going on!?" There were calls back and forth, and finally *Billboard* admitted that there had been a clerical error. The record should have advanced as Bill's tracking indicated and kept its bullet (a bullet means the record is advancing rapidly up the charts, not going down). But now the die was cast. When the music directors at the reporting stations saw the *Billboard* chart and saw the record had dropped twenty spaces and lost its bullet, they all followed suit and dumped it. It was a snowball effect, and it was impossible to recover from that "clerical error." The error at *Billboard* essentially killed the "Tryin' Like the Devil" single and made it even harder to promote the album.

After dropping Peter off, Bill and I continued onward. When we got to KKYX, the powerful *Billboard* reporting station in San Antonio, Bill and I went in and announced ourselves. The receptionist told Bill that the program director was busy. Bill politely told her we would wait, and we sat down in the lobby. The program director kept us waiting and waiting, and finally the receptionist went back to see him, to again remind him that we were still waiting. Then she returned and told Bill, "He's not going to be able to see you all today. He's extremely busy." Bill jumped up like a shot and barged back to the program director's office, and there he sat with his feet up on the desk, doing nothing. Bill was yelling at him so loud I could hear him in the lobby, "Look, I have brought one of our best new artists from Nashville to meet you, you asshole. If you can't take the time to meet with him, you can forget any more record servicing from Capitol for *any* of our artists. Capitol will not buy ads or give you any support!" Bill was so mad that the guy decided maybe it would be worth a minute of his time to meet me. But the mood had soured. After hearing Bill's conversation from the lobby, I didn't care whether I met the guy or not. The program director had already established himself as a jerk. But I played it cool, as if I had not heard the exchange from the lobby. I shook hands with him, and thanked him for meeting with me, and said I sure hoped he would consider playing my records. KKYX was one of *Billboard*'s six-point reporting stations. They were at the top of the reporting food chain, but they were always the last ones to add one of my records. They were a tough nut to crack.

Radio programmers at the big powerful stations knew they were the kingmakers. They had the advantage. The record companies could make the records, but if they couldn't get them played and the music exposed to the public it didn't much matter. The *Billboard* charts are made up from many reporting stations all across the country. The stations are weighted, from one point up to six. The stations with the most powerful signals in the biggest markets carried more weight than smaller stations with weaker signals in the secondary and rural markets. A record needed those big powerful urban stations to climb the charts. The little stations were generally eager to help, adding records quickly upon release, but they were not enough. For a hit, it needed the big guys.

The record labels did everything they could for airplay—short of payola (and I suspect that was "worked out" in some cases as well)—to get their records added to a station's playlist. There were gifts, expensive dinners, paid trips, golf tournaments, the programmer's expenses paid to radio conventions, and so on. There were advertising buys and spots for concerts, all paid for by the labels. One programmer asked me directly to buy a new dress for his girlfriend. (I didn't. I couldn't afford any new dresses for my own wife.) It was no different from a lobbyist in Washington, DC. If you have the power, use it. It doesn't have anything to do with the quality of the music, the artistry. It's business—greed, and self-interest. Anyone who has control over the exposure of an artist's music to the masses has power over the recording artist and the record label. A station's play of a record company's product was the most powerful tool for exposing the music.

Radio stations and their staff members also promote concerts and live shows. Some of the program directors made additional money that way. I'll never forget what the program director at WIVK in Knoxville told me one afternoon while he drove me to the Knoxville airport. "Remember James, no one stays on top forever. If we can't book you on the way up, we can book you on the way down." The public is fickle. It wants new artists to discover and be excited about, so the record labels must constantly be churning out new acts. Old catalog doesn't matter, unless it is something the labels can license or repackage and make money on, like Capitol did with a plethora of Beatles reissues.

Young artists must remember these things. Respond and do the favors asked. Spread it around. "I will play your records and maybe make you a star, but you will repay me in kind." That's the way it goes. That's business.

★

Today, millions of people still listen to the radio, and now they stream music in their cars. Internet marketing, social media promotion, and streaming playlists add to the advertising and promotion equation. But it's still the same game. It's all about exposing the artist's music, exploiting the product. To keep a record moving up the charts, a certain number of *Billboard* reporting stations must add a record to their playlist each week. Unless an act is huge and established, like the Beatles in their prime, it is rare for every station to jump on a record and start playing it immediately. The higher up the chart a record goes, the harder it is to get those last few stations to play it. That's when the real hardball trading takes place, and there are a lot of gigantic egos all using their leverage.

There are many record companies all releasing singles every week. To add a new record, a station must drop another record from its playlist, because they only have from twenty to forty records in rotation at any given time. All records below forty on a station's chart are deemed "extras," and they don't count toward charting. A record may be an extra for several weeks before it is even added to a playlist. A radio personality can play a few extras, at his discretion on his airtime shift, but he *must* play the rotation on the station's chart playlist. The quicker a record is added to the greatest number of stations, the faster it climbs on *Billboard*'s national chart. The longer the stations keep the record on their local charts, the longer it stays on *Billboard*'s national chart. All records go up the charts, then down the charts, until they drop off. Some radio programmers, knowing their power, were truly prima donnas, but some of them were good people. Some of them still really like music, which is the reason they got into radio in the first place. They were just like the rest of society—some good, some not so good. It was important for the label's head of promotion and the regional promotion people to regularly visit and talk with the radio programmers and establish a good bond. It is a relationship business. I am sure a lot of this is the same today with the programmers of the streaming playlists. It's just an added dimension of the same game.

None of this really has anything to do with the music. It not about the music, it's about making money through ratings, advertising dollars, and the demographics that the station's salesmen use to sell advertising. The station's format—whether it is music of one type or another, talk, sports, or news—is about holding the listener's attention between commercials. The commercials are what you *must* hear. They pay the bills. Since the deregulation of the Federal Communications Commission (FCC) radio regulations under the Carter, Reagan, and Clinton administrations, most stations today are owned by giant corporations, media syndicates. The station owners don't really care about the music. They are trying to appeal to the lowest common denominator of listener in their targeted demographic. They will change the format of a station from country to pop, or pop to country, or to talk radio or any other format in a New York minute if they feel they can do better financially. Record stores also look to the *Billboard* radio and sales charts, the press reviews, and the advertising and sales hype from the record labels to determine which records to stock in their stores. A record that is not in the store cannot be sold, and the stores can only hold so many records. There was no Amazon.com in those days, and there was no Internet or social media. At that time, radio, press, and live performance were the only vehicles to sell records. But it is hard to get live performance bookings if no one knows who you are. Radio was how that exposure happened. It is a difficult, and at times a very dirty business.

Hunter S. Thompson, the late gonzo journalist, described the music business in 1985 in the *San Francisco Examiner* with characteristic candor: "The music business is a cruel and shallow money trench, a long plastic hallway where thieves and pimps run free, and good men die like dogs. There's also a negative side."

My music was unusual for its time; some have said it was ahead of its time. That may be true, but each of us lives in our time. That's how life works. You don't get to choose the time when you are born. There was no classification then in the music business called Americana, but that is essentially what my music was. It was never hard country. It was progressive. Bill Friskics-Warren in the *Nashville Scene* a few years back called me the "Godfather of Americana." Calling me that thirty years later was indeed a compliment, but it was like closing the barn door after all the horses are out. Still, I appreciated it. It meant a lot to me that someone noticed.

My music was not slick, like so much of what Nashville was releasing in the late 1970s. But that kind of simple production also made it timeless. Sometimes, I look back and wonder how in the world I even got signed to a major label in the first place with the songs I wrote. If I had not been a carpenter and had not remodeled Frank Jones's house, maybe it would never have happened. But from the beginning, I was following my heart, following my dreams, and what Pete Seeger told me I should do, but that can get you killed in the music business unless you get really lucky.

★

After I completed the recording of *Tryin' Like the Devil* in the fall of 1975, Bill Williams scheduled another trip to Hollywood with me to meet with the Capitol executives. I still had no manager or a booking agent. In Los Angeles Bill introduced me to Stuart Yahm, who had recently left Capitol Records to start his own management company. When Stu worked at Capitol, he had been in the artist development area, the part of the label that works with the various management companies to assist in coordinating how they can mutually advance their acts.

Stu came by our hotel to meet with me. He was an unusual looking guy to say the least. He dressed pure Hollywood, tight leather pants with laces over the fly like a shoe. He was a small in stature and wore platform shoes, and although he was white, he had a big Afro hairstyle. But in talking with him I could tell he was intelligent. Despite his outlandish appearance, he was well-spoken and down to earth. He was in his early forties then, and he seemed like an honest, caring guy. He seemed to know what a manager was about, and he passionately expressed interest in helping me with my career.

I knew nothing about what a manager was supposed to do, however, so I was easily impressed. I explained to Stu that there was no money in my Capitol contract for him as a manager, and no way did I have the money to pay him for his services. I was barely able to support myself. He said he understood, and that we would work on that together. Lacking any alternative, and because Bill seemed to favor him, I said, "OK." We shook hands, and Stu began working on my behalf as my manager. He worked hard for me. I have no complaints about that.

However, in hindsight, although Stu knew the important pressure points within Capitol Records, as it turned out that was not enough. What I really needed was an established management company with connections in the concert and booking world, a manager who could put me on tour with a big established act and expose me to large audiences. Capitol, as one of the major record labels, should have been able to facilitate this. They should have set up appointments with large well-funded management companies for me to interview, but they didn't. No effort was made outside of Bill Williams's input to assist in this area. As I have said, country music was not their moneymaker, so it was not the focus of their time and effort. I should have interviewed with several people, not one person starting a new company. But I knew nothing about how any of this was supposed to work, and I didn't know the right questions to ask. So I went with, and trusted, Stu Yahm.

I liked Stu. He was a dedicated manager. I never felt he did anything that was not in my best interest, but he was new and small in the management business, and he had no influence or clout—and influence and clout are what it takes to establish an act. In looking back, the problem in associating with a small startup manager was that I was his only client. Rather than starting out on his own, Stu—for his benefit and mine—probably should have attached himself to a larger management company that had other artists paying the bills, a company that could have developed me with a roster of other named talent. But as Stu's only client I was unlikely to succeed unless I simply exploded as an artist, and with Capitol's promotion structure and lesser regard for their country division, that wasn't likely to happen. Stu was not wealthy, and although his wife, Tara, was working a day job and he had some money saved, ultimately, he would go broke working with me. We gave it a good try, but I wasn't well-known yet, and I wasn't making enough money on the road to break even without the label's tour support. There were no trust funds or inheritances in my background, and it was a challenge to just pay myself and my bandmates. Jan and I lived frugally, but we were still relying on support from the label. So much for the naive idea that one had it made when signed with a major record label.

Jan and I had a young family then, and we constantly had musicians who were as poor as we were, or even poorer, staying at our house, some for a few days and some for several months. Around this time as well, my sister, Mary Jo, moved to Nashville and stayed with us. My sister majored in music. She had a good singing voice, which, like mine, she inherited from our father. She graduated from the University of New Mexico with a BFA in voice and completed an MA in voice at the University of Colorado. She moved to Nashville to see what might be possible in the business. She performed in a musical show for several seasons at the Opryland Theme Park and did background vocal session work in the Nashville studios. She sang as a featured vocalist with a Nashville orchestra for several years. But she simply did not have the passion for music that I had, and she preferred a regular paycheck. Eventually she switched to a career in cosmetic sales.

But with the musicians and my sister, it was difficult for Jan. We had two small children. There was extra work involved in cooking, preparing meals, buying extra food, and cleaning up after people—not to mention a lack of privacy. She made sacrifices.

Without tour support, and at times housing some of my musicians, I could not afford to keep a band together and tour. Even though we kept the band small—me, bass, drums, and one lead player—we still were not able to break even on our bookings. We were playing small clubs where the audience might be nine or ten people, or a few hundred. We needed to be opening for a big established concert act, where thousands of people could have seen us and heard my songs. But that takes some powerful management. It's all about exposure.

In August 1976, The Band, another Capitol act, was playing a concert at the Greek Amphitheater in Los Angeles. I was in town and the Capitol executives invited me to the show. The amphitheater was filled with several thousand fans. The opening act for The Band on that show was Leon Redbone, a Warner Brothers act. I thought, "Why in the hell couldn't Capitol have put me on that show in front of The Band, where I could have gotten the exposure?" They could have had two of their acts on the bill. But they never had anyone in the company trying to coordinate things like that—at least not for their Nashville acts.

America is a big country. In touring, there's a lot of territory to cover. A person may be known in one region and totally unknown in another. We were fighting for radio exposure everywhere, but there were gaps in areas where radio was not playing my records, and in many parts of the country I was unknown. Stu Yahm was slowly draining his savings account by making an investment in my talent. We were generating incredible press, but everyone in the business knows that press simply doesn't sell many records. It helps (record store buyers do read reviews), but what it really takes is voluminous radio play—and even more, it takes massive audience exposure opening in front of popular big-drawing acts. Stu and Capitol were not able to accomplish this, and in the end Stu's pockets were not deep enough.

My youthful parents, Florence and Jim Talley, in Tulsa, Oklahoma, c. 1942.
Photographer unknown (author's personal collection).

The hardscrabble Carr Family on their farm near Glencoe, Oklahoma, c. 1932.
Left to right: My mother, Florence; my grandfather Og; my Uncle Clyde;
my grandmother Mary; my mother's older sister, my Aunt Ruth.
Photographer unknown (author's personal collection).   115

My parents and me in DuPont's construction camp, Pasco, Washington, 1944, during the construction of the Hanford nuclear reactor. Our tar-paper-covered trailer house is behind us. Photographer unknown (author's personal collection).

My grandparents Mary and Og Carr, who were so good to me as a boy—Tulsa, c. 1942. Photographer unknown (author's personal collection).

On our front porch at age three, Commerce, Oklahoma, May 1946. Photo by Florence Talley (author's personal collection).

On the hood of our 1937 Chevy that we drove to Washington State, c. 1946, Commerce, Oklahoma. Photo by Florence Talley (author's personal collection).

My grandparents' house in Mehan, Oklahoma, c. 1944. Photo by Florence Talley (author's personal collection).

My sister, Mary Jo, and our dog, Bob. Albuquerque, New Mexico, January 1960. Photo by Florence Talley (author's personal collection).

In my spiffy uniform as the Sandia High School drum major, Albuquerque, 1959.
Photo by Florence Talley (author's personal collection).

Performing at the Territorial House Restaurant, Corrales, New Mexico, c. 1960.
Photographer unknown (author's personal collection).

Cover photo of *Got No Bread, No Milk, No Money, But We Sure Got a Lot of Love.* Me, Jan (eight months pregnant), and Reuben James, at Vernon Talley's store near White Bluff, Tennessee. © 1973 Clark Thomas (author's personal collection).

Odetta and me during the recording of her album in Nashville. © 1973 Clark Thomas (author's personal collection).

Me and Merle Haggard at the Country Music Association Concert, Nashville.
© 1974 Clark Thomas (author's personal collection).

My brown-eyed girl, my beautiful wife, Jan, at our home in Nashville. © 1977 Clark
Thomas (author's personal collection).

With my young sons, Reuben James and Justin Louis, June 1977 at our home in Nashville. © 1977 Clark Thomas (author's personal collection).

DeFord Bailey playing left-handed guitar for me at his apartment in Nashville. © 1976 Clark Thomas (from the personal collection of David Morton).

Working on my carpenter job at Nashboro Village with Henry Huddleston (center) and Jerry LeRoy. © 1975 Clark Thomas (author's personal collection).

Me and B. B. King in Jack Clement's Studio A, Nashville, November 1976. Photographer unknown (author's personal collection).

Cover photo of *Blackjack Choir*. Left to right: Brother Burns, me, Ida Mae Shaw, Margaret Hogue, George Holden, and Henry Murphy, Herman Street, North Nashville. © 1976 Clark Thomas (author's personal collection).

At Jimmy Carter's inauguration. The Carters, me, and Jan, Washington DC Armory Show (the Georgia Party). January 20, 1977. Photo by Cavalliere Ketchum (author's personal collection).

Jan, me, and Jimmy Carter. Dinner at the White House, and my first White House performance, December 7, 1977. Photographer unknown (author's personal collection).

Cover photograph of *The Road to Torreón*. Mine and Cavalliere Ketchum's tribute to the Hispanic people of New Mexico c. 1967. Photo by Cavalliere Ketchum (author's personal collection).

Jan and me in Nashville, 1999. Photo by Jim McGuire (author's personal collection).

Performing at the dedication of DeFord Bailey's tombstone, with Roy Acuff and Bill Monroe sitting behind me, 1983. Photo by Alan Murphy (from the personal collection of David Morton).

On tour in Italy with the band. Left to right: Gregg Thomas, Italian publisher Paolo Carú, Dave Pomeroy, me, Jono Manson, Mike Noble, and our tour manager, Umberto Bonanni, in Gallarate, Italy, 2002. Photographer unknown (author's personal collection).

With progressive radio personality John Larson and two fine songwriter friends, Guy Clark and Butch Hancock, at BMI in Nashville. Photographer unknown (author's personal collection).

Performing in Utrecht, the Netherlands, September 21, 2015. Photographer unknown (author's personal collection).

My coproducer and ace musician and engineer Tommy Detamore, in his Cherry Ridge Studio, Floresville, Texas, 2007. Photo by James Talley (author's personal collection).

My grandson, Henry Talley, and our little blue heeler, Sage, Nashville, 2019. Photo by James Talley (author's personal collection).

★ ★ ★ ★ ★

Chapter 10

THE GREAT SOUTHEAST MUSIC HALL AND THE PALOMINO CLUB

The Great Southeast Music Hall in Atlanta was a place where I often performed. Atlanta is only 250 miles from Nashville, so its proximity makes it easy to perform there. The owner of the Great Southeast Music Hall was Jack W. Tarver Jr. I could not have asked for a better fan or supporter of my music. Jack was trained as a lawyer—Vanderbilt University, Duke Law School—but like so many young lawyers, after he started his practice he hated the law. Much to the disappointment of his parents, Jack gave up his law practice and opened a nightclub, the Great Southeast Music Hall. Jack was two years older than me. He was from a very wealthy Atlanta family. His father, Jackson Williams Tarver Sr., was the owner, editor, and publisher of the *Atlanta Constitution* newspaper. Jack's parents traveled in elite company and were not happy when Jack gave up the law to become a nightclub owner and a music promoter. But Jack absolutely loved music and musicians. He found the life exciting, and he loved promoting music. Unfortunately, he also partied and drank way too much.

The Great Southeast had five hundred seats, and everyone played there, artists on their way up and on their way down, from Willie Nelson, Waylon Jennings, and the Earl Scruggs Revue to all of the 1970s singer-songwriters. Everyone played the Great Southeast. I saw a young Hans Zimmer, now the famous film score composer, there one night. Jack would book up-and-coming artists at the Great Southeast, and if they became a bigger draw, he would promote a show with them at the Fox Theatre in Atlanta. If they became huge acts, like Willie Nelson did, he would book them at the Omni Arena.

I was one of Jack's favorite opening acts at the Great Southeast Music Hall. He did everything he could to help me establish myself in the Atlanta market. Unfortunately, we got little airplay in Atlanta and little support from Capitol's regional promotion staff there. Jack helped me for years, through thick and thin. However, at times I found his drinking, and his behavior when he was drinking, unbearable. The constant tension between him and his controlling parents made him unhappy much of the time. Plus, he just liked to party. It was a classic southern struggle, a little like *Cat on a Hot Tin Roof.* Jack drank to escape his demons, and everyone around him had to suffer and bear it.

As Larry Burton had once done in Nashville, Jack was constantly trying to learn the finer points of the music business. On occasion, he would come to Nashville and visit with Don Light, a Nashville manager, and pick his brain on the music business. Don had once managed Jimmy Buffett, but Buffett left Don for Irving Azoff when Azoff promised to put him on tour with the Eagles, which made him a star. Before Jimmy hit it big, I opened for him once at a club in Oklahoma City. He had just purchased his first tour bus. He was so excited about it. He wanted us all to take a tour of it. Jimmy had no pretense. He was down-to-earth and a fine singer-songwriter. For a time, Don Light also managed Keith Whitley, an incredible vocalist; but all of Don's acts left him for greener pastures.

I once played a co-bill at the Great Southeast with Townes van Zandt. We were staying at the same motel near the club, and the next morning we were out on the balcony drinking a cup of coffee and talking. In Townes's typical laid-back fashion, he said to me, "You know that song of yours, 'Give My Love to Marie'? That song got me through the winter last year." That was the way Townes talked. He was a gentle troubled soul.

Jack Tarver invited Jan and me to a Jerry Lee Lewis concert he was promoting at the Great Southeast. He had moved his club to a new eight-hundred-seat venue. Jan and I both loved Jerry Lee Lewis. When we were first married, we wore out three albums of Jerry Lee's recordings of classic country songs. For us, it didn't get much better than Jerry Lee. So at Jack's invitation, we drove to Atlanta for the show.

Carl Perkins was the opening act. Jack had once brought Carl by our home in Nashville. He was a totally unassuming, humble man. He just enjoyed driving his tractor on his farm near Jackson, Tennessee. We were looking forward to seeing Carl and Jerry Lee at the show. But when we arrived in Atlanta, Jack told us that Carl had had a small accident, a fender-bender, leaving his home in Jackson. Carl had called Jack to let him know that he was not going to be able to make it for the show.

Jack said to me, "Carl's not going to be able make it tonight. I'd like for you to open the show for Jerry Lee."

I said, "Jack, I don't even have my guitar with me."

Jack said, "Oh, hell, I'll find you a guitar!"

I said, "Yeah, that's what I'm afraid of. You'll find me something that's not even playable."

He said, "Oh, I know you play a Martin, I'll find you a good guitar."

Soon, I was backstage with Jerry Lee and his band. Jerry was sitting in a folding lawn chair on one the side of the stage, drinking straight from a bottle of vodka, and talking with his ex-wife, Myra. She was then living in Atlanta and was at the show. Jerry Lee had married her years before when she was thirteen. I went over and said hello to Jerry Lee and Myra. He was polite to me but brief. I could tell he was absorbed in talking with Myra and didn't want to be bothered. His and Myra's teenage daughter was at the show, and she would later sing a few songs.

I was not too sure about opening the show. Jerry Lee had shot his bass player only a short while before. What if he got drunk and didn't like me? He was drinking heavy that night. But Kenny Lovelace, Jerry Lee's wonderful guitarist and fiddler who had been with him for years, assured me all was fine. I had admired Kenny's playing on Jerry's recordings for years, and it was a treat to be on the same stage with him.

Jack soon returned with an old Martin D-18 for me. I don't know where he got it, but the strings on it were so old they could have been the original set! The tuning gears were all stiff, and the guitar was almost impossible to tune. It was obvious it had not been played in some time.

The show started, and I came out with my guitar. I sang one of my more rockabilly numbers, and the audience kindly applauded. But as the applause died down, and before I could start another song, there was a large lady sitting on the front row who was well into her cups, and she yelled out, "Carl! Sing 'Blue Suede Shoes'!" A little chuckle rippled through the audience. I started quickly into another song, and when I finished the audience again politely applauded. When it died down, the lady in the front row again cried out, "Carl! I come all the way down here to hear you sing, 'Blue Suede Shoes.' Won't you sing 'Blue Suede Shoes' for meeeeee?" The audience was laughing harder now, and I was growing more and more uncomfortable. I sang another song or two, with interruptions in between from the front row, and finally the lady began to get steamed. She said, "Carl, I come all the way down here to hear you sing 'Blue Suede Shoes.' If you ain't gonna sing it, I'm comin' up there!" So I finally gave up. I thought, "What the hell?" and I became Carl Perkins for a night and lit into it, "One for the money, two for the show . . . Blue Suede Shoes."

That did it for the audience. They cheered and clapped, then stood up and gave me a standing ovation. I couldn't have done better if I had planted the lady in the front row as a ringer. How could I top that? So I thanked the audience and exited the stage. I'd done enough. I had triumphed as Carl Perkins.

The show, of course, was fantastic. Jerry Lee played with reckless abandon. He played songs by Jimmie Rodgers and all manner of material I'd never heard on any of his records. He was just playing whatever came into his head and heart. Every ounce of emotion was poured out. He played the piano wildly, but flawlessly. It seemed like he was on autopilot. He went on and on. He was loving it, and with a repertoire so vast it was stunning. I'll never forget opening for Jerry Lee Lewis and becoming Carl Perkins for a night.

★

After *Tryin' Like the Devil* was released, the band and I went on a West Coast tour. It started, however, in Indianapolis at a venue called the Nashville Country Club. We were booked there for two nights. We were playing off a short stage riser, and there were some young women out on the dance floor standing on their heads. I leaned over to my lead guitar player, and said, "Well, they can't say we didn't stand them on their heads in Indianapolis."

But at the break, the club owner called and wanted to talk to me. He said, "My manager tells me that you all are playing in blue jeans and flannel shirts. You don't have matching outfits?"

I said, "No, we don't have matching outfits." At the end of the night, they cancelled our second night and stiffed us our money. Obviously, we couldn't play real country music if we didn't have matching outfits.

Our next date was over two thousand miles away. It was headlining at the famous Palomino Club in North Hollywood, *the* country music venue then in Los Angeles—and with a great name. I was looking forward to playing there. But I also wondered who in the hell does the routing on these tours—Indianapolis to Los Angeles!

We had a rented Ford station wagon from Hertz. We kept our foot on the gas across the country, driving straight through to reach Los Angeles on time. We were a short distance past Gallup, New Mexico, near the Arizona border, when the check-engine light came on and the station wagon started running extremely rough. It was missing and bucking so bad we decided we'd better turn around and try to get back to Gallup before we were stranded in the Arizona desert.

The Hertz office at the Gallup Airport was an old wooden school-teacher's desk with a Hertz sign on the front. It was in one corner of a small cinderblock building that was the Gallup Airport terminal. I left a note, along with Hertz's rental contract, on the Hertz desk and told them their car had broken down, and that it would be downtown at the Gallup Greyhound bus station with the keys over the sun visor. We drove to the Greyhound station, parked the car, and waited for the 11:30 P.M. bus out of Gallup to Los Angeles. The bus showed up just before midnight, and we got our suitcases and all the guitars, amps, and the drum set out of the station wagon and loaded everything into the baggage compartment of the Greyhound. It rolled out of Gallup around midnight.

The bus was nearly empty, and I was trying to get some sleep in the seats behind the driver. As I would switch sides of the bus, it was like getting punched in one arm and then the other all night. The other three band members were all ensconced in the back of the bus with three or four other passengers. We rolled across Arizona in the dark and finally reached the California border at Needles about sunup. There was a small restaurant in the terminal, and the driver stopped the bus for a breakfast break.

As the bus rolled to a halt, an empty Old Grandad whiskey bottle came rolling down the aisle toward me. I went to the back of the bus and found all the musicians and two or three other passengers all passed out in the back. They had been passing the bottle around all night. I left them in their inebriated slumber and went in the coffee shop for some coffee.

I later learned that when we'd loaded our gear out of the Nashville Country Club in Indianapolis, the hallway to the back door passed by the liquor storeroom. My bass player had quickly taken the bottle of Old Grandad as he was loading out his bass equipment. Since we had been stiffed at the Nashville County Club and fired because we did not have matching outfits, I had no qualms about stealing a bottle of their whiskey. But my musicians didn't offer me a drop of it!

We went to the Holiday Inn in Hollywood and went straight to sleep. I was forced to be my own road manager in those days, and I asked for a wakeup call for later in the afternoon so everyone could get ready for the performance. When it was time to go to work, none of the three *borachos* felt too good. In the Palomino audience that night were the actors Richard Chamberlain, Warren Oates, and a few other celebrities.

Leading a band on the road was new to me. I was not used to herding drunks and babysitting immature individuals. I had been used to dealing with responsible people, doing responsible things—even if it was rat control. I soon learned that I had at least two alcoholics, or near alcoholics, in the band, and it became a constant struggle. It was like herding baby chicks. But I was on such a shoestring budget that I didn't have much leverage over my musicians. It was not like I could really afford to keep a band together, and from their perspective it was like they were doing me a favor playing with me. Musicians must have tremendous discipline learning to play and master their instruments when young. It takes a lot of time and practice to play well. But some of them have no discipline whatsoever with the rest of their lives, which is what holds a lot of them back. Later in life, I saw the difference in playing with real professionals who had their act together.

We rented another station wagon and went on up the coast for several more dates in other California cities. I opened for Gene Clark's band. Gene was a founding member of the Byrds folk-rock group, and a fine singer and songwriter. He was touring then as a solo artist with his own band. Gene was quite personable, and we became good friends on that tour. We played one night in Palo Alto, and Gene heard me sing my song, "Give My Love to Marie," which was on *Tryin' Like the Devil*. Gene said to me, "I love that song and the next time I record I am going to record it." He eventually did record it, and his version is simply magnificent, with full orchestration as opposed to my very simple version of it. I had no idea it could be recorded so beautifully with such a big production.

We wound up the West Coast tour in Berkeley, California. I was able to meet Greil Marcus there, the reviewer who wrote that first glowing review of *Got No Bread*. Greil lived in Berkeley and came to the show. He joined me and the band after the performance at a local bar for some Irish coffee. He told me confidentially that I needed to replace my drummer. Hell, I needed to replace the entire band!

$\star \ \star \ \bigstar \ \star \ \star$

Chapter 11

B. B. AND THE CARTER
INAUGURATION

After my 1976 performance tour, Capitol picked up their option for my third album, which would be titled *Blackjack Choir*. It was a loose concept album of songs about the South. Since moving from the Southwest to Nashville, I had written several songs with southern themes. It's funny, but sometimes you can write more perceptively as an observer about a place you've seen for the first time, rather than what is familiar. The images are new and reflect more brightly on your mind. *Blackjack Choir* was in a way a homage to my new home in the Southland.

By the fall of 1976, I had disbanded my earlier musicians. I could not take all the drinking and insanity. I had brought Clark Pierson down from Woodstock as my new drummer. Clark was originally from Albert Lea, Minnesota. He had studio experience and was a member of Janis Joplin's last band, Full Tilt Boogie. He played drums on Janis's *Pearl* album. Clark also agreed to go on the road with me and tour after the album was released. He'd been a marine and was a solid guy. He liked to keep his boots shined. He was not married but had a woman he'd been living with in Woodstock. They had a baby daughter they'd named Pearl. I hired Mike Leech, one of the fine Memphis bassists, who'd moved to Nashville, and whom I had used on an earlier session. He and Clark made a solid rhythm section. Again, I used most of the same players I'd used on my first two albums. It was an absolute treat to hear Josh Graves and Johnny Gimble dueling it out on "When the Fiddler Packs His Case"—two masters loving playing together.

We recorded the album again at Jack Clement's Studio B. With each successive album, Capitol had given me slightly more money for recording. As usual, though, all those recording costs were advances and were evaporating my future royalties.

I had written a song for my friend Henry Murphy, my old health department compadre, called "Magnolia Boy." Henry had told me a story about how his grandfather always called him Magnolia Boy growing up. Henry said, "As a small boy, I couldn't understand why he called me that, because the magnolia flower is white, and I was Black. I asked my grandfather about it, and he said, 'Yes, child, the magnolia flower is white, but it is also sweet, just like you.'" That image stuck in my head, and I had to write a song called "Magnolia Boy" for Henry.

I have always loved the blues. It is the most honest music there is, and I've loved so many great bluesmen: Muddy Waters, B. B. King, Sonny Terry and Brownie McGee, Big Bill Broonzy, Lightnin' Hopkins, and others. I wanted to write a song that was a homage to all these bluesmen. On tour one night, I was in my hotel room about to go to sleep and the lines for "Bluesman" started to come to me, so I turned on the bedside light and jotted down: "I'm the bluesman, I've been around a long, long time. . . ." Ideas often come to songwriters just as they're falling asleep. When they do, we must get up and write them down, because they are coming from a semiconscious dream state, the unconscious mind, and we will never remember them in the morning.

We had befriended a young songwriter from New York who had moved to Nashville named Charles Silver. Charles came by the studio one afternoon while we were recording and heard the track of "Bluesman." Charles said, "You should get B. B. King to play on that song. I think he would love it." The more I thought about what Charles said, the more intriguing that possibility became. Would B. B. really consider playing on it? I put the rhythm track on a cassette tape and sent it with a letter to B. B.'s manager in New York. I asked him if B. B. would consider playing on the song with us in Nashville. It was just a young man's leap of faith. I was stunned when a couple of weeks later I got word back that B. B. would love to do it.

I was incredibly excited. I had admired his music for so many years, since I'd seen him at the Tennessee State Prison back in 1970, and since I'd first heard his music from that scratchy old speaker in Henry Murphy's 1956 Ford—Henry, the Magnolia Boy from Hattiesburg. There was more than a deep satisfaction for me when he agreed to play on my record.

B. B. flew into town and arrived at the studio for a 2:00 P.M. session. He was gracious and humble. He put on his headphones, and we started running the track for him, but Jim Williamson, the engineer, noticed a little static coming from "Lucille," B. B.'s Gibson 355 guitar. It turned out to be a bad plug on his guitar cord. B. B. said, "Does anybody have a small Phillips-head screwdriver?"

Jim brought him one, and B. B. patiently took the plug on his guitar cord apart and carefully rewrapped the tiny wires around their terminals and screwed the plug back together. It sounded fine, and we were ready to record. I have thought about that instance for years, how this great musician repaired his own guitar cord. Some petulant young rock and roller might have just said, "Somebody send out and get me a new cord." Not B. B. King. He'd picked cotton. By God, he would fix his own damned guitar cord.

We ran through the song with B. B. several times, and he laid down several tracks until he had one he was satisfied with. Then he came in the control room to listen. It sounded fantastic. We all agreed that it would certainly do, so he packed up his guitar, and we took him to the airport to fly out. He told me it was the first time in twenty years that he'd played as a sideman, since he'd played for Otis Spann in Chicago in the 1950s. He also told me that it was the first time he had ever recorded in Nashville.

I said, "Why?"

He said, "No one ever invited me before."

When he got ready to leave for his plane, we said goodbye in a hallway. He took my hand in both of his and he said, "James, you go back and listen to what we did, and if you find anything at all in it you don't like, you call me. I'll come back, and we'll do it again."

B. B. played a show not long after that at the Exit Inn, a popular club in Nashville. Jan and I went to see him. The dressing room was in a small building out back. Women were carrying in big trays of home-cooked meals and desserts. The room was so full of food and admirers that people could hardly move. Jan told B. B. about our two little boys, who were three and seven at the time, and B. B. pulled two silver dollars out of his pocket and gave them to her, one for each of the boys. We still have those two silver dollars.

Blackjack Choir was a labor of love, as were all my recordings. It was never about the money for me. It was always about the music, the art, the dreams. Yes, of course I would love to have made money on my recordings, and over the years I have made some, but that was never my primary motivation. These recordings are my creative children. They are the reason I am in this world. I just wanted to make them the best I could.

The first note on *Blackjack Choir* is played by B. B. King, the great blues-man, and the last note on the album is played by the incomparable Johnny Gimble on his fiddle. Two American musical legends, equally talented on their instruments. Both picked cotton in their youth—one in the heat of the Mississippi Delta and the other in the dry Texas dust. Both men changed their lives and made their mark through their music. I suspect that *Blackjack Choir* may be the only album where the two of them ever worked together. Riley B. King died on May 14, 2015. Johnny Gimble died on May 9, 2015. They died within five days of one another, B. B. was eighty-nine years old, and Johnny Gimble would have turned eighty-nine on May 30. It was the passing of two gigantic musical legends, the end of an era, and I had the good fortune and honor to know them both.

★

Many of the players on my early albums are no longer with us. Several of them I can't locate any longer, and I don't know whether they are still alive or not, like the great studio guitarist Jerry Shook and Clark Pierson, my old drummer. Mike Leech passed away in December 2017. But their music and their contribution to my music and my life are still there in these recordings. That's the beauty of art. It has been said, "Art alone endures, all else perishes." When I listen to these albums, as I do now and then, the memories of those sessions comes back to me, and there is still a joy in remembering those wonderful times in the studio together. They were the best years of our lives and hearing each note as it was played in those glorious days is such a joy. It still moves me.

The cover photo for *Blackjack Choir* was again taken by Clark Thomas. It is an iconic shot. It is me with some of my coworkers from the Nashville Health Department's rat control program. It was taken at a little neighborhood grocery in North Nashville—a little place where you could gamble on a number. To my right on the bench is one of our laborers, Brother Burns. On my left is Ida Mae Shaw, the health aide whose face was so badly cut in jealous rage by an ex-husband. In the center is Margaret Hogue, the great Nashville gospel singer, who was one of my health aides. Next to her is George Holden, one of the truck crew workers, and on the end of the bench to my far left is Henry Murphy, the Magnolia Boy, who first introduced me to B. B. King's music, and who taught me with such wisdom. This photograph holds a significant part of my young life and the people who taught me so much and to whom I am so indebted. They taught me what the blues was all about—and as much as any white person can learn, about what it is to be Black in America.

When *Blackjack Choir* was released, I wondered if country music radio programmers would view the cover with me and a group of African Americans and refuse to play the record. One of the sales executives at Capitol in Hollywood said, "I thought this was supposed to be a country record, why is B. B. King playing on it?" Yes, it was different, but honest. The songs came from life.

Seventeen years later, B. B.'s autobiography was released. I had not seen him in all those years. He was having a book signing at a local Nashville bookstore. Jan and I decided we would go and get him to sign a couple of books for us. We got in the line to have our books signed, and when I got up to B. B., he was sitting behind a little table. He looked up, and when he saw me, a big smile came across his face. He stood up, reached across the little book signing table and gave me a big bear hug. Then he turned to the lady from the book company standing next to him and said, "This is James Talley. He put the blues with country music. He invited me to play my first session in Nashville."

The publisher's rep was not impressed. She was more concerned that the line had stopped. People were looking out the side of the line, like, "What's going on up there?" B. B. asked me to wait, and we spoke for a short while before he had to leave. I couldn't believe it; we hadn't seen each other in all those years, but he had never forgotten our session, and of course, neither had I.

★

In the summer of 1976, Jimmy Carter was running for president. My wife, Jan, had read somewhere that Jimmy Carter liked Bob Dylan's music and she said, "If he likes Dylan, I think he would like your music." So at Jan's urging, I sent copies of my first two albums to Jimmy Carter in Plains, Georgia, with a note of support.

I didn't think much about it, but after the election in November 1976, I was at Capitol's Nashville office one afternoon checking on something. I was told there was a phone call for me. It turned out to be a lady named Joanne Goldberg, who was the television producer for Barbara Walters's show.

She said, "Barbara was down in Plains, Georgia, last night interviewing the Carters, and they were talking about the music they liked and the records they planned to take to the White House. Barbara asked them who some of their favorite artists were, and Jimmy said, 'Well, last night we were listening to my wife's favorite artist, James Talley.'" I about dropped the phone!

Joanne Goldberg didn't know who James Talley was, so like a good television producer she decided to do some checking and found out I was on Capitol Records. She called the office in Nashville to find out more about me, and since I happened to be there at the time, the receptionist put me on the phone with her. Joanne said, "I don't think we are going to use that segment in the televised interview, but I wanted you to know what Mr. Carter had said."

It wasn't long after that I was invited to play at the Carter inauguration, on January 20, 1977. The *Blackjack Choir* album had been slated for release in February 1977, but when I told Capitol about being invited to play at the inauguration, they decided to move up the release date to January. I didn't have a band together to tour at the time. I never had the money to keep musicians on a retainer. I had to assemble and rehearse a band each time I toured. So I put a band together to play the inauguration, and the week before we rehearsed in my living room for three days.

Our performance was at the Georgia party, which was at the Washington DC Armory. I invited Cavalliere Ketchum to join us, and he flew to Washington from Madison, Wisconsin, where he was teaching. I also invited Wes Pulkka, a former welfare department coworker and sculptor to attend. Wes flew to Nashville from Seattle, where he was living at the time. Cavalliere wound up taking the photo of me and the Carters backstage after the Georgia party concert that was used in Capitol Records' advertising. He also took photos of each member of our party in front of the big inauguration seal, so they would have a memento of attending.

Stu Yahm, my manager, flew in from Los Angeles with his wife, Tara. The inauguration was Stu's last official business as my manager. Stu had spent most of his savings working with me and was forced to go back to work for another record label in Los Angeles. He simply did not have the time to keep managing me and doing his job at his new record label. We parted amicably, and I was again without a manager.

Peter Guralnick came down from Massachusetts to join us, and Bill Williams came to represent Capitol Records. We shared a dressing room with Guy Lombardo and His Royal Canadians, who played the dance music at the event. After our performance we were in the back hallway of the Armory, and John Sayles, my fiddle player, came leaping down a short flight of steps, saying, "They're coming, the Carters are coming!" I took one of the newly minted *Blackjack Choir* albums, with the picture of me and my rat control pals on the cover and waited at the bottom of the steps to see the Carters. When they arrived, I presented an autographed copy to Mrs. Carter.

President Carter asked me about the picture on the front of the *Got No Bread* album. He said, "You all don't really live there, do you?" I assured him we didn't, which seemed to set his mind at ease, and I thanked him and Rosalynn for inviting us to celebrate their inauguration with them. We wished them our best for a successful administration, and they moved on to other events. It was a short intimate moment with two lovely people. Cavalliere Ketchum captured the scene with his camera, and it was over.

While we were in Washington, we had dinner with several music journalists, including Peter Guralnick, Bob Christgau from the *Village Voice*, and a few others. Christgau kept asking me questions about various political policies, and what I thought about this or that policy issue, but I kept referring his questions to Jan, who loves politics and was much better informed on all those things than I was. Christgau mentioned this in his *Village Voice* article about the inauguration—that I deferred his questions to Jan. She did know more about it than I did. She always does.

The day after the inauguration, Jan and Cavalliere went to see several tourist sites in Washington together. Wes Pulkka was charged with getting the band equipment back to Nashville, and I headed for New York City where a bevy of press interviews were waiting for me. Capitol had hired an independent publicist in New York to arrange extra publicity. That following day in New York, I had seven press interviews back-to-back. Naturally, every publication wanted to know about my experience at the Carter inauguration.

After everything from the inauguration settled down, I went back out on tour with my band. I opened several shows for Randy Newman, whose song "Short People" was out at the time. The tour was a blur with a different club each night. I had purchased a second Ford Club Wagon to hold more musicians and equipment. As usual, I had to road manage the band myself. I had a roadie to assist with the driving and equipment handling, but each morning I had to get on the phone and get the contacts where we were playing next, people's names, phone numbers, and the venues' addresses. In addition, I had to get any information on fill-in dates that were being added to the tour. I would play until 2:00 A.M., finally get to sleep around 4:00 A.M., and then be up at 10:00 A.M. and on the phone with the booking agent the next morning. I never got enough sleep. After our date at Massey Hall in Toronto with Newman, we bought two cases of Genesee Cream Ale in a Buffalo supermarket and several boxes of NoDoz pills and drove straight through to Nashville.

★

When *Blackjack Choir* was released, Capitol was planning to take out a full-page ad in *Billboard* magazine with Cavalliere Ketchum's photograph of me and Jan with the Carters. A full-page advertisement in *Billboard* is quite expensive, and since I'd had such good success with my previous *Tryin' Like the Devil* radio station tour, I thought if Capitol were going to spend that kind of money it would be better spent on another person-to-person radio tour instead of an expensive *Billboard* ad. Radio was terribly important to exposing my music. However, radio programmers do notice a full-page *Billboard* ad. It shows them that the label is behind an act. Don Zimmerman, the Capitol president came to Nashville, and I met with him. I told him I thought we'd get better mileage out of a face-to-face radio tour than a big *Billboard* ad.

Don surprised me when he said, "James, we're going to do both." We had the wonderful press, we had the momentum, we had the president's attention. I really felt the label was behind me at that point. Things were finally beginning to jell.

I flew all over the country for about three weeks, sometimes going to several cities in a day. For instance, I left Nashville one morning on an extremely early flight and had breakfast with the program director at WIL in St. Louis; then I flew to Minneapolis and had lunch with a program director there; then I flew to Kansas City and had dinner that evening with an important FM program director and his wife; then I caught a red-eye flight to Denver and arrived around 2:00 A.M. Each day was like this. It was like a politician running for national office. We were trying to cover as much of the country as possible and talk one-on-one with as many key radio people as we could. This proved beneficial to airplay. It shows that an artist cares about the people who play his records, and it also conveys to them that the label is behind the artist.

On the radio tour for *Blackjack Choir*, I was once so tired that I took off for Boston from New York, and I suddenly felt the plane braking. I thought, "Oh, my god, we're aborting a takeoff!" But the plane was landing in Boston. I had gone to sleep so quickly after boarding in New York that I didn't even remember taking off. These were grueling schedules. I did everything I could to promote my music for Capitol. I was a dedicated artist. After all, it was my life and my dream, and I wanted it to succeed.

Chapter 12

BUT ART ISN'T ENOUGH

I was in a hotel room in Boston on my second radio station tour, and I got a message that Mort Cooperman, the owner of the Lone Star Cafe in New York wanted to talk with me. I didn't know Mort, but I called him from my hotel room. He explained that he was a huge fan of my music and wanted me to play his club in New York City. I explained that I didn't have a band together right then, but I said that, when I started touring again, I would love to play his club. Therein started a long relationship with Mort Cooperman and the Lone Star Cafe in New York City, about which more later.

That spring, following the *Blackjack Choir* release, I opened some shows for Jerry Jeff Walker and his Lost Gonzo Band. I was opening then as a solo artist, just me and my guitar. I always liked Jerry Jeff's music. He was a fine singer, with an expressive baritone, and he was a good songwriter. I looked upon him as a musical kindred spirit. He was always affable and courteous to me, but during those years he was also into drugs and booze, and sometimes I didn't know which Jerry Jeff I was going to see, the relaxed affable one or the crazy one.

I met one of Jerry Jeff's managers at a show I'd opened for him in Washington, DC. He was an accountant and lived in a small town on Long Island. He said he handled the business aspects of the Jerry Jeff's management. (He collected the money.) He was professional, gracious, and seemed quite normal and sane for the music business. I mentioned to him that I needed management in a bad way, and he seemed interested. I was heading up to New York in a few days and we set up a meeting at his home on Long Island. He told me his management partner, who handled the creative part of the team, was in Austin, Texas. His name as Michael Brovsky. When we met at his home on Long Island, he said he had spoken with Brovsky about me, and Brovsky wanted to meet me. This was in the spring of 1977.

I asked Bill Williams at Capitol for a plane ticket to Austin to meet with Brovsky. Bill knew I needed management, and these guys seemed to be doing a good job for Jerry Jeff. So Bill paid for a ticket and a hotel night for me to meet with Brovsky in Austin.

When I met Brovsky, I explained that my former manager had had to drop out, and I was impressed with what he had been able to do for Jerry Jeff and Guy Clark, whom he had been managing. I told Brovsky that I thought Jerry Jeff and Guy were kindred singer-songwriters, and I wondered if perhaps he would be interested in managing me. I told him I was going in the studio in June to record my fourth album for Capitol. I explained that I would be producing it myself as I had my previous albums.

Michael fancied himself a record producer, and he said he would like to have some part in producing the new album, perhaps in the mixing. I said I would be open to working with him in any way he wanted, but I explained to him that there was no money in my Capitol contract to pay a producer. I'd produced all three of my Capitol albums to that point myself. All I was getting from the sessions was union scale through AFTRA and nothing extra as a producer. We agreed to work together on a handshake, and when I do that it means something to me. I flew back to Nashville and started preparing for my upcoming recording sessions. The album would eventually be called, *Ain't It Somethin'*, after a song I had written by that title.

To record, I put together the same team of musicians, except I used Gregg Thomas on drums. Gregg had played on my first album, and Clark Pierson was then touring with Dolly Parton. Gregg was living in Los Angeles then, and he and Marty Grebb, a talented saxophonist and keyboard player, also then living in Los Angeles, came up from Atlanta where they had been attending a music trade show. Tommy Cogbill was on bass, one of the great Memphis players who had moved to Nashville. I was thrilled that he would be playing with me. Once I worked with him, I never wanted to use another bass player. He was an incredible musician. His tone was out of this world, and he was a lot of fun in the studio. Unfortunately, only five years after our sessions, on December 7, 1982, Tommy died of a brain hemorrhage. He was only fifty years old. Randy Scruggs, Earl's second son, and simply an incredible musician, played banjo on my song "Dixie Blue." I'd played on the same bill with the Earl Scruggs Review several times at the Great Southeast Music Hall in Atlanta. Unfortunately, Randy passed away on April 17, 2018. Doyle Grisham, who was always on my sessions, and ever in my heart, played pedal steel, and the incomparable Johnny Gimble, of course, played fiddle.

There is a variety of songs on the album. It includes a very personal song about my father and his work in the plutonium plant at Hanford, called "Richland, Washington." I wrote it for my two boys, who never got to see their grandfather.

Everyone who enjoys *Ain't It Somethin'* always wants to know where in the world "Nine Pounds of Hashbrowns" came from. Well, Steve Hostak, my guitar player, had been staying with Jan and me for a while in our spare bedroom. One day for breakfast, Steve started cooking a couple of little frozen hash brown potato patties in an iron skillet. But they looked so small, and we were hungry, so we added a few more. As they began to cook, they started to expand, and before we knew it the skillet was running over with hash brown potatoes. Jan came in the kitchen and said, "Look at this! What are you guys doing?" I must confess, cooking has never been my forte, and apparently it wasn't Steve's either.

After eating our hashbrowns, I had jotted down some whimsical lyrics on a yellow legal pad. It was a spoof on the music business, which is about as stupid and excessive as that steaming skillet of potatoes. The lyrics were lying on the coffee table in the living room, where I had scribbled them down, and Steve picked them up, read them, and laughed. They weren't finished lyrics, just an idea. I put them in my briefcase for later.

One day in the studio, we had just finished the track for "Poets of the West Virginia Mines." Recording takes incredible concentration, so when we finished the song, Steve Hostak and Jerry Shook were blowing off a little pressure and started riffing back and forth on their electric guitars on one chord. The bass and drums joined in, as did I on my acoustic, and this funky groove started with everyone playing and laughing and having a good time. Then Steve said, "Hey, get those lyrics you wrote for 'Nine Pounds of Hashbrowns.'" So I quickly went to my briefcase and got my notes, and I started riffing lyrics over what they were playing, making up some of it as I went along. It was like rap or talking blues. The entire recording went on for almost fifteen minutes, before everyone had blown off enough steam and was played out. I ran out of lyrics long before that, but Jim Williamson just let the tape roll. We later added Marty Grebb and Billy Puett on their saxes to the track, and Rick Durrett played some Hammond B3, but since we couldn't justify fifteen minutes of pure guitar funk on the record, I just faded it out after the lyrics stopped. It was a lot of fun in the studio, an afterthought, like "Big Taters in the Sandy Land" was on my first album. It seems to be a favorite with many people. It's simply lighthearted fun. Sometimes you get lucky.

All the tracks and overdubs were completed for *Ain't It Somethin'* and we were ready to mix. Michael Brovsky wanted to be involved in the mixing. He flew to Nashville from Austin and, in one long night—all night, and into the morning, and with Jim Williamson and me about to give out at the controls—Michael managed to complete a mix of the entre album. He smoked pot all night and perhaps took something to stay awake. When we finished the following morning, he flew back to Austin with a copy of his mixes. Jim and I went home to get some sleep.

Michael had been higher than a kite. I'm sure he thought he had done an incredible job on the mixes, but after I got some sleep and listened to his mixes, I called Jim Williamson and said, "Jim, these mixes are terrible. I want to set up time with you and we'll go back in and remix this album."

Jim said, "I'm glad to hear you say that, because I feel the same way." Jim and I spent the next few days remixing the album with care, and I turned the project in to Capitol. I gave Brovsky coproduction credit, and I never told him we'd remixed the whole record. When the record came out, I doubt he even knew the difference.

★

When I was finishing *Ain't It Somethin'* I was also losing my main supporter at Capitol Records, Bill Williams. It is amazing how quickly the wheels can spin off of a dream. Bill had fallen in love with one of his female singer-songwriter artists. His wife, Rebecca, was completely undone. She had become a good friend of mine and Jan's, along with Bill. The affair tore the family apart. Bill was under tremendous pressure at Capitol—record promotion is not for the faint of heart. He was working extremely hard, but Capitol was not supporting him and the country division. That was hard on a person who genuinely cared about his artists. With all that was going on in his personal life as well, Bill was having troubles all around. Everything was unspooling rapidly. The whole scene was heartbreaking.

A year before, Bill had brought one of his old Texas boyhood friends, Chuck Flood, and his family up from Austin and hired Chuck as his assistant in promotion. There was no doubt that Chuck was intelligent, confident, even cocky. I was told he had a master's degree in dramatic literature, but he had been working as a bartender in Austin—one of those jobs you can get with an arts degree! Bill elevated Chuck to a responsible position at Capitol Nashville and was training him in record and radio promotion. But Bill's altruism was not repaid in kind. In the middle of Bill's complicated personal troubles, rather than being supportive and helping him, Chuck told the Capitol brass in Hollywood that everything was in disarray and Bill couldn't do his job. That might have been true at the moment, but in my opinion, it wasn't something a friend would do, or should do, to a friend—especially a friend who had given him his big break. Capitol fired Bill, and all of us who depended on his vision, guidance, and energy were adrift in uncertainty—as was Bill right then.

Bill Williams's affair drastically altered his life, his family's life, and ultimately my own. Eventually, after a few more years working in Nashville Bill decided to leave the music business. He moved back to his hometown of Waco, Texas, where his interest in music was originally kindled in his parents' mom-and-pop record store. Bill's wife, Rebecca, moved back to Austin with their girls. She was an intelligent woman and went back to college and completed a law degree at the University of Texas. She later married another lawyer. Bill started a company that sold natural stone products, and he continued to encourage local Texas musicians and songwriters. Even today, when I talk to him, he is still dreaming up new possibilities for exploiting talent in a business that he long ago left, and that left him. I find it sad. He had so much imagination and marketing talent. He could have run a big record label, made them a lot of money, and affected American music. But he didn't get the support he deserved from Capitol or from a friend. The music business is unforgiving for those who color outside the lines, and it has lost a lot of talented people as a result. But I don't give up on those who have helped me. I still love Bill Williams for all he did for me and tried to do for me—for my songs and for my family. We are still friends to this day.

However, without Bill's guidance and energy, Capitol Nashville was lost when my *Ain't It Somethin'* album was released in September 1977. It had been Bill's vision and hard work that had propelled each of my releases, and without him to push the record Capitol Nashville did nothing to promote it. It was a wasted release. No single was even released from the album. All the long hours chained to the desk writing the songs, all the money and time spent recording and mixing the project, all the musicians' contributions, everything was completely wasted. Only the artistry lives on through the years. Artists work so hard on something that means so much and then discover that the way forward is all out of their hands, beyond their control. It's disappointing, but that is an old story in the music business. It's happened time and time again to many artists. Michael Brovsky, my new manager, was not doing anything to help much either. All the essentials for success with the release were absent.

On a day in November 1977, I got a call from Brovsky. He said, "James, Capitol is not doing the job for you. I want to take you off Capitol Records and put you with a real record label." He emphasized the word "real." He explained that he had signed Guy Clark to a half-million-dollar contract with Warner Brothers.

He said, "I told Warners, 'Look at this guy, he is tall, lean, handsome, he can be your James Taylor.'"

I knew Capitol had not done a proper job promoting *Ain't It Somethin'*— it didn't take a genius to see that. I had lost Bill Williams, and without him the Capitol country promotion team had shown how truly weak they were. I was disappointed. I had worked my heart out on *Ain't It Somethin'* and I'd seen a lot of creative effort and money totally wasted. I trusted Brovsky. I thought he was an influential and powerful manager. I believed he could deliver on what he said he wanted to do for me, and I was desperate for results. The momentum for the moment had stopped at Capitol. But as my wife has told me, more than once, most of my bad decisions in life have come when I was under duress. I believed Brovsky would have my best interests at heart. He was managing some good acts. He was supposed to know the record business and be my fiduciary. That's what a manager does.

But Jan, again, has told me over the years not to be gullible. There are ruthless people in this world. They serve their own interests. They don't give a damn about you. She doesn't trust people unless they earn her trust. She's a smart lady, and she also knows my decisions affect her and our family. If I go without, so do they.

Everyone was against me leaving Capitol—Bill Williams, my wife, Frank Jones, all advised me against it. But Brovsky's confidence sold me. He said he had a deal with another label in his pocket—a label that would give me the support I deserved. So, without listening to my wife or discussing it further with Frank Jones at Capitol in Nashville, or calling Rupert Perry, Capitol's head of Artists and Repertoire on the West Coast to discuss it, I simply said, "Well, Michael, if that's what you think's best, you're the manager. Go ahead and get my release from Capitol." I was looking to the future and that new, *real* label that would do a proper job for me. Perhaps it was a deal with Warner Brothers or MCA, where his other acts were? I was certain from the way he talked that the commitment was solid.

Brovsky called Rupert Perry in Hollywood and called me back within the hour. He said Rupert told him, "No, we believe in James. We'd like for him to go in the studio in January and record another album."

Brovsky said, "I told Rupert, no, you guys aren't doing the job for him. Talley doesn't want to make any more records for you." He said, "I was adamant with Rupert."

Rupert finally said, "Well, we can't make James sing on key, if he really wants out that bad."

Brovsky then said, "James, you're now off Capitol Records."

Capitol had increased their album options. I still owed them three more albums. They were not happy, and they quickly decided to show me that an artist doesn't leave a major record label until they are ready for him to leave.

The dissolution paperwork was drawn up and sent to Frank Jones, head of the office in Nashville for me to sign. Frank liked me, he had signed me to the label, we were close. He asked me in a fatherly tone, one more time, if I really wanted to go through with it. I said, "Frank, I want to thank you for everything you have done for me. I think the world of you, but what else can I do at this point? You know how your promotion guys dropped the ball on *Ain't It Somethin'*. Brovsky says he has another deal for me."

Frank said, "Well, I sure hate to see you go, Jim." I felt horrible, but I was looking forward to my new deal at the real record label, where my work would be properly promoted.

Then, at the end of the year the real blow came, one I had never anticipated. Capitol, out of spite, as if to really show me who was boss, deleted all four of my albums from their catalog. None of my albums would be for sale for another twenty years. I had been wiped off the face of the earth as an artist. There were no albums to send out to venues to get bookings, there was nothing for sale, word of mouth would die. It didn't matter how highly acclaimed the records had been at their release. The music was just product to Capitol. They might as well have been selling plastic ashtrays. It wasn't music or art. The Capitol executives were determined to show me how the game was played, who really has the control. All my creative children were locked up forever in Capitol's vast recording vault in the basement of the Capitol Tower in Hollywood.

Jan and I waited for the call from Brovsky with word of the "real" record deal, but the call never came. I never heard from him again. I anxiously called his office, but his secretary always had some excuse why he was not available—never a good sign. I was anxious beyond belief. We waited and waited. Nothing. He had no deal in his pocket. That was a lie.

Time went on, and one week around the new year I was performing at the Lone Star Cafe in New York as a solo act. The Lone Star was a loud, noisy nightclub, a really tough gig for a solo performer. The bar, with all its noise, rattling glassware, and ringing cash registers was directly across from the stage. The heavy artillery of an amplified band was really necessary to dominate the room. But I had no money to support a band. Almost all my Capitol advances had gone out in touring expenses.

After the performance that evening, Mort Coopermen, the Lone Star owner, said he needed to talk with me. It was urgent. It was extremely late, so we went to the Empire Diner on Tenth Avenue, which stays open all night. Mort then explained that Michael Brovsky had called him that afternoon and said that he didn't have the time to work on my situation. Brovsky told him, "Look Mort, I know you and Talley are close. I'd like for you to take over managing him." Brovsky wanted off the hook.

I couldn't believe what I was hearing, but it was obvious that Brovsky had bailed. He hadn't done anything—except take me off my record label—and he wasn't going to do anything more. Apparently he had taken me off Capitol Records on a whim and a hunch. When that hunch didn't pan out and he couldn't deliver, he simply wrote me off. Jan was right. There are bad people in this world. They will hurt you and walk away. It's not their dream.

But what could Mort Cooperman do? Mort had a conscience, he believed in my talent, and he knew I had been screwed by Brovsky. So he agreed to take up the mantle as my manager. He actually seemed to look forward to the opportunity. I think he thought he could do a better job than Brovsky—which wouldn't be too hard. And what choice did I have? I was released from my record label, all my albums were deleted, and who else was going to be interested in managing me? I was back at square one. It was as if I'd never been signed to a label in the first place.

Mort owned the only country music venue in New York City. He was making money hand over fist, but to do that he was sucking up to all the record companies, asking them to host showcases, album release parties, and other promotional events at his club. He worked with the labels on that basis, but he had no clout or influence in terms of getting an artist signed to a label, and he really didn't know how to go about it. He could button-hole record executives at the club and ask for favors, but signing acts has other requirements—like a musical product that a label can sell. I told Mort up front that other record companies would not care what I had done at Capitol. Many of them would not even be aware of my work. They would assume that I had done something wrong at Capitol. Perhaps I was a prob-lem act or I would still be on the label. They wouldn't know the back story.

To get a new recording contract, another label would want to hear what new product I had for them. I told Mort what I needed to do was go in the studio right away and record a new album so we would have something to shop to the labels. But I didn't have the money, and Mort was not willing to fund the cost for new recordings, even at minimum demo scale. Product, music, was the missing piece of the puzzle. Mort thought he could schmooze his way into a new deal. I am not saying that isn't possible, but it takes a tremendous amount of influence, which he did not have. To the record labels he was simply another club owner. Mort had my best interest at heart, I never thought he didn't, but he wanted to go about it in his own way, and I was not going to change that. I had no money or other prospects at the time, so I had to work with him on his terms.

Since I was a singer-songwriter, and an unusual one at that, I was always going to be the kind of artist that a label had to create a niche for and build, like Dylan's and Springsteen's early careers. I needed the same kind of steadfast support they received from John Hammond. None of my Capitol albums were huge sellers out of the box. I had a good foundation with Capitol, but the momentum slows the longer you are inactive. Try as I might to explain these things to Mort, I couldn't get him to accept the fact that the labels didn't care what I had done before. They wanted to hear what I had for them, now! In 1978 I could have recorded an entire album at demo scale, for about nine thousand dollars, but I simply didn't have it. In those days there was no recording an album on a computer in your living room as young artists can do today.

I never saw or spoke with Michael Brovsky again after his call that day in November, when he told me I was off Capitol Records. But as my wife has reminded me many times over the years, it was my own damned fault for trusting him in the first place. I didn't know him that well to have put my confidence in him so completely. I should have seen he was an ego-driven narcissist. I should have called Rupert Perry myself and talked about the promotion failures directly. I should have told Brovsky when he suggested me leaving Capitol, "Let me think this over for a few days and get back to you."

But I didn't. I made an impulsive and abrupt decision. In the end, there was no one to blame but myself. I was an artist; I was not yet a businessman.

After leaving Capitol, with an animosity I have never quite understood, I was denigrated by Chuck Flood at Capitol Nashville to every label in town. I was blackballed. It crushed my chances for a shot with another Nashville record label. After four glorious albums, it was the end of my career as a major label artist. As time went on, that painfully began to sink in.

About nine months after I left Capitol, I saw Rupert Perry in Nashville at a Country Music Association party in the fall of 1978. He came up to me and grabbed me by the lapels of my jacket and said, "When are you going to do something!?" I should have asked Rupert then if we could meet before he returned to Los Angeles. Perhaps I could have put things back together. Rupert was a good guy and he still believed in me. I always liked him. But I didn't ask. A person can't be timid in life, he must ask! I learned that later in my life in real estate. People will do things for us if we ask them to. People don't like to turn others down if it's within their power, because they don't like their desires turned down. But we must ask. Rupert had caught me by surprise. I couldn't think fast enough, and I didn't ask. My music has always meant so much to me I have a hard time being objective about it. I failed at the business of music. I failed in everything but my art, but art isn't enough.

★ ★ ★ ★ ★

Chapter 13

PHILIP MORRIS, THE WHITE HOUSE, AND A TRIP TO MONTANA

Before Mort Cooperman opened the Lone Star Cafe, he was in the advertising business in New York. Through his advertising contacts, Mort was able to set up an October 1978 concert with Philip Morris's ad agency for me to perform at the American Grand Prix Races at Watkins Glen, New York. It was a concert for their Marlboro brand. Philip Morris had an in-house filmmaker, Julius Potocsny. He was Hungarian, extremely talented and extremely opinionated, and he knew his filmmaking. He liked me and my music, and I liked him. He filmed the Watkins Glen concert and edited it into an impressive fifteen-minute short Marlboro film. (It can be seen in two parts on YouTube.) Companies like Philip Morris were then exploring and promoting their brand with musical acts.

I put a good, tight band together for the performance. Julius filmed over two nights at Watkins Glen, using several cameras and extensive film footage. There were thousands of people out front both nights. After the concert, Philip Morris flew me to New York on their company jet for meetings with company executives. They all seemed quite pleased with the concert. There was talk of an album on the American West, and a European tour. Everything looked good for something to happen with their sponsorship, but after a while, nothing came from it. Mort never explained the reason why his plans failed, but I suspect it was because there was no record label to share in the promotion and expense. Had a major record company had this opportunity, I am sure they would have taken the bit in their teeth. Only a few years later, the big companies, like Philip Morris, 7Up, Coca-Cola, Dr Pepper, Budweiser and others, began sponsoring big concert tours with major recording artists. That's the kind of thing that good management can do for an act, but a supporting label is essential.

★

Trying to keep the boat afloat and keep the babies fed, I started going to New York to play at the Lone Star Cafe almost every other month as a single artist and going to Atlanta about once a month to play an opening slot at Jack Tarver's Great Southeast Music Hall. Jack was trying to help me every way he could. I also opened several southeastern shows for my friend John Prine, who was trying to help me.

I'd played a solo show with Steve Goodman in Rockford, Illinois, and we exchanged phone numbers. Steve was producing an album for Prine in Chicago, *Bruised Orange*. I was in Chicago performing a solo gig, and Steve and John saw I was in town. They invited me to come and sing on John's album. After that, John and I became friends.

But my openers for John were abruptly terminated by John's devoted manager, Al Bunetta. After he saw me open John's show in Athens, Georgia, Bunetta thought I was too much competition for John, and I never again opened a show for him. I understood Al's reasoning. That's why female acts often open for male acts and vice versa. John and I remained friends until he was taken in 2020 by Covid-19. He was a good friend, salt of the earth. His songs reveal everything you need to know about him. He was what he wrote and sang about, good ordinary people.

Despite my performing regularly at the Lone Star Cafe in New York and the Great Southeast Music Hall in Atlanta, Jan and I were slowly going through what little savings we'd managed to hang onto from Capitol's and BMI's advances. Most of my advance money had gone for tour support, so there wasn't much left in the kitty. Jack Tarver marshalled several of his affluent Atlanta friends, who chipped in some contributions; and Bob Beckham, a fellow Okie, at Combine Music in Nashville gave me five hundred. Bob had always loved my song "Give My Love to Marie," and I asked him if he wanted the publishing on the song for his gift.

"No," Bob said, "You keep it. Just help somebody else when you can down the line."

★

It was only a few weeks after my Capitol contract was cancelled that I got a call from Mae Axton, Hoyt Axton's mother. Mae was in the PR business in Nashville. She called me on December 6, 1977, and told me that President Carter and Rosalynn had had a state dinner cancelled for the following evening, so the president was having a Christmas party at the White House for his staff instead. Mae asked if I was available to fly to Washington and play for them the following evening—which was also the anniversary of the 1941 Pearl Harbor Attack. "I know it's short notice," she said, "but they would really appreciate it if you were available."

I had been nursing a cold but was feeling a little better, and even though I was not in great voice, a chance to have dinner at the White House does not happen every day, so I told her that my wife and I would be delighted to go. Mae put me in touch with Gretchen Poston, the White House social secretary, to work out the details. Jan and I scurried around to make plane reservations.

I called my mother in New Mexico and told her, and she said, "Now, don't you go up there to that White House in those blue jeans!" So to please Mom, we went to a men's store in Nashville and purchased some gray wool slacks. The store managed to get them hemmed for me that afternoon.

There were about eighty staff members at the party that evening. Jan and I sat at the president's table. Jan sat between the president and Rosalynn, and I sat next to Rosalynn. It was an elaborate dinner with a fancy dessert. I didn't eat much because I don't like to eat directly before I sing. As dinner was finishing, I got up to play. Mrs. Carter requested that I play my song "She Tries Not to Cry," which was on my second Capitol album, *Tryin' Like the Devil*. She told Jan that when she was traveling alone for political events, and she was alone in her hotel room at night, she would think of that poor woman in the song and it would make her tiredness and aloneness seem trivial.

I played for around forty-five minutes. One of the songs I played was "W. Lee O'Daniel and the Light Crust Dough Boys." After I played, the president said a few words thanking us. Then Bob Strauss, chairman of the Democratic Party, got up to relate his story about W. Lee O'Daniel. "I was a young man in Texas in '39, when O'Daniel ran for governor. There were a dozen Democrats in the race. Everyone said that hillbilly won't get two percent of the vote. But when the votes were counted O'Daniel had fifty-two percent and was our new governor." He went on, "These are the songs about us Democrats. They are about who we are and what we stand for."

A small United States Marine Band combo then started playing dance music. President Carter asked Jan to dance, and I danced with the First Lady. The president signed two cards of good wishes for our two boys. I asked him if he would mind calling my mother in Albuquerque. I knew, as a lifelong Democrat, she would be thrilled to speak with the president. Carter asked the White House switchboard to call her, but she was not answering. He kept trying as the night wore on, but there was still no answer. Finally, he said, "Give me her address, I will write her a note," which he did, and my mother was thrilled when it arrived. Mother had been at a church dinner in Albuquerque that night and had missed a call from the president of the United States.

I explained to Mrs. Carter during the evening that I was no longer on Capitol Records and was hoping to find another record label. I didn't go into the long explanation as to how that happened. However, in a week or two, I got a call from Phil Walden at Capricorn Records in Macon, Georgia. Phil said that Mrs. Carter had called him and told him about my situation, but despite Mrs. Carter's intervention, Phil explained that he did not feel I would be a good fit at Capricorn. He said, "We're principally a rock band label. We tried the singer-songwriter thing with Billy Joe Shaver, and it didn't work that well for us." Phil was very cordial, but his answer was no. Mrs. Carter had done all she could, which I sincerely appreciated.

Over the ensuing years I had some correspondence with President Carter. I also wrote him a letter after his loss to Ronald Reagan and received a kind note in return. Jan always attended the president's book signings in Nashville. I joined her for a few of those events as well. I always liked Jimmy Carter. He is an earnest, sincere man.

★

In the late spring of 1979, I was approached by a couple of young idealistic filmmakers in Montana. They wanted to make a film about the pollution and acid rain caused by the coal-fired power plants in Montana and on the High Plains. They were working under the auspices of the Film Fund, which had offices in New York and San Francisco. Their purpose was noble, and as concerned environmentalists they were well ahead of their time. They had discovered and liked my Capitol albums and wanted me to write some songs for the movie's soundtrack—assuming they could get the film made. The music is the last thing that goes into a film's production. They had engaged Larry McMurtry, the great Texas novelist, to write a film script for them. At this period in Larry's career, before *Lonesome Dove*, he was a regional Texas novelist—not so well known, but a fine writer with a vivid imagination and great storytelling ability. They paid my way to Montana, gave me a small fee, fed us, and put us up while we were there with them. I flew into Billings from Nashville. Larry drove to Montana from his home then near Washington, DC, where he had his bookstore, Booked Up. He was driving an old dark-gray Pontiac station wagon that had seen some serious miles. Larry was then forty-three and I was thirty-five. His son, James, was with him. James was seventeen and had his acoustic guitar with him, which he was learning to play.

We drove around Montana and northern Wyoming in a van with the filmmakers looking at various coal-fired power plants in Montana and visiting the big strip mine in Gillette, Wyoming. We saw another strip mine on the Crow Indian Reservation and saw the gigantic ore-hauling trucks and the enormous extraction draglines with buckets the size of a small house. The young filmmakers were quite serious about their project, wanting to combine a story with impactful social commentary in a film that would be explosive and have broad distribution—and that would cause people to think about pollution issues. Mike Wustner, one of the film producers was hoping for something as impactful as *The China Syndrome*, which had been released in March 1979. In a letter to me, Mike wrote, "It's just too late in human history to screw around making films with no critical substance. I think it's becoming possible to make films that entertain as well as teach, films that millions of people will see."

However, despite Mike's considerable respect for Larry's writing, I'm not sure Larry was on the same wavelength with Mike. Larry was a consummate storyteller, but he was not really into the environmental cause. His writing explored in depth and with incredible perception the relationships between people—the good and the bad, the human frailties, prejudices, and inconsistencies we all have. As excellent a writer as he was, he was not John Steinbeck or James Agee. He simply was not inclined to take on broad social causes. I think the more Larry interacted with the young filmmakers, the more he realized that this was not really in his lane, but they had engaged him, and he needed the money at the time, so he was obligated to come up with a script. We ended the week not resolving much.

But Larry went to work and completed a screenplay draft in short order. In correspondence with me that July he wrote: "I have flung myself into it—using as a working title Salty Dogs. What I appear to be writing is sort of a Hud II, only with two old people rather than one. I've only managed one shot of a coal mine in the first 30 pages and no Indians as yet—basically just writing about Archer County, like I always do. I don't know if this will sit well." Larry went to New York the first week in August to present the draft to the filmmakers, but he wrote me that week, "I've had to overwrite to get any kind of story. It is looking to me totally unmakeable, since the two characters that dominate it are both in their 70s, an age category not filled with bankable actors."

I never saw the draft screenplay, but in a letter after a phone call from Mike Wustner that fall, Mike wrote, "The present treatment needs a lot of work. At this point it lacks the depth we [all] talked about. Talking about it helps. Hopefully a group of us can get together and hash it over with the screenwriter and the director . . . if several critical thinkers come together over it, it will be shaped into a powerful script." So it appeared that the script Larry turned in was not what the filmmakers were hoping for.

Larry wrote me that November to tell me he had received Peter Guralnick's book *Lost Highway*, which I had asked Peter send to him. He also said, "The Montana Script is still in the mill—I think the young revolutionaries are discovering that the real world—if that's what Hollywood is—has slight interest in virtuous environmentalists." I had released my song, "What Will There Be for the Children?" in 1977 on my fourth Capitol album, but in 1979 the environmental movement was only just starting to resonate. The young filmmakers were indeed ahead of their time.

Before we left Montana, and after we parted from the filmmakers, I rode around with Larry and James for several additional days. We visited the Cowboy Museum in Miles City, and several other small Montana towns, reservations, and historic places. Larry loved chicken-fried steak with gravy, as I did, and it was standard fare in the little Montana restaurants, so we ate a lot of them. We went in a bookstore in Billings and Larry gave me a reading list of western literature. I purchased the books he recommended, took them home with me to Nashville and read them. Larry had considerable knowledge of western literature and history, and as a westerner myself, I have always had a keen interest in the history of the West. One of the books he recommended was *We Pointed Them North*, by Teddy Blue (E. C.) Abbott, a memoir by a real cowboy who in the 1870s and 1880s was on several cattle drives from Texas to Montana.

In that same November letter, Larry told me about his planned trail drive project. "I am having a very hectic fall—am in truth penniless and am scurrying around making speeches and buying and selling books and writing things in order to keep body and soul together. I am now embarked on my traildriving novel, which looks like it will be very long, thousands of pages in mss [manuscripts]—how I am going to be living while writing [it] I don't know. I need to do more screenwork, but I just turned down the Bob Wills story, because I don't think I could work with Jimmy Gercio." But then he said, of our weeks in Montana, "Of course I accomplished my main purpose, which was to get another close look at the trail up which my imaginary cattle will soon be walking."

After Montana, Larry was driving back to Texas to visit his mother, so I rode along with him and James down through Wyoming and Colorado. We stopped in Albuquerque, and he and James spent the night at my mother's home there. We ate Mexican food together that evening at La Placita on the Old Town Plaza with my mom. The next morning Larry and James continued on to Texas, and I exchanged my Billings ticket and flew back to Nashville.

I sent Larry my four Capitol albums, and he wrote: "I've been listening to them all day with great enjoyment." He sent me in return several autographed copies of his early novels—which he first sent to Nashville, Texas, where he said "evidently, there are no Talleys." I read them, cherish them, and still have those early works in my library. We exchanged a few letters over the years, and ten years later, in 1989, I was watching television and saw an advertisement for a miniseries called *Lonesome Dove*. It was based on the novel by the same title, written by Larry. I knew instantly from the previews that it was the trail-driving novel Larry wrote me about in his letter that November 1979. All the traveling around we'd done in Montana ten years previous became part of the setting for his novel, a powerful story that would make him a national star. I wrote and told him how much I loved the miniseries, and I have read the book a couple of times. To me, it's his masterpiece. When Larry wrote back, he didn't seem all that excited with the miniseries, but I think he simply was being modest. I still think it is a classic in western cinema.

Over the years, James McMurtry has become a fine and influential singer-songwriter in his own right out of Austin. I've only seen James once since we were in Montana together, but I hope that I imparted something worthwhile to him those many years ago as a young man starting out as a musician and songwriter. Larry and I continued to occasionally correspond over the years. He never forgot our journey together in Montana, and neither did I.

As I was writing this, I saw in the news that Larry had died at age eighty-four from congestive heart failure. I had just finished a letter to him and had put a stamp on it, which I then had to tear up. It's the end of an era. But now I hear that Larry's grandson Curtis is also a singer-songwriter.

The film from Larry's *Salty Dogs* script was eventually made into a motion picture eleven years later in 1990. After Larry's new fame from *Lonesome Dove*, I'm sure his scripts were in demand. It was called *Montana*, but the script had been rewritten into a typical western plot of an old couple in Montana where a big oil company was trying to buy their land. The husband wanted to sell, but the wife wanted to keep it in the family. It starred Richard Crenna and Gena Rowlands. It wasn't a hit. Mike Wustner was given coproducer credit, but I suspect he had little involvement. It was nothing like he had envisioned or hoped it would be. It wasn't the powerful, explosive, teaching script about the coal pollution on the High Plains, and no one contacted me to use any of my songs in it.

Chapter 14

I NO LONGER HAD ANYONE
I NEEDED TO CALL IN NEW YORK

In 1980 I performed at the Jimmie Rodgers Festival in Meridian, Mississippi. I had played the same festival a couple of years prior. It was always an enjoyable show and, Jimmie Rodgers was one of my all-time favorite artists. Peter Guralnick had flown to Meridian and he hooked up with me and Jan at the festival. On the bill that night, along with me, were John Conlee and Merle Haggard. Frank Mull, who had done Merle's radio promotion for years was there. Merle's then-piano player, Mark Yeary, told me they had been listening to *Tryin' Like the Devil* on the bus.

After the festival, Peter rode with Jan and me on our way back to Nashville. He wanted to drive through Holt, Alabama, and see one of his blues idols, Johnny Shines. Johnny was sixty-five then and recovering from a stroke. Johnny had enjoyed a long and distinguished career as a blues artist, but it was obvious he was still living the blues. The most honest music there is has never paid performers what they deserve. Johnny and his family were living in a modest brick ranch house in a country setting near Holt. He was genuinely glad that Peter had taken the time to stop by and see him. You could tell it meant a lot to him. But Peter doesn't abandon any of the people he loves. After spending a couple of hours with Johnny, we drove on. Jan and I left Peter in Birmingham to do some other research and drove on back to Nashville.

Around this same time, I ran into Merle Haggard in Nashville. He was in town recording and invited me up to his hotel room at the Spence Manor. With us that night was Red Lane, whom I'd admired for the wonderful song he wrote that Tammy Wynette recorded, "Till I Get It Right." We swapped songs and talked for hours, and the time got away from me. I came home around 4:00 A.M. It was dark in the bedroom, and I didn't want to wake up Jan, so I moved as quietly as possible; but as I entered the dark bedroom I started stumbling around and over something and making a racket. Jan had booby-trapped the room! She had set up paper grocery sacks all around the room, and as I came in, they crackled and made all kinds of noise. She was lying there laughing.

She said, "Where have you been until 4:00 in the morning?!"

I said, "I've been with Merle Haggard at the Spence Manor swapping songs!"

Since she knew that I didn't know Merle well, she said, "Oh yeah. You've been with Merle Haggard!" She didn't believe me, but it was true. She was lying in bed laughing. She has laughed about that grocery sack trap for years.

★

By 1980 I had been off Capitol Records for nearly three years, and Mort Cooperman was no closer to a record deal for me. But Mort was instrumental in getting my song "New York Town" recorded by Johnny Paycheck. Johnny was recording a live album at the Lone Star Cafe, but he didn't have a song that mentioned New York.

After all the times I'd played the Lone Star, and my many trips to New York, I had come to have a feeling for the Big Apple. It's a fascinating city, and I decided to write a song about it. Mort said, "Now, don't make it a downer, like so much of your stuff!" I kept his advice in mind and wrote "New York Town."

I produced a recording of the song in 1979 as a trial run with the notable New Jersey producer Tommy West, of Cashman and West fame. Tommy had produced Jim Croce, whose work I admired. He was looking for new acts to produce and somehow we got together. Tommy came to Nashville, and we produced "New York Town" together in 1979 using my usual crew of musicians. However, to work with me, Tommy required all the publishing rights on any songs he produced with me, and since there was no guarantee he could place what we produced, I was not willing to sign over all my publishing, unless he could get me signed to a label. He wasn't comfortable with that, so we only recorded the one song together. I liked Tommy. He was pleasant in the studio, and I thought he was a good producer. But I had been so badly burned by Michael Brovsky that my level of trust was suffering. My publishing catalog was my last asset, and without a record label it was not something I wanted to give up.

With Johnny Paycheck recording a live album at the Lone Star Cafe, Mort Cooperman called Roy Wunch, then head of CBS's marketing in Nashville, and told him about the song. It simply made sense to have something about New York on Paycheck's album. Roy asked me to bring a copy by his office, so I dropped off a cassette. He played it for Billy Sherrill, Paycheck's producer. Sherrill liked it and decided to record it with Paycheck. It was recorded in Nashville, adding the crowd noise and ambient sounds from the live show so it would match the live recordings. Paycheck's album was then released with *New York Town* as the title.

Sherrill invited me to the session, but I declined. I was paranoid he might shake me down for the publishing if I went to the session. I was very fearful of that because it was a common practice. Had I gone to Sherrill's session, perhaps he would have taken an interest in me as an artist, but I never felt Sherrill and I were on the same wavelength in terms of production, so the chance seemed slim. Still, who knows? I never met Sherrill in person. But Billy was a good producer for CBS and did his usual excellent job of producing the song in a style suitable to Paycheck—although they only used half of the song on the recording. Paycheck's version of "New York Town" was released in 1980 and it went to number one in New York for over sixteen weeks on WHN, the New York City country station. Paycheck's label, Epic Records, released the song as the B-side to the first single from the album, which pretty much killed it as a potential single for the rest of the country outside New York. The song, though, was played for years at the New York Mets baseball games. I would occasionally be watching a game and would hear it in the background.

One night Paycheck sang "New York Town" on the Tom Snyder NBC television show. That one network performance paid BMI back the remainder of the advances Frances Preston had given me in 1975. So I started receiving royalty payments from BMI—rather than statements that said, "applied on account."

★

In New York, Jerry Wexler started coming to my shows at the Lone Star and we reconnected. Jerry told me how much he loved the albums I'd made for Capitol. I told him what had happened with Michael Brovsky and the mistake I'd made in leaving the label. He said, "Everybody does stupid shit now and then, James. That's life."

Jerry was no longer with Atlantic Records, which had been sold to Warner Brothers. He was then head of the Warners' office in New York. He said, "James, I would like to sign you unilaterally out of New York" (like Willie was signed by Columbia). "But with your more country sound, I would still need the support of Warner's country division out on the West Coast. We'd need their marketing and promotion on any record we made. If I cannot get their support, a record won't make it. We'd have no success. Let me call the coast and see what I can do."

The country division of Warners then was headed by Andy Wickham, a young Brit, and a young woman named Mary Martin. Mort Cooperman had already approached Mary Martin in New York, and I knew from that interaction that for some reason she didn't care for my music. It's hard for young artists to understand, but people can't always define why they don't like something. It's just a gut feeling. Art is subjective. A person will listen and simply say, "I don't hear it." Everyone's tastes are different. But if I'd learned nothing else at Capitol, I learned that without the company's support no record will do well. In this case, Jerry could not generate the enthusiasm he felt was necessary, so no deal was struck. Neither of us was happy about it, but unfortunately, that's the way it works.

Jerry and I remained friends for the rest of his life. After his divorce from his secretary, he married a woman closer to his age, playwright and novelist Jean Arnold, and he told me he was happy. He retired to Sarasota, Florida, and we spoke often on the phone. He was incredibly supportive and said he wished he could have done more for me. I had tremendous respect for him because he *was* a music man, and because he had given me my start as a songwriter and released my first record. Music excited him. It came first. He was an exceptional record producer. He worked hard at it. He loved making records and he loved songwriters. Ironically, he sent me a postcard with a postmark of September 11, 2001, and he wrote, "You remain for me one of America's greatest songwriters." I cherish that to this day. He wanted to help me, but unlike when he was at Atlantic, Warners was a much larger company, and he was no longer the boss. Later, he sent my songs to other artists he thought should record them, including Willie Nelson. I'd had a good friendship with Willie Nelson in the 1970s. Before it was released, he played me his *Stardust* album on a little cassette player one afternoon in his hotel room in New York. I'd spent time with him in Atlanta, sang with him on stage at the Omni, and attended a recording session with him and Leon Russell in Nashville. I always hoped Willie would record one of my songs, but to date it has not happened.

★

It was 1980, and Mort Cooperman was still not having much success in securing me a recording contract. I was still playing solo dates at his club, and at Jack Tarver's Great Southeast Music Hall, but Jan and I were slowly going broke. My booking agent bailed out, saying, "Call me when you get another record deal." A percentage of what I was making as a solo performer was not attractive to a booking agent. They have to make a living too. Mort didn't have the time running a nightclub to book me, and it was hard to book myself. I was not good at it. There is a certain lack of professionalism about it—and it takes a lot of one's time. But a good booking agent is essential to keep money coming in when you do not have a record out. I was also not in a position where I could afford to lose money on the road simply to keep performing. I finally told Mort I was going to have to get a day job of some kind. Still, Mort thought he could eventually make something happen, and he started sending Jan and me two thousand dollars a month to live on. I don't know where the money came from, and I didn't ask. There is a lot of cash that sloshes around in the nightclub business. It arrived each month in two one-thousand-dollar cashier's checks. I declared it as income and paid taxes on it.

At one point, Mort decided I should move to New York, as Kinky Friedman had done. Mort felt he could better promote me if I were around close at hand. I could play at the club on a regular basis, hang out there and meet people. But that seemed dismal to me, hanging around a nightclub every night as one of the fixtures. I had a wife and two young sons in Nashville, and I simply could not do that. I told Mort that I would drive or fly to New York whenever he wanted me to play or meet, but I could not leave my family.

For a few special shows, to better showcase my music, I put a band together with the personnel I used at Watkins Glen, except I used Peter Keeble on drums and recruited Chip Hager from Conway, Arkansas, on the harmonica. Chip was a fine musician, a cousin to Mickey Newbury, and was recommended to me by Fingers Taylor, Jimmy Buffett's harp player. Chip had recently returned from deployment in Vietnam, where he'd been drafted into the US Navy. He'd spent his deployment on the Mekong River on a Swiftboat. His mother told me that he was in bad emotional shape when he returned from the war, and that playing music had saved him. Chip definitely had PTSD from the war, which was occasionally visible in his behavior and feelings. His family owned a jewelry store in Conway. He was a fine jeweler, an avid outdoorsman, and a talented harmonica player. Chip passed away in 2008. He was a great performer.

I played four shows with this band, two at the Lone Star Cafe and two at the Great Southeast Music Hall. We recorded all the shows on high-quality chrome cassettes from the soundboard. The house sound mixers at both clubs were exceptionally good. Miraculously, I was able to resurrect those tapes in a Nashville studio in 1994 for a live CD that was released in Germany by Bear Family Records. It was called *James Talley: Live*.

This was one of the best bands I ever had. They were all talented musicians and were professionals. Unfortunately, I had no other place to go with them. There were no other bookings, and I simply could not afford to keep them together. I later used some of them on some demo recordings, but eventually John Salem, the piano player, and Bill Hawks, the bass player, gave up on Nashville and returned to Wichita. Larry Chaney, the excellent guitarist, remained in Nashville for several years and then moved to Austin where he has had a good career in music. Chip Hager returned to Conway, Arkansas, to his family's jewelry business. It was a shame. They were a great band.

Mort Cooperman kept trying but was never able to understand, or perhaps accept in his mind, that recording new material was the essence of what we were trying to accomplish. That was the key. Record companies sell product. Without the product, no labels were ever going to be interested, and the longer I went without a recording contract the colder I became as viable artist. With all the Capitol product deleted, I was essentially like a new artist. As 1982 approached, I was already thirty-eight years old, and in the perpetual youth culture of the music business, it became less and less likely that a new contract would ever happen. Mort kept sending us money every month, and I'm sure, in his mind, he felt that compensation should relieve some pressure on him to perform. It helped me and my family, yes, but it did not advance my career one iota, and Mort seemed to work less and less as time went on. It was not a sustainable management plan.

The money from Mort came every month for exactly two years, which amounted to forty-eight thousand dollars. That's no small testament to his faith in me as an artist, but at some point, without any success, a person's enthusiasm wanes. If he had taken one-fourth of that money starting out with me, and we'd produced a new album, he would have had something to present to his label contacts. Sending the money covered his guilt for not getting the job done, but again, it was not a sustainable plan.

One afternoon the phone rang at the house, and it was Mort. He said, "James, we're having an internal audit of our books at the Lone Star. I can't continue sending you money. I'm sorry." But he said, "I've met someone else who is interested in managing you. I'd like for you to come to New York and meet him."

Mort was bailing out. He'd done all he could under the circumstances, and all he was willing to do. There probably was no "internal audit," at least not one that would have found the money from those cashier's checks; but it didn't matter. In the final analysis, as much as we both wished it were different, Mort had not accomplished any more than Michael Brovsky. The difference was, at least he had tried. Mort cared, but the result was the same. Either I was simply not marketable, or he'd gone about it in the wrong way. As Peter Guralnick said in his book *Lost Highway*, my career was like I'd been exhibited as a prize fish and then thrown back into the ocean. The disappointing thing was that after that last trip to New York to meet the prospective new manager, I never heard from Mort again, not once. That hurt. He wrote me off the same as Michael Brovsky.

I went to New York to meet the new potential manager Mort had found. We met at the Lone Star Cafe with Mort. His name was Eddie Irving. Mort sat with us for a few minutes to make the introduction, then he bowed out and left me with Eddie. I don't know where Mort found Eddie, but he was a piece of work. He was overweight, extremely needy, and terribly insecure. He was the son of Val Irving, who was retiring from the legitimate management business in New York. I never met Val. One of Val's last acts was Robert Merrill, the opera singer who sang the national anthem at Yankee Stadium. Val had managed the careers of Audrey Meadows, Peggy Lee, Eddie Fisher, and other big-name performers in his day. Eddie Irving wanted to be a manager like his father. He claimed to know Frank Sinatra and said he had Vegas connections. He was going to get Sinatra to record my songs. He wanted to live large. He talked big and flashed a lot of money, but it did not take very long before I realized he was absolutely nuts.

Eddie flew to Nashville to meet Jan and our boys. His manner was a caricature of an old school gangster. He brought gifts for everyone. For my wife it was a big bottle—not a small one—of Givenchy perfume; for my youngest son, he brought two teddy bears, not one, which he called night bear and day bear. For my oldest boy, he brought the biggest Swiss army knife available, complete with a leather holster. He flashed a roll of hundred-dollar bills that was nearly impossible to wrap a fist around. Everything with him was over the top. He so wanted to be loved. My wife told me right away, "This guy is crazy!"

But I was desperate and grasping at straws. What else did I have? Let it play out, I thought. In my heart, though, I knew this was not going to work. My wife reads people, she knows.

In New York, Eddie would pick me up in his new Chrysler K-Car, the model supposedly that Frank Sinatra had, and the one Ricardo Montalban advertised on television, with the "Corinthian leather" seats. Eddie had a Black chauffeur who picked up the car from the garage and drove us around. The car was always spotless and waxed. Eddie would often stop by a place, I believe it on was Seventh Avenue. He would park at the curb, quickly run in, and return with a huge wad of hundred-dollar bills. Ultimately, I asked him what business that was where he kept getting all this cash, and he nonchalantly said it was a brothel—"Beautiful young girls, from NYU, working their way through college. I have three of these places," he proudly said, "Would you like some entertainment?"

"No," I said, "I have a beautiful wife at home. Thanks."

Eddie installed a separate WATS telephone line in our house in Nashville, so he could talk with me. Long distance was still expensive then. He would call late at night and talk for hours about his dreams and all that he wanted to do for me. I would be lying on the floor talking with him, dead tired, and trying to stay awake. The next time I flew to New York, he again went by his brothel for cash, and I asked him, "Eddie, how do you run a business like this in New York, without the . . ."

"You mean the mob?" He said.

"Yes," I said.

"Oh, we give them a third of the action for protection." He said it like it was nothing. I thought to myself, "Who are they protecting him from?"

I returned to Nashville, and Jan and I had a long talk. We were small average folks, people trying to live their lives and pursue a few fragile dreams. We had never met anyone like Eddie. He was manic, bombastic, and totally nuts! Jan and I had enough sense to know that if I kept working with him, and he was indeed involved with the New York mob, then we would eventually also be involved with them. I had seen *The Godfather*, and I didn't want to be part of any of that. It wasn't healthy. Jan wasn't thrilled with Eddie's involvement in prostitution either. His business associates in New York could potentially be quite dangerous. Better to end this relationship sooner rather than later. So we made the decision to end it before we became further involved. I hadn't signed any agreement with Eddie, so I called him and explained that my wife and I simply were not comfortable continuing with him any longer. I thanked him for his interest and belief in me, but I didn't want to get involved any further with him. I was just a guy singing and writing songs. I had a beautiful wife and two little boys that I loved. He spent considerable time on the call trying to change my mind, but in the end, I told him it was a final decision on our part, and we ended it.

The one good thing that Eddie did accomplish for us, however, was that he somehow muscled CBS Records in New York into paying me the mechanical royalties they owed me for Johnny Paycheck's recording of "New York Town." The big labels were famous then, in the pre-computer age, for holding back the mechanical payments they owed to small independent publishers. The first time Eddie flew down to Nashville, he arrived with a check from CBS for over forty-two hundred dollars. That sure "helped the church," as they say down south. Eddie never paid the phone company for the WATS line. They came and took it out, but I no longer had anyone I needed to call in New York.

★ ★ ★ ★ ★

Chapter 15

THEY DON'T MATTER ANYWAY

It was 1982. I was still floundering around trying to figure out how I was going to sustain my music career and make a living. Jan had gone back to work at the Tennessee Department of Human Services as a child welfare caseworker—difficult and emotional work. Our boys were seven and twelve by then. Children grow. They don't wait for you to get your act together. I told Jan that to make things easier on her I would take over cooking supper. I did it for about a week, and the boys pleaded, "Mama, will you please do the cooking!"

That January 1982, I went to Boston to tour with John Lincoln Wright's band—John Lincoln Wright and the Sour Mash Boys. Jim Rooney had introduced us a few years prior. John was kind enough to invite me to play with him and his band, and he paid me generously. He didn't have to do it, but he respected my work and wanted to help. John was in his mid-thirties then and had just married a wonderful woman named Vickie. She was a true New Englander, a Yankee lady. She was plain in her appearance, with an infectious smile and a pleasant manner. She was a delight, and a stabilizing influence on John, and they were truly in love.

John Lincoln, whom Vickie called Lincoln, was small in stature, maybe five foot six inches tall, but he had a powerful baritone with a great register. He wore a big Stetson most of the time, which made him seem taller. He was a confirmed liberal. He was an excellent songwriter and a commanding band leader. He had a lot of charisma, and local musicians wanted to work with him. He and his band played all over New England. John would stay with Jan and me when he came to Nashville to pitch his songs to music publishers.

John was a man of fixed routine. He was also an alcoholic, which ultimately killed him at age sixty-four. But he never got drunk. He just kept a steady buzz going all day long. Each morning he would start off with two cups of strong black Louisiana coffee, then read the *Boston Globe* on a large table in his kitchen. Once his two cups of coffee were gone, he would open a cold Ballantine Ale from the refrigerator, which he would sip very slowly while continuing to read his paper. Once that Ballantine was gone, he would open another. He would sip on it the same way until it was gone. Then he'd open another. It might take him an hour, maybe two, to drink one can. It was like taking his medicine. His faculties never seemed diminished, and he always seemed patently alert. It was just enough buzz to keep him on an even keel. But as he grew older, the booze took its toll.

Each afternoon we would walk through the snow and slush to the Plough and Stars, an Irish bar on Massachusetts Avenue across from Harvard. We would order one of their home-made sandwiches and John would order a pint. There we would meet Desmond O'Grady, the Irish poet, who was a writer in residence at Harvard. I got to know Desmond well and thought of him fondly. He came to many of our shows and became quite enamored with my songs. He thought of me as a fellow poet. We drank Irish whiskey together each afternoon.

We played all over New England. John always delivered an excellent show. It was an entertaining mix of his own songs and country standards. He would open the show with a set, then I would play a set of my songs with his band. Then John would return with another short set to close out the evening. I have seen a lot of country shows, including Merle Haggard's and Willie Nelson's, and I must say, John's performances were right up there among the best. He was an excellent entertainer and songwriter. He knew how to please an audience and was very personable with his fans.

★

In 1982 Paul Volcker, the Federal Reserve chairman, was trying to quash the nation's incredible inflation by restricting the nation's money supply. The prime interest rate spiraled to over 20 percent. The economy was in the toilet. I approached Curb Records' Dick Whitehouse, who in the past had expressed appreciation for my recordings.

I asked Dick if I paid for the pressing, would he help me release "Are They Gonna Make Us Outlaws Again?" on Curb Records as a single. With the troubled economy, it seemed like "Outlaws" might resonate with people.

I had originally released the song on my second Capitol album, *Tryin' Like the Devil*, in 1976 after gas prices spiked during the first Arab oil embargo. Capitol had released it as a single at the time.

Dick thought it was worth a try and said we could release it on Oak/ Curb, an independent label that he owned with Ray Ruff, his main promotion man. Dick said Ray would work the record for us. So I pressed up enough copies for radio in blue vinyl, with a red and white label to give it added attention. Curb shipped it out to radio, but Ray didn't seem to work too hard on it, and without a major label's promotion not much happened with it. It reinforced how tough radio always is without the push from a big label.

By the late summer of 1982, I needed income from any source I could find. A friend of mine, Joe Dougherty, had a trendy high-end cookware store called The Cook's Nook in the affluent Green Hills section of Nashville. Joe was from Birmingham, Alabama, and had originally come to Nashville to be a songwriter. But after a few years he gravitated to this other business, which provided a more stable income. He started small, but his business grew rapidly. He was doing well, and he decided to open two more stores in shopping malls at opposite ends of town. Since I still had my Ford van, he hired me at ten dollars an hour to haul stock between his three stores.

As the Christmas season of 1982 approached, Joe needed extra sales help and asked me if I would be willing to work at his main store and sell coffee. He carried a large line of various specialty coffees. Since I had sold retail at Montgomery Ward and at Meyer and Meyer in Albuquerque in my youth, retail selling was nothing new to me. And I needed the money.

I've always enjoyed a good cup of coffee, so I drank samples of the various flavors and started experimenting with blends—mixing and recommending. The customers loved it. They thought I was some kind of coffee guru, but I was just shooting from the hip. At the end of the Christmas season, when we took inventory, Joe said, "I don't know what you did, but you've sold more coffee than Juan Valdez," a fictional character then in a television coffee commercial.

But the emotional part of this arrangement was difficult for me. By doing this retail work I'd been exposed. I was now selling coffee for ten dollars an hour—after being written up in newspapers from coast to coast and hailed in glowing reviews as a great singer-songwriter. I'd been compared to Woody Guthrie, Bob Dylan, and The Band. I'd played at the White

House for the president of the United States; but Capitol Records had deleted all my albums. I *was* that prized fish that had been exhibited and tossed back in the ocean. That Christmas, I'd sold coffee to people I knew in the music business. I thought, "What must they think of me?" My failure had been exposed. But I needed the money, and Joe was kind enough to help a friend.

One evening after Christmas, we'd closed the store and the two of us were alone and drinking a cup of coffee in the stock room. I told Joe how hard this was for me. He looked directly at me and said, "Jim, you've accomplished more than 99 percent of the dreamers who ever came to this town. You don't have anything to be ashamed of."

★

In the summer of 1983, I had the opportunity to go into the real estate business. I'd met a scoutmaster who had a small one-man real estate company. He wanted to attend the World Scout Jamboree in Canada that summer and spend time camping with his scouts. He needed someone to answer the phones and keep the office open while he was away. He agreed to pay me two hundred dollars a week. I was too old, and my back problems had grown worse over the years. I couldn't go back to the carpentry work I'd done ten years earlier, so I agreed to work for him.

This led to my going into the real estate business, which I did for a number of years. I started making good money and I had the freedom, with a flexible schedule, to continue with my music. I eventually became a CCIM (Certified Commercial-Investment Member), the highest certification in commercial-investment real estate. With a fine art degree, it was like nothing I had ever been exposed to. It was challenging. But after earning the designation, I could crunch numbers with someone who had an MBA. In my last years in the business, I was selling apartment complexes. As I started making money, I urged Jan to quit her stressful welfare work. She got a real estate license and started working with me. She did residential work. She had better instincts in residential real estate than I did. She was incredible at matching buyers with the right properties. I used to tell people she could find houses under rocks.

But understand, real estate is about money, sometimes a lot of money. At first it was hard for me to adjust to all the zeros in those numbers. But I became good at the business because I was honest with people, and because

I could think creatively and solve problems. But real estate was never precious to me like my music. It wasn't a passion. I could be detached, objective, and cold about it. It was only money. That was hard for me with my music. Music was my passion, my heart and soul, my feelings. It was art. I could never treat it with the same objectivity I did real estate. Though I was sidetracked for several years from my true love, I'm glad I had the opportunity to work in real estate. I learned a lot about business and people.

I had a good friend, John McCarthy, a Nashville accountant. We each had two sons about the same age, and we met when our boys were in the same Boy Scout troop. One morning, I was sitting in the car with John in front of his office, and I said, "John, I feel so low sometimes. I was an acclaimed singer-songwriter and recording artist, played for the president, and now I have my name and home phone number on signs in people's yards. It is incredibly depressing at times."

John turned to me, and I will never forget what he said: "Jim, you have nothing to be ashamed of for doing what you had to do to take to care of your family, and anyone who thinks any less of you for doing that wasn't your friend anyway. And they don't matter."

It was the support of my friends like Joe Dougherty, John McCarthy, and Peter Guralnick, who always reminded me to "keep the faith," that got me through those difficult sidelined years of my life. That, and the intelligence and support of my beloved wife, Jan—and the determination instilled in me by my old Okie mother.

★ ★ ★ ★ ★

Chapter 16

BEAR FAMILY, THE CAPITOL REISSUES, AND CIMARRON RECORDS

In 1984 Richard Weize from Bear Family Records in West Germany visited me in Nashville. I had met Richard through a country music radio personality in Germany, Walter Fuchs. Walter was "Mr. Country Music" in Germany. He wrote several books about country music in German, in which I was well represented. He was on the air for decades with country music programs on German radio. Walter loved my music, and when my first Capitol album was released, he sought me out in Nashville, and we became lifelong friends.

Richard Weize, on the other hand, was unusual, sometimes a difficult guy to like. One German friend said he was a cross between a hippie and a Nazi. He was abrupt, opinionated, hard of hearing; he talked loudly, and he didn't seem to bathe too often. But he was on a mission with his Bear Family Records label to preserve all the great music that he loved, which was rockabilly and country music. His label became the place where collectors could find the recordings that the major American labels had long ago deleted from their catalogs. He had a stable of music collectors and music appreciators in Europe who would buy nearly everything he issued on Bear Family. He would obtain a license, at ridiculously low fees, from the major US record labels to reissue their old masters. The labels were not doing anything with them anyway, so whatever they received in license fees was all gravy. Richard would take a digital tape recorder and sit for days in their record vaults transferring the old recordings to digital cassettes. He would secure the old artwork as well, and his reissues were impressive with elaborate packaging and thick booklets of information, photographs, and artwork.

The problem was, he never paid any of the artists, including me. He released beautiful boxed sets of multiple albums, and later boxed sets with multiple CDs. His licenses with the record labels were for release in Germany, but he sold the product all over the world. He treated all the artistic work as if it were public domain, which it wasn't. As an artist, if you wanted to collect your money from Bear Family, you had to sue him in Germany, and it would cost you more than you would ever collect. Richard knew that. It was easy to run a record company if you never paid the artists for their music. But to give him some slack, he did keep wonderful, essential, music in print, which the major labels deemed to be of little or no value. He also provided artists like me, whose work he deemed worthy and who had no other outlet, a place where their music could be released.

When Richard visited us the first time in Nashville, he couldn't understand why a US record label hadn't signed me. He loved my music. Why was I being ignored? Why were my Capitol albums no longer in print? He couldn't believe I was not releasing new product. "Where are your new recordings?" I explained the unfortunate circumstances regarding my leaving Capitol Records and told him I was selling real estate for a living. He then asked me if I had anything new that I could play for him.

I brought out some tapes I'd recorded in a studio in Somerville, Massachusetts, with John Lincoln Wright's band, and a few other songs I'd managed to record in Nashville. I had eight sides completed in total. Richard listened to the recordings, then said that he wanted me to come to Germany and perform at Bear Family's fifteenth anniversary concert in 1985. He agreed to pay Jan's and my way to Europe and gave me a small fee. Since Jan and I had never been to Europe, this sounded exciting. And he said if I could record just three more songs, along with the recordings I had, he would release an album of those songs in conjunction with his fifteenth anniversary concert.

I managed to record three more sides: "Montana Song," "Ready to Please," and "We're All One Family," with Ron Cornelius as my coproducer at Pete Drake's Nashville studio. This gave me the recordings to complete my first Bear Family album. The album was called *American Originals.* It was my fifth album and the first album I released after I left Capitol. It had been eight years since I'd released an album. Bear Family released it in Europe at their fifteenth anniversary show. It was also the first album I released on compact disc (CD). Bear Family released it in both vinyl and CD format. I owned the master recording, as I did with everything Bear Family ultimately released. In the production I was trying for a more contemporary sound—less fiddles and dobros—which I thought was what the American labels wanted at the time. Nashville music was starting its transition into a harder sound. The album has some very good songs on it, including my version of "New York Town," but it is not well-known in the United States because it was never released here.

No written license agreement was ever executed with Bear Family to use my masters. It was simply a handshake. After meeting Richard, Jan, said, "You'll never see a dime from that guy." She was right again, as she usually is.

We went to Germany for the concert. I rehearsed and played the show with some excellent German musicians. Jan and I purchased Eurail passes, and after the performance we traveled all over Germany, Austria, and Switzerland. We visited our friends Hans Ziemann in northern Germany and Walter Fuchs and his wife, Marianne, in Buhl in the south. It was a fun trip.

As the years went by, I was far from rich, but I'd made enough money in real estate that I had some peace of mind and the time to think more about what I loved—my music and songwriting. In 1987 I started working on some new recordings at the Sound Emporium with a fine Nashville drummer, Tommy Wells, as my coproducer and Gary Laney as the engineer. These recordings would eventually become a CD titled *Love Songs and the Blues.* The tracks were not yet completed or mixed, and I was short on cash to complete the project, so I set it aside for a while. But Rick Durrett, my longtime piano and keyboard player from my four Capitol albums, worked a deal with a studio and helped me complete the recordings. It was released on CD in Europe by Bear Family. Again, it has some fine songs on it, but it never got much attention over here as it was never distributed in the United States.

By this time in my music career, I had no contacts at the major labels, and I had no management to represent me. I was forty-three years old, and my heyday as an artist with a major label was behind me. But my passion for writing and recording was not. If an artist chooses to make music, or paint, or write novels, it doesn't matter how old he is. It doesn't matter whether the popular music business, in its constant search for youth and new talent, accepts an artist. I kept making music because it was what I loved to do. Success, I came to realize, is not defined by money or fame but by the quality

of the entire body of work a person has created. I don't have music that I
am ashamed of, that has been created for strictly commercial purposes. I
have produced or coproduced all my work, and I have always approached it
as art, attempting to make it as good as possible and my productions as
timeless as possible.

★

In 1991 Richard Weize again visited Jan and me in Nashville, as he had
done almost every year since his first trip. He asked if he could see Cavalliere Ketchum's photographs again from *The Road to Torreón* project. I
showed him the photographs and again we listened to the demos, which
he'd heard on previous trips. After looking through the prints and listening to the recordings again, he said, "This project really needs to be
released. Is there any chance you could afford to record it?" He wasn't willing to pay for the recordings (he never was), but if I would produce the
music, he would release it in a CD boxed-set edition with a book of Cavalliere's photographs—the same as I and John Hammond had envisioned
twenty years before.

With Richard's commitment to release the project on Bear Family,
which I knew would be an expensive package, I borrowed some money and
set to work to record the songs. Unlike when Michael Brovsky left me high
and dry in 1977, I was comfortable enough by that time financially to record
the project. I knew I'd likely never see any money from it—which I never
have—but that's not the point. It was always a labor of love for me, written
with the same urgency that Woody Guthrie wrote his songs. I wanted to see
it released. I recorded it with Gary Laney at the Sound Emporium, with
Dave Pomeroy as my coproducer. Dave is a good friend and one of the best
bass players in Nashville. Doyle Grisham and my other usual musicians
played inspiring music for it. It was a sterling assemblage of talent, and a
marvelous interpretation of my earliest songs from the Southwest.

The project was released in 1992, and Bear Family outdid themselves
on the packaging. It was presented with a beautifully designed white box,
with one of Cavalliere Ketchum's signature photographs on the cover, and
the photographic book and a CD inside. For a time, Beth Hadas at the University of New Mexico Press imported and sold the package in the United
States. It is still available on Amazon.com as a German import, or directly
from the Bear Family Records website.

The Road to Torreón was the third album project I made with Bear Family for European release. I could not have been happier with their presentation. I only wish that such a beautiful package could have been issued in the United States. It's a shame that something so American had to be released in a foreign country. It was a dream that came to fruition twenty years after I had first presented it to John Hammond in 1972. It is the tribute to the Hispanic people of New Mexico I'd always hoped for.

I issued one more release with Bear Family in 1994, *James Talley: Live*. It was the live recordings made from soundboard tapes recorded in the early 1980s at the Lone Star Cafe in New York and the Great Southeast Music Hall in Atlanta. The sonic quality is somewhat lacking because of the way it was recorded, but the energy of a youthful James Talley with a great band is there.

John Walsh, whom I had met in Washington, DC, when I played a concert at the Smithsonian and who was then executive editor at ESPN and a big supporter, was at the Lone Star Cafe the night we recorded. He wrote a heartfelt comment for me to print on the back of the album:

> Every so often the American entertainment culture mines a treasure. James Talley's interpretation of the country's sociological landscape through simple and revealing storytelling is a melodic treasure chest we can now enjoy once again. The spirit of the songwriting is from the heart and of the earth. It's a Woody Guthrie snapshot of many good people trying to find their way. Listen and you'll hear about the world around you. Listen carefully and you'll learn something new about that world.

I have not seen John in many years, but I will always hold him dear in my heart. He was inducted into the Sports Broadcasters Hall of Fame in 2017.

★

Because Capitol Records had deleted the four classic albums I'd recorded for them in the late 1970s, I decided by the early 1990s to see if I could find a way to get those albums back in print. Willie Nelson had used a music attorney in Atlanta named Joel Katz who had obviously done great things for Willie's career. So I contacted Joel. I drove to Atlanta, and we had lunch. I explained that it seemed logical to try resurrecting my career with Capitol because they had my four original albums in their music vault. They had all been highly acclaimed at the time of their original release. Twenty years had passed, and perhaps any animosity toward me had left the building. Joel said that he'd always liked my Capitol albums when they were released, and he agreed to help me.

Nothing moves quickly in the record business, but eventually Joel called. He said he had spoken with Hale Milgrim, then the president of Capitol Records. Hale had agreed to re-sign me and start releasing my prior catalog along with new recordings. Joel had some clout! I was simply ecstatic. It was 1993, I was then almost fifty years old, and I was thrilled with the news. But a little more time went by, and I got another call from Joel. Hale Milgrim had been abruptly terminated, and now Gary Gersh had been installed as the new president at Capitol. Katz said he really didn't know Gersh that well and had no relationship with him. I was dead in the water.

Hale Milgrim was a true music man, someone who absolutely loved music. He was close to my age and had some understanding of my history. Gary Gersh was a new young executive in his thirties, who had only been in the music business since the 1980s. He knew nothing of me or my work. He was a young gun hired to jazz up the Capitol roster, and he was much more attuned to rock and rap than anything country.

Nevertheless, I decided to keep directly pursuing Gersh at Capitol, and I started writing him letters. He agreed to see me at the Capitol Tower in Hollywood, so Jan and I flew to Los Angeles for the meeting. Jan had never been to the West Coast before, so we planned a little West Coast vacation after my meeting with Gersh.

When I met with Gersh, he was quite cordial, and he indicated that perhaps we could release my first two albums on CD and see how they did. I don't know if he had listened to the music in preparation for the meeting or not, but things seemed to go well. But not much happened, and things languished. I kept speaking with Analee Canto, who had been Hale Milgrim's secretary before he left. She was still at the label and was trying to work the back channels for me. Katy Bess, another executive secretary, was also trying to help. Never discount the help that support staff can provide. They may not be able to help that much, but they can surely hurt you if they choose—and they are never paid what they are worth.

I kept carefully crafting letters to the chief executives at Capitol, and I wound up with quite a stack of correspondence over ten years. Finally, Capitol contacted me and said that they were starting a new catalog division that would specialize in releasing masters from their tape vault. This seemed like a great idea to me. There is so much wonderful music languishing in the basement of the Capitol Tower that is worthy of being heard. (Now, in the digital age, all the major labels should make available their extensive vault material. There's almost no cost to releasing it digitally on a streaming platform.)

I was turned over to Capitol's new catalog company, and I flew to Los Angeles to meet with the new president of the catalog division. That was in 1995, and I had just completed my album *Woody Guthrie and Songs of My Oklahoma Home* the previous fall in Santa Fe. The people at the catalog company were excited about my Woody Guthrie project. They loved the recording and wanted to release it and start reissuing my Capitol catalog. I excitedly returned to Nashville. It seemed like maybe the planets were starting to line up. A couple of weeks went by, and I got a call from one of the assistants to the catalog division president.

He said, "James, are you sitting down?"

"What is it?" I said.

"Well," he said, "I hate to tell you this, but Capitol has decided to close the catalog company and we've all been fired. You can forget about us releasing your Woody Guthrie project and your other music. It's not going to happen now."

By that time, Gary Gersh had been dismissed, and another president had taken over at Capitol. Every three years there was a new president. It was like musical chairs. So I started writing letters to the new president. I was finally turned over to Capitol's attorneys in business affairs, their legal department.

I spoke on the phone with Capitol's chief lawyer, John Ray. He seemed like a decent guy and wanted to help if possible. We talked for a few minutes, and I said, "John, let me ask you something, do you have any children?"

"Yes," he said, "I have three daughters, why?"

I said, "How would you feel if those girls were taken from you and locked in prison, in a dark dungeon, and you could not see them, you could not talk to them, or hear them speak? You could not love them, and they could not love you back. How would that make you feel?"

"Well, not too good," he said. He was stammering and taken aback.

"Well, Capitol Records has taken my creative children, whom I loved, nurtured, and gave years of my life to. Capitol has taken them from me and locked them in prison, deep in your music vault for over twenty years, and no one can hear them speak. No one can hear them or enjoy their voices. Those are my creative children. I love them, I devoted years of my life to them, and I want to hear them speak again. I want Capitol to either reissue those albums, or I want you to give them back to me so I can reissue them myself."

John understood and was sympathetic. He got the metaphor. He said, "Give me a couple of weeks, James. Let me talk to some folks here at the label and see what I can do."

John called me in a week or two and said he had spoken with several people at the company, but he simply could not generate any interest in re-releasing them. He was sorry. (Record companies rely on new product, not catalog.) But he said, "I will work out an agreement with you. You will have the exclusive rights to your masters, and you can reissue them or license them to other entities if you choose. Everything must go through you. Capitol cannot license them directly to anyone else. That is the best I can do, but you will have your masters back."

An agreement was drafted and sent to me for my review by one of John's young associate attorneys, David Lessoff. In the agreement, however, there was a clause whereby Capitol, if they chose, still retained the right to reissue the albums in the future on one of their imprints. They could not license them to any third party, any other company or individual without going through me. If they chose to reissue them, it had to be on one of their corporate imprints. I said to David on the phone, "Let me be sure I understand this. If I spend my money, my time, my effort and energy to release these masters, and if I do by some chance make something happen with them, then you want the right to take over, release them, and cut me off at the knees. Do I understand this correctly?"

David said, "Well, I guess that is about right."

I said, "Well, I don't think Capitol is ever going to do anything with these masters, but here's the deal: Capitol deleted these albums out of spite over twenty years ago, and every six months I get a statement from Capitol that says I still owe them $382,000. If they had kept these albums in print, where I could have gone out and performed and promoted them, Capitol would now have four gold records on their wall, and that debt would be paid! So if they want to retain the right to reissue these albums, after my decade of trying to get them to do it, then I think that $382,000 debt needs to go away."

"Well, why is that?" David asked.

"Because" I said, "they have already taken a tax write-off for that amount years ago, the same as a bank writes off bad assets, and by removing the albums from catalog, they gave me no way to repay the debt.

David said, "I understand. Let me talk to John Ray and I will get back to you."

David called me back the next day and said, "OK, that debt has gone away. If we ever reissue those albums on one of our imprints, you will be paid from the first unit sold."

"OK," I said, "We have a deal."

★

I resigned myself to the fact that I was never going to receive a dime from Bear Family Records. They were essentially using my masters for free. They did not release recordings in the United States unless you imported them. So in 1999, with the Internet taking off, I purchased two website domains (www.cimarronrecords.com and www.jamestalley.com) and started my own Cimarron Records label. I wanted to see my Capitol masters reissued.

But it is expensive for an individual, with no economy of scale, in a consignment business, where you don't get paid by the CD distributor until the product actually sells in the store, and the store sends them the money. There are many costs involved in a CD release, even without the recording cost: design, artwork, printing, packaging, CD duplication, press and publicity, radio promotion, postage, and shipping. The only money saved in a reissue release is the studio time and musicians. I also wanted to issue the new albums I was recording. Therefore, it took me until 2005 to finally release the thirtieth-anniversary reissue of *Got No Bread*. In 2017, I reissued a fortieth-anniversary reissue of my second Capitol album, *Tryin' Like the Devil*, in CD format.

As of this writing, I still have not released *Blackjack Choir* and *Ain't It Somethin'*, my third and fourth Capitol albums as CD releases, but they are both available now as streams. Streaming is the distribution method of today. Physical sales have slowed tremendously, but I still sell custom CDs and downloads on my website (www.jamestalley.com). Burnside Distributors in Portland, Oregon, distributes my physical CD product to brick-and-mortar stores and Internet stores that still sell physical product.

David Lessoff left Capitol Records some years ago and has gone on to other music industry positions in the digital space, but we still stay in touch and have remained close friends since his days at Capitol Records. John Ray has retired from Capitol. In the record company consolidations of recent years, Capitol is now one of the many labels under the Universal Music Group, which is part of the French music conglomerate Vivendi. It's a changed world. My fragile little dreams remain out there somewhere in the cloud, a footnote within the Internet music galaxy. It's still all about the money. The music is just product.

★

After starting Cimarron Records in 1999, I released two new albums that I recorded in Santa Fe, New Mexico: *Woody Guthrie and Songs of My Oklahoma Home* and *Nashville City Blues*. These were both recorded at Stepbridge Studios in Santa Fe, which was owned by Tim Stroh, of the Detroit Stroh's Beer family. Tim was a music enthusiast and an excellent recording engineer. His Santa Fe studio was well appointed, with first-rate recording equipment. It was in an old adobe building in downtown Santa Fe. Gregg Thomas, my old drummer, who was then living in Santa Fe, coproduced the projects with me. John Griffin was the excellent bassist. Richard Hardy, a local Santa Fe musician and silversmith, lent a dusky sound to the recordings with his 1920 Gibson mandocello (an incredible instrument) and his mandolin and mandola. John Potrykus played dobro and pedal steel. We kept it simple. The sessions were completed in November 1994. Due to the delays at Capitol Records, my Woody recording was not released until late 1999, when I started Cimarron Records.

The Woody album came off with a true authentic acoustic sound. We kept the music as true to Guthrie's original feeling as possible, except that it had the advantage of modern sonic quality, something that was missing from Woody's original recordings. Once again, I was thrilled when the reviews started coming in. Neil Strauss in the *New York Times* said the recordings completed Guthrie; Bill Friskics-Warren in the *Nashville Scene* called me the Godfather of Americana; and in a stunning Amazon.com review Jerome Clark wrote:

> Those of us who know Woody Guthrie's music can be excused for wondering why we should be asked to listen to James Talley's covers rather than Guthrie's readily available originals. The answer is in the listening. Talley's interpretive gifts are such that very soon

into the CD the issue fades into inconsequentiality. This is, let there be no mistake, a Talley, not a faux-Guthrie, record. Talley's readings are subtle, nuanced, original, unexpectedly moving. No one—and I've heard them all—has done "Deportee" and (especially) "This Land Is Your Land" better. Where the latter is concerned, you'd think you'd never heard this well-traveled song before. Talley reinvents it and goes deeper into its American heart than any artist, including Guthrie, has ever managed to do. If there were any justice in this world, it would be played on every radio from California to the New York Island.

I returned to Stepbridge in the fall of 1995 to record *Nashville City Blues.* I used the same personnel that I used on the Woody Guthrie sessions, adding Jono Manson on electric guitar and some background singers, Denise Brissey, Joan Griffin, and John Nieto. Gregg Thomas was again the drummer and my coproducer. Tim Stroh recorded and mixed the project. I did not complete the mixing, however, until 1998, due to a delay in recovering from back surgery.

After we recorded the album, I played the song "Nashville City Blues" for Jack Tarver, my old friend and supporter in Atlanta. Jack said, "Well, if you want to destroy your music career in Nashville, go ahead and release it."

I said, "What music career in Nashville are you talking about, Jack? I'm selling real estate for a living, remember!" I went ahead and released it. Screw it!

Nashville City Blues came out in the summer of 2000, on the heels of my Woody Guthrie release, and I got word that Amazon.com had named me their Folk Artist of the Year 2000. The reviews on *Nashville City Blues* were heartwarming, as they had been with my Woody Guthrie CD. Peter Guralnick wrote, "I feel like you made this album for me."

Marc Greilsamer for Amazon.com wrote:

Talley is resilient . . . the concept of dreams arises in nearly every song . . . "the dream is the spark," whether it comes true or not. "Dreaming," he writes, "is a way of coping with man's discontent." Similarly, the "blues" is a way to come to grips with man's discontent, and here he uses the blues in all of its permutations. . . . *Nashville City Blues* is about the healing effects of the blues, its loyal companionship and its knowing sympathy.

Following the release of *Woody Guthrie and Songs of My Oklahoma Home* and *Nashville City Blues*, I started touring again as a solo act. I was tired of wrangling musicians on the road. Our two sons were grown, and Jan and I enjoyed traveling to various states and European countries together. When I was a young man, and an artist on Capitol, our children were small, and it was difficult for her to travel with me. It felt good to have her with me on these tours, where we could do a little sightseeing between performances. She did exhaustive research on each tour and road-managed all the trips.

I continued to play scattered dates in Atlanta, Massachusetts, New York, Oklahoma, California, Alaska, West Virginia, North Dakota, and other states. I did a small midwest tour with my friends in Switchback, Marty McCormack and Brian FitzGerald.

At this point in my life, I understood how the music business worked. I didn't expect to feel the earth move with the release of either *Woody Guthrie and Songs of My Oklahoma Home* or *Nashville City Blues*. Without a major label's support, and their publicity, radio promotion, and sales, the chances were slim that anything significant could happen. But it was still fun. I was writing, recording, and performing again for people who appreciated my artistry.

Bill Wence's radio promotion company in Nashville promoted my CDs to the new Americana-formatted radio stations, and we had good success at radio. But here's how that business model works: the CDs go out to radio and the press, and the album goes up the music chart for six weeks, then down the chart for six weeks. Then it's pretty much over for that album. There are no singles to keep the exposure going for a year. The reviews come in and are still wonderfully supportive. But this business model holds no real return for all the time and money it takes to write the songs, record the music, hire the publicity and promotion people, and manufacture the CDs. It has to be a labor of love. It's like the old joke says: "A musician is the only person that will put five thousand dollars' worth of gear into a fifteen-hundred-dollar car, drive five hundred miles to play a fifty-dollar date!" Staying on the road for two hundred dates a year might sell enough CDs to break even, but that means hauling a CD inventory everywhere and being on the road constantly—and now, of course, people are streaming their music anyway.

At my age I can no longer punish my body doing all that road work. When I tour now, I like to have some fun. That's why a lot of my touring over the past twenty years has been in Europe. Jan and I never tire of traveling and seeing the world, but at our age it must be done leisurely. But at least, now, with the plethora of Internet music sites, YouTube, and all the streaming platforms, the music is readily available. It's no longer in the basement at the Capitol Tower in Hollywood.

I have tried my whole life to make essential music, music that matters and is timeless, music that will find an audience now and forever—like Jimmie Rodgers or Woody Guthrie have. It's been almost fifty years since I recorded my first album, and thankfully people are still listening.

★ ★ ★ ★ ★

Chapter 17

A CREATIVE OASIS IN SOUTH
TEXAS, AND THOSE WHO CAN'T

In the year 2000 Bill Bentley, in publicity at Warner Brothers Records in California, mailed me a CD. Bill had written an article about me back in 1976, when I performed at the Armadillo World Headquarters in Austin. He was then just starting out as a young music reporter for the *Austin Sun*, a little weekly music paper. Bill was young then, with hair down to his waist. Twenty-five years had passed, Bill had moved to Los Angeles, cut some hair, and wound up in publicity at Warner Brothers Records. We've stayed in touch. The album he sent me was *The Return of Wayne Douglas*. It was the last album that Doug Sahm recorded, and under his real name. It was recorded in 1999, just before his death from a heart attack, and was released in 2000. It was a great record with quality songs and musicianship. The sonic quality of the record was impressive. I had been wanting to return to the essentials of my early albums, with fiddles and steel guitars, for some time. That was what I loved. I emailed Bill. He said the project had been engineered and produced in Floresville, Texas, outside of San Antonio, in a little studio owned by Tommy Detamore, the pedal steel player on the album. The rhythm section was solid, and the fiddle player on the album, Bobby Flores, was outstanding, like a young Johnny Gimble.

I had been considering recording a "best of" album from the songs on my four Capitol albums, and I wanted that southwestern sound. This seemed like the perfect ensemble to provide it. As it turned out, Tommy Detamore was aware of my earlier work on Capitol. We set a date in December 2000 for me to come to Floresville and record an album with him and his musicians: Dan Dreeben on drums; David Carroll on bass; Tommy on electric guitar, pedal steel, and engineering; and Bobby Flores on fiddle, guitar, mandolin, and harmony vocals. Ron Huckaby was on piano. Al Gomez was on trumpet, and Ponty Bone, whom I'd known since the late 1970s when he was with Joe Ely's band, drove down from Austin with his accordion. Joe Ely joined me for a duet on "W. Lee O'Daniel and the Light Crust Dough Boys."

Jan and I made plans to go to San Antonio for a couple of weeks. Tommy called the musicians together before we started and said, "James has come all the way from Nashville because he heard what you guys have done, so let's not disappoint him." I got the sound I wanted, and I began to love Tommy's little studio and its isolation in the wilds of south Texas.

The first album I recorded with Tommy was titled *Touchstones*. Tommy was not only a great steel player, but he was also an incredible engineer and mixer, and one of the most pleasant and unflappable people you would ever hope to work with in the studio. As they say, "He has great ears." Those 2000 sessions were also the first time I had recorded an album using all-digital technology. Once an artist works digitally, I don't think he will ever desire to go back to analog recording. The mixing and editing capabilities simply do not compare.

Touchstones was well received at radio. Bill Wence's promotion company took it to the top ten on the Americana radio chart, and the reviews were laudatory, as has fortunately been the case with most of my albums over the years. God bless the music reviewers.

My music was finally out of the darkness and could be introduced to a new, younger audience. Sadly, however, Tommy called me a few years ago with news that the little Cherry Ridge Studio burned down. That was heartbreaking, because Tommy had created an oasis in the Texas countryside that was perfect for creative work.

★

All my music career I had wanted to record a live concert using the best recording equipment, and with a great band. I've always felt that delivering one's music to a live audience is the way music should be judged. There is more energy and intimacy in a performance before a live audience. It's a two-way communication. The audience and the performer feed off each other. I had recorded my live shows at the Lone Star Cafe in New York and the Great Southeast Music Hall in Atlanta, but because of the way those performances were recorded, the energy was there, but the sonic quality was not.

In 2002 I was invited to perform in Italy, where I had a number of avid listeners, who had been drawn to Bear Family's European releases, especially the boxed set release of *The Road to Torreón*. That's the one benefit I received from Bear Family, they did expose my music in Europe. Paolo Carù owned a record shop in Gallarate, a small town outside of Milan and published an Italian music magazine, *Buscadero*. Paolo published several reviews and features of my music in his magazine by the Italian music journalist Marco Denti and others.

Jono Manson, who had played on *Nashville City Blues*, had been touring in Italy for several years, and in 2002 gained the interest of Simone Grasse, an Italian music promoter in Sarzana. Simone wanted to promote a tour with me and my American musicians. We recorded a live CD from the performances. Dave Pomeroy was on bass, Gregg Thomas was on the drums, and Mike Noble was on electric guitar. Mike had been stationed in Italy at the Aviano Air Base when he was in the US Air Force, and Dave Pomeroy was born in Naples when his father was stationed there in the service. We all looked forward to going to Italy.

The promoters were great. Umberto Bonanni was our excellent tour manager. After the last date in Chiari, a big banquet was held for us. It was amazing hospitality. I must confess, I have never had a bad meal or a bad glass of wine in Italy. The people were incredibly gracious. Jan flew over after the last performance and we spent another two weeks touring northern Italy, going to Rome, Florence, and Venice. It was a beautiful trip.

Jono Manson digitally recorded the concerts and mailed me the hard drives when we returned to the United States. I took them to Tommy Detamore's studio in Floresville to complete them. Tommy and I and mixed and edited the concerts into two CDs' worth of material. In 2004 I released the first CD from these recordings, entitled *Journey*. The sound was excellent, as was the musicianship. We edited and mixed the remainder of the Italian recordings in 2006–2007 for a second CD, which was entitled *Journey: The Second Voyage*.

Each of the *Journey* CDs has several of my newer songs on them—songs that are not found on any of my other CDs. I am especially proud of my song "I Saw the Buildings," which was my response to the 9/11 attacks on New York City and Washington, DC. It took me time to get my head around that tragedy. I simply marvel that here we are in the twenty-first century still arguing and killing each other about whose vision of the afterlife—a mystery no one knows—we should subscribe to. I tried to tell the heartbreak of 9/11 and the great mystery in my song, "I Saw the Buildings." Listen especially to Dave Pomeroy's inspired bass solo at the end of the song. It never ceases to amaze and move me.

Also on *Journey* is "The Song of Chief Joseph." This is a long narrative song about the Nez Perce War of 1877. It tells the story of Joseph and his people, the Nez Perce tribe of northeastern Oregon, who were forced onto reservations in America's genocidal Indian wars of the late nineteenth century. When the Nez Perce surrendered after a five-day shootout, Chief Joseph issued his famous statement, "From where the sun now stands, I will fight no more forever." We all have our heroes in history, and Chief Joseph is certainly one of mine. Whenever I am feeling down, I think of the suffering he and his people went through, and whatever my problem is seems insignificant.

When I returned from Italy in 2002, there was a message on my answering machine from an attorney in New York telling me that Moby had recorded my song "She's the One." He did a small rewrite and changed the title to "Evening Rain." The song was in the soundtrack of the movie *Daredevil*, starring Ben Affleck and Jennifer Garner. After a wonderful trip to Italy, that was frosting on the cake.

In 2007 I started recording some new songs at Dave Pomeroy's Ear-wave Studio in Nashville. We recorded the basic tracks for "Santa Fe Blues," and a new version of "She's the One," which was on my second Capitol album, *Tryin' Like the Devil*, from 1976. I took the tracks we'd recorded to Tommy Detamore's Cherry Ridge Studio in Texas to complete them. In addition to Tommy's regular crew, I used Floyd Domino on piano, whom I had known and worked with when we were on Capitol together and he was a member of Asleep at the Wheel. This CD would be called *Heartsong*, and at this writing is the last album I have released.

★

In 2010 Jan and I went to Germany to perform at the Buhl Bluegrass Festival for Walter Fuchs. I worked with an excellent European band, Four-Wheel-Drive, which was headed by Joost van Es, an incredible fiddler from the Netherlands. After the festival, Jan and I went to Lyon, France, for a performance at the invitation of Jacques Spiry, a local music aficionado. We performed a municipally sponsored date in Spain at El Port de la Selva on the Catalonian coast, arranged by my friend in Girona, Lluis Sala, one of the most intelligent and sincere people I've ever met. We ended the tour in

Frankfurt, Germany, at a performance sponsored by Olaf Purkert. It's a pleasure to play my music for people and to know that they have been moved by my perspective. That's why you write songs in the first place, to share.

Jan and I have returned to Europe and the United Kingdom several times over the years. Old fans come to the shows with my early Capitol albums for me to autograph. In Paris I performed at the American University, la Fondation des Etats-Unis, and spoke on the history of American folk and country music. I had some planned remarks for my talk but somehow left them at the hotel, so I had to use Cavalliere Ketchum's "Navajo Rug" method for my presentation—I winged it. Jan found my presentation quite humorous as I fumbled through it. The event was arranged by my longtime French friend and supporter Gérard Meffre. French journalists who had written about my music for years were at the show. It was a joy to finally meet so many of them. Regardless of the town or the country, it always means so much to share with people who love good songs.

★

The Vietnam War was the defining tragedy of my youth. At our home in Medanales, New Mexico, I had a neighbor down the road who I noticed always flew the American flag and the POW flag on a tall flagpole on his property. I was walking with my dog one afternoon and met him mending his fence. His name was Frank Archuleta. Frank was an army ranger with two deployments in Vietnam. He was a member of the 173rd Airborne Brigade—"The Sky Soldiers." Frank had two Silver Stars, five Bronze Stars, and six Purple Hearts. He was very modest about his decorations, and I didn't learn of them for some time after meeting him. He was in that horrendous pre-Thanksgiving battle in 1967 for Hill 875 at Dak To, where his company had been surrounded and overrun. One hundred men were killed and nearly as many helicopters were shot down.

I would stop at his house while walking with my dog and we would sit and talk under his covered patio in the dry New Mexico air. We became good friends. But every conversation with him within a few minutes led to Vietnam. After fifty years he still had PTSD. He lived by himself and had a little support dog. He said his wife could not live with his PTSD and nightmares. They had been separated for many years. He said he spent eighteen months in the hospital in Denver after his last wounding—three AK-47 rounds. He went to college on the GI Bill and completed a bachelor's degree and eventually a masters. He retired from the Denver Fire Department, where he was once honored as Fireman of the Year. His family used to herd sheep on the land where our rural subdivision is located in Medanales.

He felt comfortable talking with me and appreciated me listening to him. I cared about him and what he said. He told me it meant a lot to him. In August 2017, just before returning to Nashville, I went to the VA Hospital in Albuquerque with him and performed an impromptu acoustic performance in the waiting room. It pleased him greatly.

I told him I was going to write a song for him. It took me some time to get it right. In the song I tried to capture his feelings about the war, how he felt about his return from the war, and how he was shamed for being an American soldier. On his return to San Francisco, protestors threw eggs and tomatoes at him and the other veterans from behind a chain-link fence as they deplaned. A young co-ed at the University of Colorado called him a "baby-killer."

I was not supportive of the war. It was a big mistake, but I never denigrated the young men who served in that conflict. I never understood people's reasoning on that.

One afternoon on his patio I was visiting with him, and some of his veteran pals who lived nearby came to visit. They were taking sips of whiskey and raising their glasses and toasting, "For those who can't!" I asked him the next day when I stopped by what "For those who can't" meant. He said it was for those who were killed in the war, and who can't be here with us having a drink. I thought about that and all the things we had discussed over our summers together, and I found my image for the song, "For Those Who Can't."

I started the song at my house in New Mexico that summer of 2017, but I finished it after I returned to Nashville in the spring of 2018. When I was satisfied with it, I mailed a copy of the lyrics to Frank. He was so proud of it. He took the lyrics to the postmistress in Medanales and asked her to make several copies for him. He called me in Nashville and wanted to know when I would be back in New Mexico. I told him in a few weeks, and that I would play the song for him when I got there. But about a week before I was ready to leave for New Mexico, I got a message from one of my neighbors: Frank had died of a stroke. He was seventy-four. He never got to hear the music to his song.

★ ★ ★ ★ ★

Chapter 18

AND THAT'S HOW I WILL FINISH

In 2019 John Thomson in Scotland arranged a tour for me in the United Kingdom. It wasn't long after Jan and I returned to Nashville from that tour that Covid-19 hit in February 2020. In the long months at home, I decided to write this memoir. It is now summer 2021. Jan and I have both had our Covid vaccinations and we are now visiting our home again in rural New Mexico.

I am gratified there are radio people all over the world who love and play my music. Walter Fuchs is now retired, but Herbert Fischer in Denmark plays one of my songs in every broadcast. Hermann Lammers Meyer in Germany still plays my music. There are radio people in Italy, the Netherlands, Australia, New Zealand—all over the world—and in the United States, who continue to program my songs. I've had two more songs in television shows in the past year and another one in a movie. I am still writing songs, but with the Covid-19 pandemic it has not been a good time to record. Hopefully soon, though, I will release another album with some of my new songs. I remain eternally grateful for all those who have helped me along the way and continue to share my music.

★

When *Got No Bread, No Milk, No Money, But We Sure Got a Lot of Love* was reissued in 2005, I received an email from a listener, Mary McCollum. She said: "Thanks for the songs you have written and recorded, especially for the Got No Bread album I had back in '75. The title track from that album has played in my memory for thirty years through good times and bad. Always bringing me hope that 'this too shall pass.' Three kids and one grandchild later, it plays on."

For a songwriter, it doesn't get any better than that. That's the reason for art, to move people, to help them feel and think. It's not about the money. That's not why we do it.

I started out wanting to be a painter and I wound up painting with words and music. The colors are there, and the brushstrokes of my life. But my paintings don't fill the walls of a museum. They are carried in the heart and are streamed in the mystery of the Internet cloud. That's my gallery.

And my songs didn't just appear out of the ether. They came from somewhere. I worked for them and earned them. They came from my life, from everything I've seen, felt, and touched in life, just as Pete Seeger told me Woody Guthrie's did. They came from my life as a young boy, living along the great Columbia River in Washington. They came from the stories and the times I spent with my grandparents and relatives in Oklahoma. They came from my youth in New Mexico, with my love of the American West, its beautiful skies, mountains, and deserts, and its citizenry of Anglos, Hispanics, and Native Americans. They came from my summers as a horseman and wrangler, wearing boots and spurs, in those beautiful Sangre de Cristo mountains in northern New Mexico. They came from the suffering and despair I witnessed as a welfare caseworker, which so disturbed me and changed forever my view of life in America. They came from my association with and the education and enlightenment I received from my Black coworkers in Nashville's public health rat control program. They came from my labor as a carpenter, working alongside good, hardworking people who were trying to find their way, put food on their table, a roof over their heads, and make the payments on their pickup trucks. They came from the money and greed I witnessed, and the good people I helped, in the real estate business. They came from my years of reading, and my love of books, of history, poetry, art, and language—and from the love of my wife and family.

Everyone at some point in life looks back and tries to reconcile their successes and failures. No, I didn't become a star. I probably had too much of an artistic bent for that anyway. Commercial record labels don't have much patience for "artists." The return isn't quick enough. They want "acts." I made a mistake in leaving Capitol Records. The effects were painful for me and my family. I put my faith in the wrong people; and yes, after my career cratered, I was bitter for a while. I went for several years without writing a song.

But then I realized that whether I had a big record company behind me or not, my writing, my painting with words and music was what I did. I simply could not stay away from a creative life. I am a songwriter who loves his craft. I realized that I was proud of the artistry of my life. My work had been well reviewed and revered. I was encouraged and supported by friends and other songwriters, musicians, and music journalists. I had to continue with whatever means I had. I am proud of the social themes expressed in my work. That's how I started out and that's how I'll finish. I've tried, like Woody Guthrie, to write about my generation, my country, and the lives of my countrymen. Songs can give us a lot. Humorous songs give us laughter and relief. Sad songs give us strength. They let us know we are not alone. I see all my songs as love songs because they are about life and people, and life in its essence is about love—giving love and receiving love. It's the most important thing in life. It never goes out of style. I am not religious, but I think Jesus was onto something when he told us "Love one another."

Not being a star kept me close to ordinary people. I've come to understand and appreciate that. No one recognizes me when I go to the supermarket. But my life is good. I have a wonderful wife, two marvelous sons, a loving daughter-in-law, a handsome grandson, and a little blue heeler furgirl named Sage. I have an adobe home in rural New Mexico, where I can look at the mountains from my patio and hear the coyotes barking and talking coyote-talk under the starlight on a nearby hill. In the mornings I drink my coffee on my patio and watch the ravens swoop and call, with blue light glistening from their shoulders as they land on the tops of the dark juniper trees. I have my shelves of books, and old friends I can call. I have the love of many good people all over the world, who listen to my songs, and who now magically call up my creative children and hear them speak on digital rivers of music. My work that was once silenced in the vaults at Capitol Records for twenty years is now free. I am a songwriter. I'm still trying like the devil, and I know dreams are out there in a world full of joy and sadness. *Try to see the paint on the tractor and keep the faith!*

ACKNOWLEDGMENTS

In telling my story, I thought maybe my successes and failures might give some guidance and inspiration to others pursuing a creative life. It is important to remind ourselves that regardless of the ups and downs in our life's pursuits, we must continue to believe in ourselves and our dreams, no matter how fragile those dreams may appear at times. There is much to gain, and love, in the pursuit of dreams.

In that regard, there are some people I must thank for their help in seeing these dreams and this publication realized. First, my five-decades-long friend and half-fast mandolin player, Steve Price, in New York City. Steve has published over thirty books in a long career and was for many years a working editor in the New York publishing world. I sent him the first fifty pages of the first draft and he extoled "Keep the descriptions simple and direct. You're not writing a novel. You must hold people's attention and keep them turning the page." Steve, I've tried.

I worked with William F. Cass at Philmont Scout Ranch in the summer of 1962. I was an eighteen-year-old horseman in those days, and we have stayed in touch ever since. Bill has published several books about the ranch, and he graciously went through this manuscript for me more than once, keeping my chronology straight and making many worthwhile suggestions on how to improve the text.

Tom Wilk, a friend, author, and journalist in New Jersey, has reviewed my music over the years. He worked as a newspaper copy editor and feature writer for close to thirty years at the *Courier-Post* in Cherry Hill, New Jersey. Tom went through the manuscript with his eagle eye and highlighted many textural errors and kept me honest.

Beth Hadas in Albuquerque, my dear friend and a longtime advocate of my music, offered to review the manuscript for me. Beth, until she retired about a decade ago, had long been the director of the University of New Mexico Press. I have admired many of the authors and titles she has edited through the years. We met back in the mid-1990s when she agreed to import *The Road to Torreón* and make it available through the UNM Press. Beth gave me so much of her time and encouraged me throughout. Her advice and suggestions were vital in improving the manuscript. She told me, "You must kill your darlings. You simply cannot put in every detail." So I became a killer of darlings! There were dead, bloody, and cut darlings all over the floor!

This book would never have been realized but for the advocacy and encouragement of Kent Calder, the guitar-playing editor at the University of Oklahoma Press. Kent initially encouraged me, feeling the book would fit well into the Press's American Popular Music Series. In numerous emails and phone conversations Kent guided me in shaping the manuscript into publishable form. He knows, too, how much it means to me to have my story published by the University of Oklahoma Press—because so much of my family's life and history are part of the state of Oklahoma. So with the help of Steve Price, Bill Cass, Tom Wilk, Beth Hadas and Kent Calder, here is the book as it now appears. I cannot thank each of them enough for almost turning me into a writer. I must also thank Pippa Letsky for the fine job she did with my final copy edit, and the entire family of gracious and caring people at the University of Oklahoma Press for helping me tell my story. You are all appreciated to the hilt!

Thanks go to Clark Thomas for his wonderful photographs. Clark graciously documented so much of my early life when we were both young and starting out. Thanks to Jim McGuire for his photos. Jim has taken so many stunning photographs of music people in his long career. Both are now retired and (I hope) living the good life.

Thanks go to David Morton, another half-century friend, for helping me recall many of my interactions with DeFord Bailey, the photos, and keeping that record accurate. And of course, thanks to my old compadre of sixty years, Cavalliere Ketchum, for his lifelong friendship and his incredible photographic art. And thanks Cavie for helping me select that old 1949 Willys. Man! I wish I still had that truck!

Thanks go to Peter Guralnick, the consummate writer and appreciator of American music, and my dear friend for these many decades. When I told Peter I was writing this book and asked if he would be interested in writing an introduction for it, he said, "Count me in!" Peter, I thank you. I have kept the faith!

Lastly, thanks go to Jan, my beautiful and brilliant wife of fifty-three years. She was the first one to read the draft and helped me recall many incidents, stories, and facts—and did her best to kept me honest. Never an easy task! If anyone knows this story as well as I do, it is her. Thank you, darling.

Thanks also to so many wonderful friends, musicians, listeners, and appreciators of my music and songs over the years. You have touched my life, my heart, and given me so much to treasure—near home, and all around the world. I love you all.

JAMES TALLEY DISCOGRAPHY

Albums by James Talley now available on Cimarron Records, Inc.

Got No Bread, No Milk, No Money, But We Sure Got a Lot of Love
Original Capitol Recordings, Torreón Productions, 1975.
Cimarron Records issue no. 1001, thirtieth-anniversary reissue by Cimarron
Records, 2006.

>Songs:
>W. Lee O'Daniel and the Light Crust Dough Boys
>Got No Bread, No Milk, No Money, But We Sure Got a Lot
>   of Love
>Red River Memory
>Give Him Another Bottle
>Calico Gypsy
>To Get Back Home
>Big Taters in the Sandy Land
>No Opener Needed
>Blue Eyed Ruth and My Sunday Suit
>Mehan, Oklahoma
>Daddy's Song
>Take Me to the Country
>Red River Reprise

Tryin' Like the Devil

Original Capitol Records Recordings, Torreón Productions, 1976.
Cimarron Records issue no. 1002, fortieth-anniversary reissue by Cimarron
Records, 2016.

> Songs:
> Forty Hours
> Deep Country Blues
> Give My Love to Marie
> Are They Gonna Make Us Outlaws Again?
> She Tries Not to Cry
> Tryin' Like the Devil
> She's the One
> Sometimes I Think about Suzanne
> Nothin' but the Blues
> You Can't Ever Tell

Blackjack Choir

Original Capitol Records, Torreón Productions, 1977.
Cimarron Recordings issue no. 1003.

> Songs:
> Bluesman (with B. B. King)
> Alabama Summertime
> Everybody Loves a Love Song
> Magnolia Boy
> Mississippi River Whistle Town
> Daddy Just Called It the Blues
> Up from Georgia
> Migrant Jesse Sawyer
> You Know I've Got to Love Her
> When the Fiddler Packs His Case

Ain't It Somethin'
Original Capitol Records, Torreón Productions, 1977.
Cimarron Recordings issue no. 1004.

Songs:
Ain't It Somethin'
Only the Best
We Keep Tryin'
Dixie Blue
Not Even When It's Over
Nine Pounds of Hashbrowns
Richland, Washington
Middle 'C' Mama
Old Time Religion
Poets of the West Virginia Mines
What Will There Be for the Children?

American Originals
Torreón Productions, 1985.
Originally released without license by Bear Family Records, Germany.
Cimarron Records issue no. 1005.

Songs:
Find Somebody and Love Them
Bury Me in New Orleans
Baby, She Loves a Rocker
Whiskey on the Side
Are They Gonna Make Us Outlaws Again?
A Way to Say I Love You
New York Town
Open All Night
Montana Song
Ready to Please
We're All One Family (All Over the World)

Love Songs and the Blues
Torreón Productions, 1989.
Originally released without license by Bear Family Records, Germany.
Cimarron Records issue no. 1006.

> Songs:
> Your Sweet Love
> Whatever Gets You through Your Life
> I Can't Surrender
> He Went Back to Texas
> Working Girl
> Little Child
> Up from Georgia
> All Because of You
> A Collection of Sorrows
> 'Cause I'm in Love with You
> May Your Dreams Come True

The Road to Torreón
Torreón Productions, 1992.
Originally released without license by Bear Family Records, Germany.
Cimarron Records issue no. 1007.

> Songs:
> Maria (The Road to Torreón)
> Ramón Estebán
> H. John Tarragón
> Demona
> La Rosa Montaña
> She Was a Flower of the Sunburnt West
> The Rosary
> As I Waited Out the Storm
> Little Child of Heaven
> Does Anybody Know Why Ana Maria's Mama Is Crying?
> I Had a Love Way Out West

James Talley: Live
Torreón Productions, 1994. Recorded live at the Lone Star Cafe in New York
City and at the Great Southeast Music Hall in Atlanta.
Originally released without license by Bear Family Records, Germany.
Cimarron Records issue no. 1008.

Songs:
Tryin' Like the Devil
Woman Trouble
Whiskey on the Side
Dixie Blue
W. Lee O'Daniel and the Light Crust Dough Boys
Not Even When It's Over
Nothin' Like Love
Find Somebody and Love Them
Survivors
Bluesman
I Can't Surrender
We Keep Tryin'
Are They Gonna Make Us Outlaws Again?
Give My Love to Marie
Alabama Summertime
Take Me to the Country
Take a Whiff on Me

Woody Guthrie and Songs of My Oklahoma Home
Torreón Productions, 2000; recorded in 1994 in Santa Fe, New Mexico.
Cimarron Records issue no. 1009.

Songs:
Belle Star
Dust Pneumonia Blues
East Texas Red
Do-Re-Mi
Deportee (Plane Wreck at Los Gatos)
Vigilante Man
I Ain't Got No Home
Roll on Columbia
Ladies Auxiliary
Gypsy Davy
Red Wing
Pretty Boy Floyd
Talkin' Dust Bowl
More Pretty Gals Than One/Poor Boy
Dust Bowl Refugee
Pastures of Plenty
Oklahoma Hills
Grand Coulee Dam
So Long It's Been Good to Know You
The Sinking of the Reuben James
This Land Is Your Land

Nashville City Blues
Torreón Productions, 2000; originally recorded in Santa Fe, New Mexico, in 1995 and mixed there in 1998.
Cimarron Records issue no. 1010.

> Songs:
> Nashville City Blues
> Down on the Corner
> Don't You Feel Low Down
> Rough Edge
> Baby Needs Some Good Times
> Streamline Flyer
> When I Need Some Love
> If It Wasn't for the Blues
> You Can't Get There from Here
> So I'm Not the Only One
> House Right Down the Road
> Workin' for Wages
> I've Seen the Bear

Touchstones

Torreón Productions, 2002; recorded in Floresville, Texas.
Cimarron Records issue no. 1011.

> Songs:
> Tryin' Like the Devil
> Sometimes I Think about Suzanne
> Calico Gypsy
> Bluesman
> W. Lee O'Daniel and the Light Crust Dough Boys
> Not Even When It's Over
> Forty Hours
> Deep Country Blues
> Are They Gonna Make Us Outlaws Again?
> Richland, Washington
> Nothin' but the Blues
> Up from Georgia
> To Get Back Home
> What Will There Be for the Children?
> When the Fiddler Packs His Case
> Give My Love to Marie

Journey

Torreón Productions, 2004; recorded live in Italy and mixed in Floresville, Texas.

Cimarron Records issue no. 1012.

Songs:
W. Lee O'Daniel and the Light Crust Dough Boys
Bluesman
My Cherokee Maiden
That Old Magic
Tryin' Like the Devil
Sometimes I Think about Suzanne
La Rosa Montaña
The Song of Chief Joseph
Richland, Washington
Somewhere on the Edge of the World
When I Need Some Love
I Saw the Buildings
Up from Georgia
We're All One Family

Journey: The Second Voyage

Torreón Productions, 2008; recorded live in Italy and mixed in Floresville, Texas.

Cimarron Records issue no 1013.

> Songs:
> Down on the Corner
> Little Egypt Land
> Someone Who Loves You
> Deep Country Blues
> Forty Hours
> Give My Love to Marie
> Hear That Lonesome Whistle
> Nothin' but the Blues
> Sea of Cortez
> Open All Night
> Streets of Babylon
> Nashville City Blues
> Calico Gypsy

Heartsong

Torreón Productions, 2008; recorded in Nashville and Floresville, Texas.
Cimarron Records issues no. 1014.

Songs:
North Dakota Girl
I Will Come to You
They Can't Kill Love
When Mama Ain't Happy
World of Broken Hearts
Are They Really Different?
Santa Fe Blues
She's the One
The Girls from Kelowna
Cold Blooded Killers
Whiskey and Beer
When It Was a Love Affair
Big Thunder
The Most Influential Teacher
If Only You Had Stayed
Song for Shiloh

INDEX

References in italic typeface indicate illustrations.

Made in the USA
Las Vegas, NV
07 June 2023

73102565R00139